The Resurrection Fact

Responding to Modern Critics

EDITED BY

John J. Bombaro

AND

Adam S. Francisco

BOOKS

NEW REFORMATION
PUBLICATIONS

An imprint of 1517 the Legacy Project

The Resurrection Fact: Responding to Modern Critics

Published by:
New Reformation Publications
PO Box 54032
Irvine, CA 92619-4032

Printed in the United States of America

Publisher's Cataloging-In-Publication Data
(Prepared by The Donohue Group, Inc.)

Names: Bombaro, John J., editor. | Francisco, Adam, editor.
Title: The resurrection fact : responding to modern critics / edited by John J. Bombaro and Adam S. Francisco.
Description: Irvine, CA : NRP Books, New Reformation Publications, an imprint of 1517 the Legacy Project, [2016] | Includes bibliographical references and indexes.
Identifiers: ISBN 978-1-945500-54-1 (hardcover) | ISBN 978-1-945500-55-8 (softcover) | ISBN 978-1-945500-56-5 (ebook)
Subjects: LCSH: Jesus Christ—Resurrection. | Resurrection—Biblical teaching. | Bible. N.T.—Criticism, interpretation, etc. | Christianity.
Classification: LCC BT482 .R47 2016 (print) | LCC BT482 (ebook) | DDC 232.97—dc23

NRP Books is committed to packaging and promoting the finest content for fueling a new Lutheran Reformation. We promote the defense of the Christian faith, confessional Lutheran theology, vocation and civil courage.

Dedicated to Melinda and Rachel
and our respective children

Sophia, Marie, Anna, and Luca

and

Tim, Kiahna, Elena, and Robert

ἕτοιμοι ἀεὶ πρὸς ἀπολογίαν παντὶ τῷ αἰτοῦντι ὑμᾶς λόγον, περὶ τῆς ἐν ὑμῖν ἐλπίδος

—1 Peter 3:15

Contents

Contributors

Clinton J. Armstrong (MA, Washington University; MDiv, Concordia Seminary, St. Louis; PhD, University of California, Irvine) is Associate Professor of History and Theology at Concordia University, Irvine. He is the author of *General Epistles*, volume six of the *Reformation Heritage Bible Commentary*, and a contributor and collaborator on other studies relating to history, language, and classics.

John J. Bombaro (MDiv Concordia Theological Seminary; MTh, University of Edinburgh; PhD, King's College London) is senior pastor at Grace Lutheran Church in San Diego, California, and a chaplain with the United States Navy. He is a regular contributor to *Modern Reformation* and the author of *Jonathan Edwards' Vision of Reality* (2012).

Andrew R. DeLoach (BA, University of California, San Diego; JD, California Western School of Law; FCA, International Academy of Apologetics, Evangelism, and Human Rights) is an attorney in Pasadena and Adjunct Professor at Concordia University, Irvine, and Trinity Law School in Santa Ana, where he is also professor-in-residence for the summer International Human Rights program in Strasbourg, France. He is a regular contributor to *Modern Reformation* and the *Journal of Christian Legal Thought*.

Adam S. Francisco (MA, Concordia University, Irvine; DPhil. University of Oxford) is Professor of History at Concordia University, Irvine. He is the author of *Martin Luther and Islam: A Study in Sixteenth Century Polemics and Apologetics*, the coeditor of *Making the Case for Christianity: Responding to Modern Objections*, and a contributor to a variety of other works covering Islam and Christian apologetics.

Carolyn Hansen (BA, Yale University) was born and raised in San Diego, California. At Yale, she studied intellectual history and wrote her senior thesis on the politics of grounding human rights in natural rights. She was the captain of Yale's Nordic Ski team and the chairman of the Conservative Party in the Yale Political Union. She currently lives in Washington, DC, pursuing a career in law and public policy.

Angus Menuge (MA and PhD, University of Wisconsin, Madison) is Professor of Philosophy at Concordia University, Wisconsin. In addition to dozens of scholarly articles and reviews, he is the author of *Agents Under Fire: Materialism and the Rationality of Science* (2004), and editor of *Reading God's World: The Scientific Vocation* (2004) and *Christ and Culture in Dialogue: Constructive Themes and Practical Application* (1999).

Jonathan Mumme (MDiv Concordia Seminary, St. Louis; Dr. Theol. University of Tübingen) is Assistant Professor of Theology at Concordia University Wisconsin. He is the author of *Die Präsenz Christi im Amt: Am Beispiel ausgewählter Predigten Martin Luthers, 1535–1546*, coeditor of *Feasting in a Famine of the Word: Lutheran Preaching in the Twenty-First Century*, and serves on the editorial board of *Lutherische Beiträge*.

Craig Parton (MA, Simon Greenleaf School of Law; JD, Hastings College of Law) is a trial lawyer and partner at Price, Postel and Parma in Santa Barbara, California, and the United States Director of the International Academy of Apologetics, Evangelism, and Human Rights (www.apologeticsacademy.eu). In addition to numerous articles and essays, he is the author of *Religion on Trial* (2008) and *The Defense Never Rests: A Lawyer among the Theologians* (2015).

Mark A. Pierson (MA Concordia University, Irvine; MDiv, Concordia Theological Seminary) has taught theology and philosophy at the high school, undergraduate, and graduate levels and is currently pursuing a PhD in New Testament Studies at Fuller Theological Seminary. His published essays have appeared in *Learning at the Foot of the Cross, Theologia et Apologia: Essays in Reformation Theology and Its Defense*, and *Making the Case for Christianity: Responding to Modern Objections*.

Introduction

John J. Bombaro

He who would preach the Gospel must go directly to preaching the resurrection of Christ. He who does not preach the resurrection is no apostle, for this is the chief part of our faith. . . . The greatest importance attaches to this article of faith. For were there no resurrection, we would have neither comfort nor hope, and everything else Christ did and suffered would be in vain.[1]

—Martin Luther

The resurrection of Jesus Christ is *the* Christian assertion, according to Luther. In this, Martin Luther said nothing new. Even the Old Roman Creed, the predecessor to the Apostles' Creed, differentiates between Christ being raised on the third day and the future general resurrection of all believers. The resurrection was the fundamental confession of Christians from its inception. Paul received the Gospel of Jesus Christ's atoning death and justifying resurrection for sinners—both Jews and gentiles—only a year or two removed from those very events, saying that it was already by that time, say, 34 or

---

[1] Martin Luther, *D. Martin Luthers Werke*, Kritische Gesamtausgabe (Weimar: H. Böhlaus Nachfolger, 1883), 12:268; Ewald M. Plass in *What Luther Says: A Practical In-Home Anthology for the Active Christian* (St Louis, MO: Concordia Publishing House, 1959), 1215.

35 AD, *the* tradition, *the* creed, *the* Gospel. The Gospel he received and was proclaiming was an announcement of particular historical events concerning a particular historical person—Jesus of Nazareth. *This* historical Jesus is one and the same person with the crucified and risen Christ. That was the Christian message, bold though it be.

So bold in fact was the Gospel of Christ that only nineteen years after the execution of Jesus, his message caused such unrest among the Jews of the imperial capital that the emperor had to intervene.[2] This was because the followers of *Chrestus*,[3] as Pliny identifies the object of Christian worship,[4] were claiming that Christ Jesus is *the* Caesar, the Lord of the cosmos, to whom every knee would bow and every tongue confess. The kingdom of God, according to them, pertained to how Jesus Christ ruled under the noses of the Caesars by the forgiveness of sins and in the power of the Holy Spirit. That *that* was a reality, a real kingdom, a true state of affairs, was substantiated— vindicated as a claim—by the bodily resurrection of Jesus Christ: hence Paul's missionary endeavors of Gospel proclamation that God has been victorious over sin, death, and the kingdoms of this world through Jesus Christ's blood atonement and bodily resurrection. Paul was stating that the entire world of both Jews and gentiles was under a new governor, and that meant humanity belongs to God twice over—first because he created us and second because he has redeemed us through the work of his Son. "For none of us lives to himself, and none of us dies to himself," states Paul epigrammatically. "If we live, we live to the Lord, and if we die, we die to the Lord. So, then, whether we live or die, we are the Lord's. For to this end Christ died and lived again, that he might be Lord both of the dead and of the living" (Romans 14:7–9). The resurrection of Jesus Christ

---

[2]Martin Hengel, *Between Jesus and Paul: Studies in the Earliest History of Christianity* (Minneapolis, MN: Fortress Press, 1983), 49.

[3]"The name 'Christ' does not appear among the Jews in Egypt, in Rome, in Cyrenaica, or in Josephus. The title and name ὁ Χριστὸς was totally incomprehensible for Greeks and Romans; the itacistic pronunciation of η as ι gave the slave name Χρῆστος." (Ibid., 167 n. 9).

[4]Pliny the Younger, "Pliny to the Emperor Trajan," in *Letters*, Book 10, Letter #96.

proclaimed by the New Testament authors therefore raises questions of a renewed ontology as well as of a renewed epistemology.

And raise questions it does.

The resurrection does not put an end to doubt. Rather, it seems to invite it. The Gospel accounts themselves are clear that the disciples were initially uncertain about how to understand the empty tomb. Luke 24:37–38 says that when Jesus appeared to the disciples, doubt or hesitation arose in their hearts that wasn't easily dispelled until some of them touched his hands and feet or at least were given the opportunity to do so (John 20:17, 24–29; 1 John 1:1–2). However it may have been for each of them, they were compelled, transformed by their encounters with the risen Christ Jesus.

Advance the conversation from the first century to the present day, and where there was once doubt turned to joy, there now exists a skepticism that has turned to cynicism regarding the bodily resurrection of Jesus Christ and, by extension, any claim to his lordship, not only outside the church but also by those claiming to be of the church. Resurrections don't happen, which means the resurrection of Jesus didn't happen either.

Why is there so much contemporary skepticism about the resurrection? Part of the reason pertains to the triumph of David Hume's repudiation of miracles and the association of intellectual respectability with Humean skepticism that has become tethered to a physicalist world view. Matthew Lee Anderson writes, "One rule of our current intellectual climate, in fact, is that we should doubt everything first. Only then, if it is somehow left standing in the end, should we go on to believe it."[5] A totalizing claim like the resurrection and consequent worship of Jesus would require monumental proof. Wayne Booth advances this idea when he says,

> [Our contemporary dogma] teaches that we have no justification for asserting what can be doubted, and we are commanded by it to doubt whatever cannot be proved. In that view one never is advised to see the capacity for belief as an intellectual virtue. Though few have ever put it quite so bluntly as the young [Bertrand] Russell in his more

---

[5]Matthew Lee Anderson, *The End of Our Exploring: A Book About Questioning and the Confidence of Faith* (Chicago, IL: Moody, 2013), 51.

prophetic moments, to doubt is taken as the supreme achievement of thought.[6]

From this platform of post-Enlightenment scientific rationality (in which Hume remains a major player), there's nothing spiritual, only the empirical; there's no theology, only anthropology. And so intellectual commitments to physicalism or materialism, sometimes called naturalism, rule out supernaturalism as a consideration and with it, the miracle of resurrection.

But the resurrection is proclaimed as a fact of history and throughout history, reaching back to the eyewitnesses of the event itself—the authors of the New Testament. And so we must conclude with Oxford mathematician John Lennox that the world of *scientific* inquiry does not encompass all *rational* inquiry, since its principles do not translate into the domain of historical inquiry. As Eric Metaxas writes: "Yes, science has limits. It can describe the universe of matter and energy, but it cannot *account* for that universe. Ludwig Wittgenstein said, 'The great delusion of modernity is that the laws of science explain the universe for us. The laws of nature *describe* the universe . . . but they explain nothing.'"[7] It appears, then, that aside from Hume's presuppositions, there has been a category error at play. The scientific method could not explain a claim like the resurrection (much less rule it out, especially given our "open universe") since it is a historical claim. Historical inquiry, then, would be the preferred method of inquiry for the New Testament assertion of Jesus's resurrection, being much more akin to the principles of jurisprudence, where testimony and evidence are weighed and considered in terms of their explanatory force for occurrences under consideration.

In this light, we see that convincing reasonable people that something happened and "proving" that something happened are not the same thing. And if we are talking about a miracle like the resurrection of Christ Jesus, we cannot "prove" that it happened

---

[6]Wayne C. Booth, *Modern Dogma and the Rhetoric of Assent* (Notre Dame, IN: University of Notre Dame Press, 1974), 101.

[7]Eric Metaxas, *Miracles: What They Are, Why They Happen, and How They Can Change Your Life* (New York: Penguin Books, 2015), 26.

any more than a prosecutor can prove someone committed a crime. Instead, what is required not only for belief but also for action is to substantiate the resurrection beyond a reasonable doubt. That is to say, when the doubting or skepticism becomes unreasonable, implausible, or untenable, the reasonable person yields to the proposition at hand—namely, that Christ is risen from the dead.

Skeptics, however, regenerate in every generation, sometimes parroting old arguments, sometimes bringing new ones. In this volume, we find both kinds. Consequently, these are great times to be engaged in apologetics or simply knowing the reasons behind Christian truth claims. Monthly, it seems fresh insights emerge from New Testament studies, archeology, philology, cultural studies, and other disciplines. Two trends are of particular importance: (1) scholars almost universally are dating the New Testament documents earlier, and (2) they are now placing Jesus in his Jewish milieu, not a Greek one. This has had a profound impact upon our present conversation. With scholarly acknowledgement of a compressed time frame for the emergence of Christianity—where Paul is now seen as a ground-floor participant, and there is significant overlap between the oral and written traditions of the earliest Jewish Christians—there simply isn't enough time for a "big fish" story to develop regarding the resurrection or the "making of Christology." As Richard Bauckham explains:

> The earliest Christology was already the highest Christology. There is no "the making of christology" as if it had undergone an arduous evolutionary process. There was a Christology of divine identity from the beginning. "Not only the preexistent and the exalted Jesus but also the earthly, suffering, humiliated and crucified Jesus belong to the unique identity of God, then it had to be said that Jesus reveals the divine identity—who God truly is—in humiliation as well as exaltation, and in the connection of the two. God's own identity is revealed in Jesus, his life and his cross, just as truly as in his exaltation, in a way that is fully continuous and consistent with the Old Testament and Jewish understanding of God, but is also novel and surprising."[8]

---

[8]Richard Bauckham, *God Crucified: Monotheism & Christology in the New Testament* (Grand Rapids, MI: Eerdmans, 1998), viii.

One can speak meaningfully of Easter only if one knows that here, the Jewish man, Jesus of Nazareth, is raised—someone who in his human life, with its activity and suffering and crucifixion, is not just any interchangeable person from history or imagination. As Martin Hengel states it: "The cause of Jesus had a future only on the basis of Easter."[9]

This brings us back to defending the central claim of Christianity—that the crucified Christ is risen. This is the Gospel. For Paul, St. Augustine, Luther, and all Christian believers, there is no consolation prize, no plan-B scenario. These are the words of eternal life, and Christ is that life—indeed, he is the resurrection and the life. This assertion must be defended because it is a public procla- mation, a public theology, concerning a public figure in public places regarding public events. The nature of Christianity is that it consists of a public truth claim: God was in the world reconciling the world to himself through Jesus Christ. Christians, then, must assume the burden of having to respond to those who raise objections against it. But one cannot *prove* that Jesus Christ was raised from the dead, just as one cannot prove that Caesar crossed the Rubicon. Our defense, then, consists of arguments regarding (i) the actual burial and sub- sequent empty tomb, (ii) the appearance to the witnesses, (iii) the governing narrative and political-religious context, (iv) the Gospel accounts of Jesus's life and sayings related to his death and resurrec- tion, (v) the phenomenon of the extraordinary rise of the church in its location and with *this* Gospel, (vi) the hostile witness accounts regarding Christ and the phenomenon of the church, (vii) the litur- gical and devotional practices of the earliest Christians worshipping the living Christ (whose tomb was not venerated), (viii) the maximal claim of a bodily resurrection being the earliest claim in the earliest records, (ix) the continual assertion by the disciples and apostles that the living Christ was with them in the Eucharist and governing them by his Spirit, and (x) the issue that those with, as Craig Parton says, the means, motive, and opportunity to produce a body or expose a conspiracy never emerge.

---

[9]Hengel, *Between Jesus and Paul*, 61.

The modern objectors of the bodily resurrection selected for this volume hail from a variety of disciplines and backgrounds and include historians, New Testament scholars, philosophers, and professors. They are notable and influential authors. Our contributors likewise evidence a spectrum of vocations and backgrounds but share a common Christian faith as disciples of Jesus Christ.

Our first contributor, a New Testament scholar, Mark Pierson, opens by asking the fundamental question, "[D]id Jesus experience a physical resurrection from the grave—an authentic supernatural occurrence in which the God of Israel restored his servant Jesus to life—or not?" The answer presents an unmistakable either/or scenario: If so, then this solitary fact verifies the most basic claim of Christianity; if not, then "Jesus remained dead on the third day, [and] the gospel proclamation of forgiveness and eternal life through him is baseless and patently false." Apologists, he observes, have taken three approaches (expose antisupernatural presuppositions, defend resurrection appearances, and articulate the significance of the empty tomb) to answering resurrection gainsayers. He notes, however, that now deniers circumvent the either/or resurrection dilemma and robust Christian defense of the same by eliminating the fact that Christ ever entered the tomb.

Pierson thus finds former Baptist minister Robert Price repudiating the historicity of Jesus of Nazareth, Muslim commentator Louay Fatoohi distorting the historical facts about Jesus's death by crucifixion, and media-celebrated Bart Ehrman speculating that Jesus's remains were left to decompose on the cross. In contesting them, Pierson exposes their inconsistent methodologies and logic that derail an honest consideration of Christ Jesus to bring the question of the resurrection back to the forefront of the Christian proclamation.

Adam Francisco, a historian, exposes an undermining methodological error in the work of New Testament skeptic Bart Ehrman. His chapter, "Can a Historian Explain the Empty Tomb with the Resurrection of Jesus?" focuses on an excursus entitled "The Historian and the Problem of Miracle" in Ehrman's standard college text for introductory New Testament courses: *New Testament: A Historical Approach to the Early Christian Writings*. Exploiting the problems of David Hume's ill-reasoned antisupernaturalistic philosophy, by which Hume manipulates the conversation on miracles by defining them according to the parameters of his own materialistic world view, Francisco shows that Ehrman's deference to Hume's definition and analysis of a miracle are the undoing of his own historical method, even though he grants that "miracles can and do happen."

Methodologically, Ehrman begins where Hume ends and extrapolates that historically substantiating a miraculous event is problematically compounded by our ability to *know* if a miracle took place in the past. Miracles, he says, are an insurmountable epistemological problem for the historian. Ehrman avers, "If accepting the occurrence of a miracle requires belief in the supernatural realm, and historians by the very nature of their craft can speak only about events of the natural world (which are accessible to observers of every kind) how can they ever certify an event *outside* the natural order— that is, a miracle—occurred?" Francisco rightly notes Ehrman's "bait and switch" or, better, switch-and-bait tactic. Ehrman has used Hume's definition to set the miraculous event *outside* spatiotemporality and thus into the realm of the unknowable.[10] Consequently, the resurrection is precluded from a range of possible answers to the empty tomb. But Hume's self-serving definition of a miracle is altogether unsatisfactory and has been rejected as a category error. With that rejection is the misapplication of its domain of occurrence—not *outside* (in the eternal realm) but *inside* time and space precisely as a *historical* event. What is more, the historian shouldn't dismiss an event because the *cause* may be indiscernible (in this case, God), but should rather collect and evaluate data *that* an event has occurred— namely, that the tomb was empty—and then ask the next question: *why was it so.* Francisco then takes us to the evidence—namely, the New Testament documents themselves, which of course have been abandoned by Ehrman as a viable explanation for why the tomb was empty. And it is there Francisco shows that Ehrman plays the part of a partisan philosopher rather than an impartial historian "by

---

[10]A generation later, Immanuel Kant would denominate the realm of the unknowable (into which he placed three "ideas"—God, the self, and essences) as the noumenal realm, in juxtaposition to the phenomenal (empirical) realm, i.e., the domain of science.

restricting historians to consider only what he deems probable *apart from consideration of the evidence.*"

Lutheran pastor and apologist John Bombaro identifies John Dominic Crossan as the progenitor of "progressive Christianity"— an alternative way to deny by affirming the resurrection of Jesus Christ. This movement acknowledges a historical Jesus but one differentiated from the ahistorical "Christ of faith." With Jesus divorced from the "Christ" of the bodily resurrection, room is made for alternative interpretations of the resurrection as either "apparitional" or mere literary device.

Crossan, however, goes a step further by claiming that the resurrection is really to be understood as a parable with metaphorical meaning rooted not in the New Testament but in a prototypical "cross gospel" source and its derivative *Gospel of Peter*, both of which he asserts were extant before the Gospels and Paul's writings. By taking redaction criticism to a new level through a determination of the kind of texts he wishes to engage, Crossan fashions a progressive Christianity devoid of supernaturalism, replete with parabolic meaning relevant and applicable to contemporary political, social, and economic issues. Bombaro shows that Crossan doesn't *discern* the forms; rather he *determines* them through texts (both imagined and real) that have no support in the scholarly community in terms of their relationship to early Christianity, let alone its origins.

Moreover, Crossan, like Ehrman and Price, has antecedent naturalistic commitments that predetermine his approach to the New Testament and, especially, the resurrection. For him, miracles do not happen, and so a bodily resurrection never happened as a fact of history. Jesus, then (inaccessible through the expressions of the Gospel writers), was just a mortal human being crushed by the political juggernauts of his day. He is neither the Christ of God nor the second person of the eternal Trinity. As such, argues Bombaro, this "Christ" of Crossan is nothing less than an *antichrist* ("other than Christ"). Consequently, "progressive Christianity" has no biblical Gospel of Jesus Christ and thereby ceases to be Christian.

With all seriousness and yet a good dash of playfulness, seasoned attorney and noted apologist Craig Parton explores what kinds of questions might actually be asked of the legal authorities who witnessed the crucifixion or encountered the risen Christ, were they themselves put in the witness stand. In his chapter "The Case against *The Case against Christianity*: When Jerusalem Came to Athens," Parton uses both his imagination and skills of deposition and examination to create a forum to hear "live testimony" from a panel of "historical persons who have been dead" for centuries. The panel, consisting of none other than Sanhedrin justices Gamaliel, Joseph of Arimathea, and Nicodemus, and jurist Paul of Tarsus, is scrutinized—cross-examined, as it were—by contemporary atheist philosopher Michael L. Martin. Parton gives voice to their defense in the domain of jurisprudence.

Parton is concerned about the nature of the charge against Jesus, that capital punishment was administered and verified, and that testimony was conveyed to the penmen of the four Gospels. Joseph and Nicodemus, whose testimony would have been inscrutable as Jewish legal authorities, certified that Jesus was in fact dead and placed in Joseph's own family tomb. The death and burial of Jesus were confirmed by high legal authorities, and this fact should not be underestimated, especially when the New Testament authors were careful enough (and daring enough) to actually name participants in and witnesses of Jesus's trial, crucifixion, and entombment. Since the entire affair took place in and was framed by the principles and procedures of jurisprudence, Parton argues in the voices of the legal participants of Jesus's passion week that Michael Martin fails to remain consistent with his treatment of New Testament evidences.

"Are Christians justified in their confession of the bodily resurrection of Jesus Christ?" asks philosopher Angus Menuge. Atheist scholar Matthew McCormick answers this epistemological question in the negative—Christians are not, since there's insufficient evidence, particularly for the notion of "miracle." McCormick details his reasons for rejecting the miraculous and for why secularists like himself are better equipped to assess the date from an unbiased perspective in his *Atheism and the Case against Christ*. But Menuge detects fissures, presuppositions, assumptions, and bad reasoning throughout McCormick's critique of Christian belief. He deftly shows the inadequacy of McCormick's philosophical method by exposing the latter's misunderstanding of the relationship between faith and evidence, as well as his own biases that include a tendentious handling of the evidence and his own willingness to "embrace a highly implausible naturalistic explanation of the resurrection appearances."

German higher criticism facilitated a modern-day reorientation from "true north," as New Testament scholar Jonathan Mumme puts it. True north was the Christian belief in a bodily resurrection from the dead, in which a material continuity between the deceased and resurrected Jesus Christ was maintained. This event was the capstone to the victory of God and the dawning of his new creation. The resurrection fact thereby oriented biblical and therefore authentic Christianity for future generations. But the antisupernatural exegetical tradition of the eighteenth-and nineteenth-century higher critics posited a host of alternative theories so that today, the resurrection may be seen as no longer central and defining for what may be more broadly termed "Christianity." Mumme argues, however, that outside of the "true north," corporeal resurrection of the once-crucified Jesus Christ, readers of the New Testament are left to saunter aimlessly about the grid of "Christianity," "with little more than conflicting guesses at who Jesus is and what he did."

Imbibing the spirit of the German higher critical movement but desiring to work with the narrative of the New Testament is Dale Allison. He melds aspects of contemporary scholarship in the field of psychology, particularly the phenomenology of apparitions, with the New Testament's witness to a resurrected Jesus, taking the proclamation that "Christ is risen" into a different interpretive direction. Apparitional belief, scientifically acknowledged today, inevitably gave rise to resurrection claims by the authors of the New Testament.

Jonathan Mumme, however, disputes both the plausibility and the probability of Allison's "apparition" proposal by showing how uninevitable Jesus's resurrection was for Palestinian Jews. Resurrection has a specific New Testament meaning, with its origins drawn directly from ancient Jewish beliefs and its own matter-affirming anthropology *and* soteriology. The word *resurrection* designates one and only one option for what happens after we die. Apparitional existence wasn't one of them for the Jews, but resurrected bodily existence was. Drawing off the definitive work of N. T. Wright, Mumme shows that "the word *resurrection* always means bodies."[11] Allison's apparitional Jesus, then, tells the wrong story among the wrong people using the wrong definition. It is little wonder, then, that the grid of Christianity is turned upside down by Dale Allison. Given Jewish beliefs about their future and anthropology, the cause of Jesus had a future only on the basis of a bodily resurrection—true north, according to St. Paul in 1 Corinthians 15, without which we are lost in this world.

A much-neglected but ever-rewarding apologetic is revived for contemporary readers by C. J. Armstrong and Andrew DeLoach from the writings of C. S. Lewis. In 1945, J. R. R. Tolkien wrote to his son Christopher about the "beauty" of the biblical story, lamenting that skeptics in the name of modern science were jeopardizing the cultural significance and value of Genesis *as a story* in their repudiation of the Torah's creation account. In his letter, Tolkien told his son that

> Lewis recently wrote a most interesting essay (if published I don't know) showing of what great value the "story-value" was, as mental nourishment—of the whole Chr[istian] story (NT especially) . . . His point was that they do still in that way get some nourishment and are not cut off wholly from the sap of life: for the beauty of the story, while not necessarily a guarantee of its truth, is a concomitant of it, and a *fidelis* is meant to draw nourishment from the beauty as well as the truth.[12]

Tolkien unknowingly refers to Lewis's published essay, "Myth Became Fact."[13] Lewis understands the Gospel accounts of (especially) Jesus's virgin birth as "mythic." But what distinguishes fairy-stories (to use Tolkien's term) from the mythic elements of the Gospels is that

---

[11]N. T. Wright, *Simply Good News: Why the Gospel Is News and What Makes It Good* (San Francisco, CA: HarperOne, 2015), 47.

[12]J. R. R. Tolkien, "96 To Christopher Tolkien," in *The Letters of J. R. R. Tolkien*, ed. Humphrey Carpenter and with the assistance of Christopher Tolkien (New York: Houghton Mifflin Company, 1981/2000), 109.

[13]C. S. Lewis, "Myth Became Fact," in *God in the Dock: Essays on Theology and Ethics*, ed. Walter Hooper (Grand Rapids, MI: Eerdmans, 1944/2001), 63–67.

the Christian story moves from the beauty of the poetic and imaginative into the reality of authentic human history: "Now as myth transcends thought, Incarnation transcends myth. The heart of Christianity is a myth which is also a fact," says Lewis. "The old myth of the Dying God, *without ceasing to be myth*, comes down from the heaven of legend and imagination to the earth of history. It *happens*—at a particular date, in a particular place, followed by definable historical consequences."[14] By grounding the mythic story (and stories) about God in the Incarnation of Jesus Christ, Lewis paves the way to understanding the mythic miracles of incarnation and atonement and resurrection as poetic manifestations precisely in the domain in which we live and move and have our being. The miracle of the resurrection, like the incarnation, does not cease to be a myth even though it has become a fact—*that*, he says, is the miracle of Christianity.

Armstrong and DeLoach fete out Lewis's meaning of Christ Jesus as "Perfect Myth and Perfect Fact" and so expose the genetic fallacy used by so many skeptics who simply dismiss the New Testament accounts of the resurrection because of their pejorative categorization of it as myth. Of course Christians believe in a myth, but that myth became fact. As Armstrong and DeLoach argue, myth, like poetry, may *better* convey reality than abstraction or factoids possibly can. Thereby truth becomes manifold. Skeptics have lost the rhetorical weapon of "myth" against Christianity because it has been rightly and soundly reappropriated by Lewis but also Tolkien and Chesterton.

Furthermore, Armstrong and DeLoach are not content to allow the Christian proclamation of the resurrection to be absorbed into and relativized by the "mystery religions," as is so frequently and carelessly done by scholars and teachers through their anthropological "comparative religions" approach to Christianity. As our authors show, an honest and insightful comparison between ancient mythology and Christianity actually has few points of contact and exhibits no Christian dependency; indeed, in some cases (e.g., Plutarch), the Greek author arrives on the scene a century or two after the birth of

---

[14]Ibid., 66.

Christianity. No, Christianity already has an antecedent in biblical Judaism, and the bodily resurrection of Jesus Christ brings the surprising and yet fully appropriate and compatible fulfillment of the promises of Israel's God.

Finally, Carolyn Hansen confronts the disputed work of Gerd Lüdemann, who argues that supernatural and literalistic resurrection is entirely out of step with modern learning and science. Instead of real-world encounters with a tactile and true postresurrection Jesus Christ, Lüdemann asserts that the earliest leaders of Christianity were struck by the trauma of having lost their inspirational leader and so desiring the successful establishment of his "kingdom," experienced profoundly moving *visions* of Jesus alive and reigning. These were encounters entirely of a psychological nature, not physical manifestations. This is how the "Jesus is Lord" movement began, he explains—namely, with traumatized disciples envisioning Jesus "living" after his crucifixion and living on through their passion to see the kingdom of God come. In this way, the apostles' "resurrection" visions of Jesus become a metaphor for hope in this life that provided a catalyst for conversion, evangelization, and devotion to Christ among his earliest followers.

Hansen straightforwardly contradicts Lüdemann's theses by substantiating that the New Testament witnesses operated in a Semitic philosophical tradition that was *intensely tactile* and defined by a biblical narrative in which God was providential and miraculously active in space and time. It was the apostles' deep commitment to a Jewish worldview that provided them with resources to recognize the difference between trauma-induced visions and a bodily resurrection. Indeed, biblical Judaism had a profound understanding of material reality and, relatedly, its antithesis in terms of nonphysical entities. What the earliest Jewish Christians proclaimed was a bodily resurrection, and no one more so than Paul who was himself "a Pharisee, descended from Pharisees" (Acts 23:6).

A defense of the resurrection consists not only of a response by way of negation (e.g., Christianity is not *this*) but also through positive affirmations (*this* is Christianity). In what follows, the reader will find both. However, it is our hope that the final word retained by our readers would be the one that stands *for* something rather than *against* something. Together, our words stand for something positive, not negative—namely, the good news that the one true God has now taken charge of the world, in and through Jesus and his death and resurrection. We freely acknowledge that this life-affirming assertion is the narrative that defines our lives and, indeed, determines all lives. For it isn't merely a narrative about salvation but also about creation—specifically, a new creation. The power that tyrannized the old creation has been broken, defeated, overthrown. With the resurrection of Jesus Christ, God's kingdom is now launched, and launched with power and glory, here on earth.

According to the New Testament, faith responds to this Gospel, whether spoken or written. Paul would answer, "Faith comes by hearing and hearing from the word of Christ" (Romans 10:17). Here, faith is the response of the ear to the spoken word. John would answer, "These things are written that you may believe that Jesus is the Christ" (John 20:30–31). Faith, then, is a response to the word of God; it is not a response to history, or to historical reconstructions, or even arguments really. Moreover, it is the claim of the New Testament and the reality of experience that the Gospel is self-authenticating. This faith comes by the activity of the Holy Spirit. The incarnation, the atonement, and the resurrection are not merely redemptive ideas; they involve a real man at a specific time and place who was crucified, buried, and on the third day raised in resurrection life. Faith that saves is faith in *this* Christ, according to the same Jesus Christ.

In the first century, the resurrection fact faced both Jewish and Greek audiences with a challenge—the challenge of a new reality and each person (and their family's) relation to it: Christ *is* the risen Lord. And since facts are by definition "something that happened," and this happening was witnessed, proclaimed, and recorded, the fact stands for all generations, entreating all to share in this glorious faith.

1

Defending the Fundamental Facts of Good Friday and Easter Sunday

Mark A. Pierson

What really happened on that first Easter Sunday? That is, did Jesus experience a physical resurrection from the grave—an authentic supernatural occurrence in which the God of Israel restored his servant Jesus to life—or not? If so, this solitary fact verifies the most basic claim of Christianity: God was in Christ reconciling the world unto himself, not counting people's sins against them (2 Corinthians 5:19). It also puts Jesus in the unique position of having power over death, making him the sole solution for humanity's most pressing problem (see John 5:25–26; Revelation 1:18). Yet the converse is likewise true: if Jesus remained dead on the third day, then the Gospel proclamation of forgiveness and eternal life through him is baseless and patently false. These stark ramifications were clearly identified by the apostle Paul, who rested the entire Christian position on the veracity of this single event: "If Christ has not been raised, our preaching is useless and so is your faith" (1 Corinthians. 15:14). In other words, if Jesus never rose, Christians believe in a fairy tale and it is time they grew up.

The import of this question for believers and unbelievers alike can hardly be overstated. We need to ask, then, whether the evidence of history confirms or contests the assertion that Jesus is risen, indeed.

Getting into the History of the Matter

Historically speaking, apologetic efforts regarding Jesus's resurrection have typically fallen into one of three categories.[1] First, there have been attempts to expose the various problems found in naturalistic explanations for why Christians came to believe in a risen Jesus.[2] While many alternate scenarios have been suggested (deceptive disciples, mass hallucinations, psychological delusions, plagiarism from the mythologies and mystery religions of paganism, wish fulfillment, alien involvement, etc.), the viability of each falls short either in terms of internal coherence or in correspondence with the established evidence (or both). Second, the resurrection appearances themselves have been defended.[3] References to the risen Christ found both in the New Testament and elsewhere[4] have received extensive scrutiny concerning their historical value. As a significant part of this category, special attention has been given to the eyewitnesses, whose vantage point is unmatched and who (temporally speaking) had everything to lose and nothing to gain by

---

[1]Gary R. Habermas, "The Resurrection of Jesus Timeline: The Convergence of Eyewitnesses and Early Proclamation," in *Contending with Christianity's Critics: Answering New Atheists and Other Objectors*, ed. Paul Copan and William Lane Craig (Nashville, TN: B&H, 2009), 113.

[2]For a concise analysis of the most popular opposing theories, see Gary R. Habermas and Michael R. Licona, *The Case for the Resurrection of Jesus* (Grand Rapids, MI: Kregel, 2004), 81–150.

[3]Included here is the contention of the earliest apologists that Jesus's resurrection was foretold in the Old Testament. See Avery Cardinal Dulles, *A History of Apologetics*, reprint (Eugene, OR: Wipf & Stock, 1999), 2–5, 24–25, 44, 81.

[4]In addition to the nine traditional New Testament authors, another thirty-three writers made reference to Jesus within 150 years after his life (including church fathers, Gnostics, and secular non-Christian sources), most of whom either mentioned Jesus's resurrection appearances outright or implied familiarity with the claim. See Gary R. Habermas, *The Historical Jesus: Ancient Evidence for the Life of Christ* (Joplin, MO: College Press, 1996), 187–241; Paul Rhodes Eddy and Gregory A. Boyd, *The Jesus Legend: A Case for the Historical Reliability of the Synoptic Jesus Tradition* (Grand Rapids, MI: Baker, 2007), 165–99.

persisting in their belief that they really saw Jesus alive again.[5] Third, apologists have focused on the significance of the empty tomb. If the location of Jesus's grave was known, it is simply inconceivable to think it remained occupied while the first Christians proclaimed his bodily resurrection in Jerusalem—that is, to those who could have easily visited the tomb and seen its status for themselves. In turn, substantiation of the empty tomb frequently forces skeptics to explain the pesky detail of Jesus's missing body, which has generally led back to the first category, where purely naturalistic explanations for what happened have been found unconvincing, usually due to a total lack of evidence.

The two topics we will address in this chapter overlap with all three of these categories. First, we will look at what happened to Jesus on Good Friday—namely, whether in fact Jesus of Nazareth expired via crucifixion and was subsequently entombed. This will make up the bulk of our study. While the question of what happened on Easter itself is paramount, the death of Jesus must first be established before there can be any meaningful claim of a resurrection. Indeed, some modern, radical skeptics have argued that he never was crucified, never died, and never was buried, allowing them to dismiss the Easter message as fiction. Theses untenable assertions will be refuted. Second, we will consider the contention that the resurrection narratives in the Gospels contain contradictions, such that Matthew, Mark, Luke, and John cannot be considered historically reliable. The truth of the resurrection, then, rests in part on these two issues.

A noteworthy feature shared by these two lines of inquiry is their dependence on the historical record apart from any presuppositions about the nature of miracles. We shall see elsewhere in this volume that one's methodology for discovering what occurred in the past invariably determines one's outcome.[6] If antisupernaturalism

---

[5]On the value and assessment of eyewitness testimony relating to Jesus, see Richard Bauckham, *Jesus and the Eyewitnesses: The Gospels as Eyewitness Testimony* (Grand Rapids, MI: Eerdmans, 2006), 5–11; Eddy and Boyd, *The Jesus Legend*, 269–91.

[6]See chapter 2 by Adam Francisco, "Can a Historian Explain the Empty Tomb with the Resurrection of Jesus?," and chapter 8 by Carolyn Hansen, "Tactile and True."

is embraced as an axiomatic assumption, such that paranormal explanations are automatically ruled out *no matter how strong the evidence is in favor of them*, then bad philosophy and ideological commitments will have corrupted good history, and the truth will potentially be missed.[7] Certainly if miracles do not happen, then the miracle of the resurrection never happened either; but we can only know there is absolute uniform experience against the supernatural if we know *a priori* that all reports of miracles are false. Yet how can we conclude that all individual miracle claims are untrue unless we first know that suprahuman activity is positively impossible? Thus we are arguing in a circle.[8] The systematic prohibition against historians ever considering the possibility that God chose to intervene in our world is simply unwarranted.[9]

That our particular subjects can be examined while remaining open-minded about the possibility of miracles may appear more obvious with our first topic than the second. Most people would certainly agree that Jesus's crucifixion, death, and burial can be understood in purely naturalistic terms. The Gospels themselves affirm the plain character of these precise events, irrespective of certain peripheral, supernatural details or the authors' interpretive comments.[10] Regarding disagreements between the accounts, however, there would seem to be the glaring problem that they all affirm Jesus was *miraculously* restored to life. Yet it is important to note that we will be considering whether or not the narratives are so grossly inconsistent with one another that they should be written off *for that reason alone*. Since the exact moment of Jesus's resurrection is not, in

---

[7] For extended assessments of historical methodologies in relation to the miraculous, see Michael R. Licona, *The Resurrection of Jesus: A New Historiographical Approach* (Downers Grove, IL: InterVarsity Press, 2010), 29–198; Craig S. Keener, *Miracles: The Credibility of the New Testament Accounts* (Grand Rapids, MI: Baker, 2011), 1:83–208.

[8] C. S. Lewis, *Miracles*, reprint (New York: HarperCollins, 2001), 161–62.

[9] Even though this fact is well known and the premise is logically sound, it frequently remains ignored by skeptics.

[10] That the evangelists and New Testament authors discern and underscore theological meaning in the reported events concerning Jesus of Nazareth does not negate the bare historicity of those events.

fact, recorded in the Gospels, our query need not directly entail what caused people to think they saw Jesus alive again. We will only consider the charge that these four texts *contradict* each other in what they report as having happened on Easter.

Before we begin, a general note must be made about the Gospels as trustworthy sources. Apologists have routinely demonstrated the reliability of these texts when evaluating them according to the standard procedures used to assess the value of any work of ancient history. Space constraints prevent us from making that case here,[11] but it is worth noting that even many unbelieving scholars have admitted that Matthew, Mark, Luke, and John are the best historical sources we have about Jesus.[12] Therefore, we will operate under the assumption that the Gospels remain historically reliable witnesses unless our investigation shows otherwise.

"He Was Crucified, Died, and Was Buried"

The above heading comes from the Apostles' Creed and is confessed by countless Christians every week. We will now attempt to ascertain whether these tenets are merely a matter of faith, or are also a matter of fact.

He Was Crucified, Indeed

There are two primary groups of people who reject Jesus's crucifixion. On the one hand, there remains a small band of extreme skeptics who deny that Jesus was a figure of history at all. Naturally, then, they also dismiss any claims about his execution. On the other hand, most

---

[11]For a summary of this case, see Mark A. Pierson, "The New Testament Gospels as Reliable History," in *Making the Case for Christianity: Responding to Modern Objections*, ed. Korey D. Mass and Adam S. Francisco (St. Louis, MO: Concordia, 2014), 35–66.

[12]Examples include Bart D. Ehrman, *Jesus: Apocalyptic Prophet of the New Millennium*, reprint (Oxford: Oxford University Press, 2001), 22; Michael Martin, *The Case against Christianity* (Philadelphia, PA: Temple University Press, 1991), 43–44; Michael Grant, *History of Rome* (London: Weidenfeld & Nicolson, 1978), 258–59.

practicing Muslims disbelieve it because Qur'an 4:157–58 expressly states that Jesus was taken up to God (*Allah*) without experiencing death. We will now consider a chief line of argument from each of these two positions.

The most popular contemporary voice claiming Jesus never existed belongs to Robert Price. Price is a biblical scholar,[13] a member of the Jesus Seminar,[14] and a former Baptist minister who has incessantly attacked Christianity for decades. While his contentions can seem endless, they rest on a handful of methodological assumptions about the study of history. Of these "commandments," as he calls them, none is more favored by Price when rejecting Jesus's existence than the criterion of *double dissimilarity*.[15]

The criterion of double dissimilarity is one of many tools used by scholars to assess the authenticity of historical reports.[16] Regarding Jesus in particular, it seeks to identify material in his narrated words and deeds that is unlike anything found in either contemporary Judaism or the subsequent Christian movement. The rationale is that if an expression, teaching, or action is without parallel, then it is more likely to have originated with Jesus himself instead of having been borrowed from another source and attributed to him. While this principle makes a certain kind of sense, it is also exceptionally and unnecessarily restrictive, for it can only reveal a Jesus who is patently un-Jewish and unchristian. As a comparison, one might consider what sort of historical Martin Luther we are left with

---

[13]To my knowledge, Richard Carrier is the only other living scholar with an earned graduate degree in a relevant field who denies Jesus's existence. (Price has a Ph.D. in New Testament studies, while Carrier's doctorate is in classics.)

[14]For a critique of the Jesus Seminar, see Luke Timothy Johnson, *The Real Jesus: The Misguided Quest for the Historical Jesus and the Truth of the Traditional Gospels* (New York: HarperCollins, 1996).

[15]Robert M. Price, "Jesus at the Vanishing Point," in *The Historical Jesus: Five Views*, ed. James K. Beilby and Paul Rhodes Eddy (Downers Grove, IL: InterVarsity Press, 2009), 55–83. Relatedly, Carrier's work rests entirely on employing Bayes's theorem as a necessary methodological approach to the historicity of Jesus.

[16]See Robert H. Stein, "Criteria for the Gospels' Authenticity," in *Contending with Christianity's Critics*, 88–103.

if the reformer cannot sound anything like the medieval Catholicism that preceded him or the Lutheran Church that came after him. Clearly, the value of this tool is limited.

Price expands this criterion to such an extent, however, that it loses its value completely. In addition to late Judaism and early Christianity as traditions against which Jesus material must be checked for similarities, all of Hellenism is included as well.[17] Meaning, nothing can be considered authentic about Jesus if it bears resemblance to virtually anything in the entire ancient Mediterranean world! For example, not only does Price render Jesus's betrayal by Judas ahistorical because Julius Caesar was also betrayed by a friend,[18] but he also explains away Jesus's death on a cross by citing the *near-death experiences* of certain characters in ancient romance novels.[19] What is more, with such a broad database for making comparisons, Price feels free to find composite characters wherever he wishes and employ them to his predetermined ends. Joseph of Arimathea, for instance, is dismissed as a combination of King Priam from Homer's *Iliad* and the Hebrew patriarch Joseph, since both asked for permission to bury someone close to them.[20] Indeed, the most routine, commonplace events pertaining to Jesus are rendered fictitious by this method. Not even the women weeping over his death can be accepted as true because it too closely resembles episodes in both Jewish and pagan literature where women also mourn over divine or heroic figures.[21] Parallels can thus be found everywhere, with Price taking the slightest resemblances as unmistakable evidence of fabrication on the part of the New Testament authors.

---

[17]Robert M. Price, *The Incredible Shrinking Son of Man: How Reliable Is the Gospel Tradition?* (New York: Prometheus, 2003), 16–17.

[18]Robert M. Price, *Jesus Christ Superstar: The Making of a Modern Gospel* (self-published: eBookIt.com, 2011).

[19]Robert M. Price, *Deconstructing Jesus* (New York: Prometheus, 2000), 213–26.

[20]Price, "Jesus at the Vanishing Point," 74.

[21]Price, *Deconstructing Jesus*, 213–26; idem, *Jesus is Dead* (Parsippany, NJ: American Atheist Press, 2007), 192.

This modified version of the double dissimilarity criterion is so difficult to satisfy that it becomes "all devouring," allowing Price to claim that absolutely no facts can be established about Jesus.[22] Yet it also makes it nearly impossible to know anything about *anyone* from history. In fact, it makes details about Price himself doubtful. Questions were raised about Jesus's existence before Price,[23] and people have more recently made claims like those found in writings bearing his name. One could suggest, then, that Jesus being a real person was never challenged by Price himself, but rather certain material found in other sources was retooled and attributed to him. Moreover, his personal story of falling away from the faith and becoming an anti-apologist is hardly unique, which, if we apply his own standard consistently, should raise questions about the very existence of one Dr. Robert Price.

The most egregious aspect of all this, however, is the simple fact that Price has twisted the purpose of the criterion of double dissimilarity. It was not framed to show *in*authenticity, as though failing to pass the test renders a given tradition historically unreliable. That is, if material about Jesus is also clearly found in the Judaism of his day or in primitive Christianity, the result is not a negative verdict but simply the observation that, according to this criterion, it cannot be traced back to Jesus himself. Other means may still succeed in establishing its historicity. Double dissimilarity, rather, functions positively and can only *increase* confidence that a passage is authentic.

Accordingly, Price is simply wrong when asserting, "The burden of proof would seem to belong with those who believe there was a historical man named Jesus."[24] On the contrary, ancient sources composed by disparate groups (Jews, Christians, Gnostics, Greeks, Romans) living soon after the person and events in question affirm that Jesus existed. The vast majority of modern scholars have also insisted that Jesus was a figure of history with no serious doubts. Add to this the fact that Price's handling of the criterion of double

---

[22]Price, "Jesus at the Vanishing Point," 60.

[23]Cf. Martin, *The Case against Christianity*, 37.

[24]Robert M. Price, *The Christ-Myth Theory and Its Problems* (Cranford, NJ: American Atheist Press), 15.

dissimilarity is flawed, and the burden of proof falls on the one who not only rejects the universally accepted position but also does so on faulty grounds.[25]

In Islamic theology, there is no doubt that Jesus was and is real. He is believed to have lived in first-century Palestine as a preacher of good news, the son of Mary, whose disciples thought he was a prophet and the Messiah. For most Muslims, however, these simple facts are not established by examining the historical record; instead, they are accepted as undeniable truths *because they are stated in the Qur'an.* This is also why Jesus's crucifixion is disbelieved. As mentioned above, Qur'an 4:157–58 clearly teaches that Jesus was never nailed to a cross. Any claim to the contrary, then, is unequivocally rejected because it opposes the (supposed) Word of Allah.

This approach, in which ideology undermines historical facts, is typified by the popular Muslim apologist Louay Fatoohi.[26] In his most comprehensive work on the identity of Jesus, Fatoohi largely manages to feign objectivity by citing the findings of liberal scholars against the integrity of the Gospels; yet he also reveals his own bias with a telling admission. He says, "I need to make it clear that this book follows the Qur'anic approach. Any information . . . that is relevant to the subject of this book will first be presented and then explained from the Qur'an's point of view. Presuming that the Qur'an is the Word of God, this book seeks to show the consistency of the Qur'anic story of Jesus and its alignment with historical facts."[27] Thus it is no surprise when, in *The Mystery of the Crucifixion,* Fatoohi denies every mention of Jesus's execution found in Christian writings as a fabrication, based on his religious commitment to a seventh-century text.[28] He also throws

---

[25]This basic point is even made by Bart D. Ehrman, *Did Jesus Exist? The Historical Argument for Jesus of Nazareth* (New York: HarperOne, 2012), 38–39.

[26]For a concise critique of Fatoohi's arguments, see Adam S. Francisco, "Defending the Deity of Jesus in the Face of Islam," in *Making the Case for Christianity,* 95–113.

[27]Louay Fatoohi, *The Mystery of the Historical Jesus: The Messiah in the Qur'an, the Bible, and Historical Sources* (Birmingham, AL: Luna Plena, 2007), 41–42.

[28]Craig Parton makes the point that such "testimony" as found in the Qur'an, some six centuries removed from the original witnesses to Jesus, would be

out all references found in Jewish, Greek, and Roman sources as well, an obvious indication that his conclusions are not based on accepted scholarship but on his presuppositions about the Qur'an. His weak reasoning is especially exposed when he claims no non-Christian sources can be accepted if there is even the *possibility* they were somehow influenced by Christians.[29] But historians determine what happened in the past based on *probability*, not possibility.[30] Otherwise, evidence becomes irrelevant and personal preference is the final arbiter.

What Fatoohi readily accepts as a reliable source instead, of course, is the Qur'an.[31] Yet it is extremely unlikely that any non-Muslim historian would give preference to this single work, coming at least five hundred to six hundred years later than the earliest relevant witnesses, over the consensus found in roughly sixty documents whose authors were both friendly and hostile to Christianity.[32] Once Muslim ideology is removed, the question of Jesus's fate is easily answered: he was crucified.

He Died, Indeed

While it may seem like a foregone conclusion that Jesus's crucifixion ended in death, some have argued otherwise in hopes of providing a naturalistic explanation for the resurrection appearances. This has been called the "apparent death theory" or "swoon theory." One version entails Jesus passing out or slipping into a coma and being mistaken for dead; the other suggests the soldiers were bribed and took him down from the cross before he expired. In either case, Jesus recovered, and the impression was given (with the help of his pierced

---

inadmissible as hearsay in a modern court of law.

[29]Louay Fatoohi, *The Mystery of the Crucifixion: The Attempt to Kill Jesus in the Qur'an, the Bible, and Historical Sources* (Birmingham, AL: Luna Plena, 2008), 69–84.

[30]See C. Behan McCullagh, *Justifying Historical Descriptions* (Cambridge: Cambridge University Press, 1984), 4.

[31]Interestingly, while the New Testament documents are undergoing a twenty-eighth critical edition for scholarly study, there remains to this date not a single scholarly critical edition of the Qur'an.

[32]See note 4 above.

hands and feet) that he had risen from the dead.[33] The primary problem with this theory is that it discounts the lethal nature of Jesus's scourging and crucifixion.[34]

When a victim was flogged by the Romans, a whip with several thongs was used with iron balls or sharp objects tied at intervals on each strand. The person was stripped naked and fastened to an upright post such that his entire backside was exposed and scourged. Soldiers repeatedly delivered blows with full force, causing violent contusions and lacerations. Eventually the skin would be torn away in various places, exposing veins, arteries, underlying muscles, intestines, and even bones. The purpose of this torture was to bring the victim to the point of physical collapse, just short of death.[35] Had Jesus been scourged only, he still would have been exceptionally weak, a fact attested by the Gospels reporting that someone else was compelled to carry Jesus's cross for him (Matthew 27:32; Mark 15:2; Luke 23:26).

Crucifixion as a means of death was intended to maximize a person's anguish. The word "excruciating" is derived from this experience and literally means "from the cross." While the initial nailing of one's hands and feet was indeed painful, the major problem was asphyxiation—or, being unable to breathe. As a victim hung suspended on a cross, his positioning would make it difficult to exhale unless he first pushed himself up on his pierced feet. To inhale, he would then have to lower himself by resting his body weight on his pierced hands. Repeating this action over and over again would cause severe pain, with muscle cramps and spasms making the act

---

[33]This theory was more popular in previous centuries, yet its persistence is attested by the 2003 BBC documentary film, *Did Jesus Die?*

[34]The skeptic David F. Strauss, *The Life of Jesus for the People* (London: Williams and Norgate, 1879), 1:412, vehemently rejected this theory on the grounds that a half-dead Jesus would neither be able to exit his sealed tomb nor convince people he was the Lord of life.

[35]On the nature of Roman scourging, see William D. Edwards, Wesley J. Gabel, and Floyd E. Hosmer, "On the Physical Death of Jesus Christ," *Journal of the American Medical Association*, 255.11 (March 1986): 1457; Craig A. Evans and N. T. Wright, *Jesus, the Final Days: What Really Happened* (Louisville, KY: Westminster John Knox, 2009), 30; Licona, *The Resurrection of Jesus*, 303–04.

of breathing increasingly difficult.[36] This lengthy suffocation process was so brutal that there is only one recorded instance of a Roman victim surviving after being taken down mid-crucifixion; yet unlike Jesus, that individual was not scourged prior, and he received the best medical care available.[37]

Roman centurions were accustomed to seeing people die by crucifixion, knowing that if someone no longer pushed himself up to breathe, he was very likely dead. It was a common procedure, however, to ensure the demise of the victim with a spear wound to the heart.[38] As reported in John 19:34, this is what happened to Jesus, causing a flow of blood and water to pour from his side, likely because the pericardium sac around his heart was ruptured.[39] In these and other details, the Gospels' reports of Jesus's treatment at the hands of the Romans comports with what we know of their first-century practices.[40] The medical evidence as examined by modern-day physicians also confirms that Jesus was definitely dead when taken down from the cross.[41]

He Was Buried, Indeed

One of the most recent scholars to reject Jesus's burial is the notorious unbeliever, Bart Ehrman.

Formerly a fundamentalist, Ehrman has challenged nearly every aspect of traditional Christianity and regularly produces popular-level books against the integrity of the New Testament. In his denial of Jesus's burial, Ehrman (in typical fashion) relays his

---

[36]Edwards, Gabel, and Hosmer, "On the Physical Death of Jesus Christ," 1461.

[37]See Habermas and Licona, *The Case for the Resurrection of Jesus*, 301–02.

[38]Quintilian, *Declarationes maiores* 6.9.

[39]Habermas and Licona, *The Case for the Resurrection of Jesus*, 102.

[40]Evans and Wright, *Jesus, the Finals Days*, 28. The Gospel accounts also report that verification of the death of Jesus took place, not only by the crucifying Roman soldiers at Golgotha (John 19:31–35) but also by Pilate himself before he would release the body to Joseph of Arimathea (Mark 15:44–45).

[41]See the extensive analysis of Frederick T. Zugibe, M.D., Ph.D., *The Crucifixion of Jesus: A Forensic Inquiry*, 2nd ed. (New York: M. Evans, 2005).

personal journey from belief in what Scripture says to his current position of agnosticism. When he first heard the suggestion that, like a common criminal, Jesus's body was left for scavenging dogs to devour,[42] Ehrman thought it was "excessive and sensationalist." But after doing a bit of research himself, he could no longer affirm the Gospels' assertion that Jesus was entombed by Joseph of Arimathea. "My view now," Ehrman concludes, "is that we do not know, and cannot know, what actually happened to Jesus' body."[43] Just how compelling, then, is the historical case *against* Jesus's burial?

It must be noted from the outset that Ehrman's argument primarily rests on his view that "the Gospels cannot simply be taken at face value as giving us historically reliable accounts" about Jesus. His reasons are as follows: (1) The Gospels were composed too late to be considered credible; (2) because they are anonymous (with their traditional names having been added later), they cannot have come from eyewitnesses; (3) stories about Jesus were changed, invented, and exaggerated long before the Gospels were written, with no way to control the information; and (4) the authors were motived by theological concerns and therefore were not interested in giving historically accurate information.[44]

These points have been answered in detail by other New Testament scholars and apologists, such that we need only address them briefly here. (1) Ehrman himself claims Matthew, Mark, and Luke were written roughly thirty-five to forty-five years after Jesus.[45] This remains within the lifetime of eyewitnesses—both friendly and hostile ones—who would have corrected or protested any glaring inaccuracies about what Jesus did and said. It is also a remarkably short interval between the events and their being committed to writing

---

[42]See John Dominic Crossan, *Jesus: A Revolutionary Biography* (San Francisco, CA: HarperOne, 1994), 172–76.

[43]Bart D. Ehrman, *How Jesus Became God: The Exaltation of a Jewish Preacher from Galilee* (New York: HarperOne, 2014), 157.

[44]Ibid., 88–93.

[45]Ehrman, *Jesus*, 48.

when compared to other works of antiquity.[46] Our major sources on
Alexander the Great, for example, come hundreds of years after his
death; yet historians accept them as generally reliable. (2) While the
Gospels were originally anonymous, their contents can still be traced
back to eyewitnesses. Around AD 80, a man named Papias acquired
information on who wrote the first two Gospels, relying on the testimony of those who knew Jesus's disciples. He concluded that Matthew
wrote his own account, and Mark recorded Peter's words.[47] The Gospel
of Luke contains a preface (1:1–4) wherein the author stressed how he
carefully investigated everything and relied on eyewitnesses. The fourth
Gospel explicitly states its author was an eyewitness (John 21:20–24).
(3) Ehrman claims people told stories about Jesus akin to the childhood game of "telephone," in which the very transmission of information facilitates its distortion.[48] Various studies of oral cultures
have shown, however, that the retelling of major events and their
significance remained constant, due in part to key individuals possessing a common memory of what happened (as Jesus's disciples
would have).[49] (4) Theological concerns do not automatically result

---

[46]Or indeed works of modern times. One cannot but think of biographers
whose lives are/were contemporaneous with their subjects. How much more
reliable they are when biographers personally know their subjects and live in
the same regions and experience the same customs, conversations, and events!

[47]On the dates involving Papias, see Bauckham, *Jesus and the Eyewitnesses*,
15. Bart D. Ehrman, *Jesus Before the Gospels: How the Earliest Christians
Remembered, Changed, and Invented Their Stories of the Savior* (New York:
HarperOne, 2016), 111–18, mainly dismisses Papias because not everything
he reported was accurate, and because a church father living two centuries
later considered him unintelligent. A strong case, however, that Papias's information on the first two Gospels originated with the apostle John is made by
Robert H. Gundry, *Mark: A Commentary on His Apology for the Cross* (Grand
Rapids, MI: Eerdmans, 1993), 1026–45.

[48]Ehrman, *Jesus*, 51–52; cf. idem, *How Jesus Became God*, 93; idem, *Jesus
Before the Gospels*, 190.

[49]In Ehrman's latest work, *Jesus Before the Gospels*, he appears to cite and
interpret scholars in such a way that his long-held skepticism toward the
Gospels is vindicated. Eddy and Boyd, *The Jesus Legend*, 237–308, deal with
many of the same topics and scholars, yet their extensive treatment reveals a
faithfully preserved pre-Gospel oral tradition.

in bad history writing any more than *anti*-theological concerns do. Whereas Ehrman thinks the Gospels are a form of propaganda,[50] the classicist Richard Burridge has shown how similar they are to Greco-Roman biographies, a genre in which authors intended to communicate factual history.[51]

Specifically regarding Jesus's claimed burial, Ehrman suggests the following scenario. After Jesus's demise, his followers began to have mystical (or imagined) encounters with a heavenly, glorified Jesus. While this Jesus was merely raised as a spirit, Christians soon began to claim that he was raised physically, with the same body that died on the cross. Eventually, the empty tomb was invented as a means to prove that Jesus had risen in bodily form. This led to the burial story, since there must first have been an occupied tomb.[52] In short, the burial of Jesus was a key component in Christians' attempt to bridge the gap between their uncanny postmortem experiences of an exalted Jesus and the public knowledge of Jesus's crucifixion.[53]

While the problems with this theory are manifold, we will contest two key points of Ehrman's argument. First, Ehrman finds evidence in what the earliest known creed about Jesus *does not* say. In 1 Corinthians 15:3–4, Paul reiterated the essence of the Gospel message: "For I delivered to you as of first importance what I also received: that Christ died for our sins in accordance with the Scriptures, that he was buried, that he was raised on the third day in accordance with the Scriptures." While Jesus's burial is indeed mentioned, Ehrman thinks this part is fictional because it fails to mention either a tomb or the person who supposedly buried Jesus, Joseph of Arimathea. Due to the important apologetic role the empty tomb came to play, Ehrman assumes Paul "surely would have included" these

---

[50]Ehrman, *Jesus*, 30.

[51]Richard A. Burridge, *What Are the Gospels? A Comparison with Greco-Roman Biography*, 2nd ed. (Grand Rapids, MI: Eerdmans, 2004); see also Eddy and Boyd, *The Jesus Legend*, 259–68, 309–36.

[52]Ehrman, *How Jesus Became God*, 168–83.

[53]Compare this conjecture with the observation of historian Michael Grant, *Jesus: An Historian's Review of the Gospels* (New York: Scribner's, 1977), 176: "The historian cannot justifiably deny the empty tomb . . . the evidence necessitates the conclusion that the tomb was found empty."

details if he had known about them. What is more, Ehrman notes how Paul went on to give specific names of people who saw the risen Lord, making the absence of Joseph, a prominent member of the Jewish Council, all the more conspicuous.[54]

This is an argument from silence, with Ehrman relying on guess-work to reach his conclusions, all the while ignoring the genre of creedal transmission that constitutes 1 Corinthians 15:3–5. He nearly admits as much when, after raising the question of why the author omitted this information, he says, "*My hunch* is that it is because he knew nothing about a burial of Jesus by Joseph of Arimathea."[55] A hunch is merely speculation, and one person's hunch is as good as another's. Perhaps there is no mention of Jesus being "buried *in a tomb*" because the phrase is redundant, like someone today saying "buried *in a grave*" or "cremated *into ashes*." Perhaps Paul thought it far more significant to name key witnesses of Jesus's miraculous res-urrection than to name people like Judas, Caiaphas, Pilate, or Joseph, who merely participated in Jesus's earthly fate. Indeed, there could be many legitimate reasons why the creed left out these details. Thus it is irresponsible for Ehrman to treat the absence of evidence as evi-dence for his own views.[56]

The second major problem with Ehrman's position is his assess-ment of what the Romans normally did with the corpses of people they crucified. While he remains agnostic about what ultimately happened in Jesus's case, Ehrman cites various ancient documents to suggest that the body of Jesus either was never buried or was placed into a common grave reserved for criminals. In fact, he argues, Jesus's body probably remained on the cross for some time to decompose. This is because the Romans, not the Jews, had executed him; and the Jews were powerless to keep the cruel Romans from desecrating Jewish burial customs and laws. Ehrman adds that Pilate would certainly not have allowed a cru-cified victim to receive a decent burial.[57]

---

[54]Ehrman, *How Jesus Became God*, 141–42, 153.

[55]Ibid., 142; emphasis mine.

[56]Cf. David Henige, *Historical Evidence and Argument* (Madison, WI: University of Wisconsin Press, 2005), 175–76, 184.

[57]Ehrman, *How Jesus Became God*, 160–63.

Craig Evans, a New Testament scholar who has written at length on both Jewish burial practices and the Roman world in which Jesus lived, forcefully and convincingly disputes Ehrman's analysis. Regarding Ehrman's portrayal of Roman policy regarding the nonburial of crucified victims, Evans says it is unknown just how regular a practice it was to leave corpses up for an extended period of time. Regardless, numerous exceptions can be found in written sources. For example, Roman law reads, "The bodies of those who are condemned to death should not be refused their relatives . . . [and] should be given to whoever requests them for the purpose of burial" (*Digesta* 48.24.1, 3).[58] The Jewish historian Josephus also observed: "The Jews are so careful about burial rites that even malefactors who have been sentenced to be crucified are taken down and buried before sunset" (*Jewish War* 4.317).[59] Add to this the fact that the Jewish Council was required to bury the body of anyone it condemned to death (as it had Jesus), and it makes perfect sense that one of its members, Joseph of Arimathea, would be charged with the task.[60] Thus Ehrman's use of the sources is insufficient.

Finally, in 1968, the bones of an ancient Jewish male were found inside of an ossuary (a container for skeletal remains), with an iron spike still protruding from his right heel bone and a piece of wood adhering to the spike. Clearly he had died on a cross. Since ossuaries were used to gather up the bones of someone whose flesh had decayed after being buried, this specimen provides tangible evidence that burial was permitted at times for victims of crucifixion. Furthermore, the ossuary and its contents date to the late AD 20s, which is when Pilate himself was governor. Pilate, then, having condemned this individual to a cross like he did Jesus, must also have granted permission for the internment. Ehrman is aware of

---

[58]Quoted in Craig A. Evans, "Getting the Burial Traditions and Evidence Right," in *How God Became Jesus: The Real Origins of Belief in Jesus' Divine Nature: A Response to Bart D. Ehrman*, ed. Michael F. Bird (Grand Rapids, MI: Zondervan, 2014), 76.

[59]Quoted in Ibid., 78–79.

[60]Ibid., 80–81, 87–89.

this archaeological evidence[61] but conveniently omits it when arguing that Jesus would not have been entombed. Based on this and
other glaring oversights, his conjecture about the early creed, and his
unconvincing case against the Gospels as reliable sources, Ehrman's
dismissal of Jesus's burial flies in the face of the historical record.

Easter: Four Narratives, One Reality

We now turn from Good Friday to Easter Sunday to consider if
the reports of what happened contain contradictions. It should be
remembered that we are bracketing out the question of whether miracles are possible and are merely taking the accounts as they stand.

Quality, Not Quantity

Bart Ehrman has also claimed the Gospels are "filled with
discrepancies . . . on nearly every detail in their resurrection narratives." This is a common objection to the truth of Easter: how can
we accept the historical fact of the resurrection if the Gospels contradict each other on the historical particulars? Ehrman is so confident that these differences can instill doubt, he invites people to read
the four Easter stories while asking simple questions, such as: Who
went to the tomb first? Was the stone rolled away when the women
got there? Did they see one man, one angel, two men, or two angels?
Did the women tell the disciples what happened or not? Where did
the disciples see Jesus—only in Galilee or only in Jerusalem? Ehrman
thinks that after people see so many problems, they will either be
forced to admit the Gospels are untrustworthy, or people will have to
do "a lot of interpretive gymnastics" to harmonize them.[62]

Before we see if attempts at harmonization require as much
fudging as Ehrman imagines, an important point regarding historiography needs to be made. The veracity of the core event(s)
in historical reports is not jeopardized when inconsistencies exist
involving peripheral details that are of little significance. In other

---

[61]Ehrman, *Jesus*, 224.

[62]Ehrman, *How Jesus Became God*, 134.

words, to think that apparent conflicts regarding relatively minor points of a narrative disprove the central fact(s) is "bad historiography."[63] This is especially the case when the sources have been shown to contain generally reliable data. Four brief examples from history help illustrate this point.

First, the ancient Greek historian Thucydides was bothered by the fact that not all written accounts of the Peloponnesian War were in agreement. Since he had served as a general during the war, however, these incongruities could not dissuade him from knowing whether the war occurred or who won. Second, the great fire of Rome in the first century was recounted by three primary sources (Tacitus, Suetonius, and Dio Cassius), which differ on some intriguing details. Did Nero order the city to be burned? If so, did he send men openly or secretly to set the fire? Did Nero watch Rome burn, or was he thirty-five miles away at the time? If the former, from what location did he witness the fire? Despite the varied answers found in our sources, no serious historian would doubt that Rome actually burned. Third, survivors of the *Titanic* contradicted each other about whether the ship broke in two or remained intact. This may seem like a strange point of contention for eyewitnesses, but that the *Titanic* sunk was not disputed by anyone. Lastly, there is perhaps no recent historical event about which more disagreement exists than the death of President John F. Kennedy. Conflicting theories, testimonies, and evidences abound, with new books being published regularly that attempt to set the record straight. And yet, the chief event of Kennedy's assassination in Dallas via gunfire remains an accepted fact.[64]

This same principle of historiography should be applied to the Gospels. Virtually every question Ehrman raises about discrepancies in the Easter narratives pertains to peripheral details; yet the core of each account lines up remarkably well with the others, thus strengthening their credibility on the central event of Jesus's resurrection.

---

[63]David Baggett, "Resurrection Matters," in *Did the Resurrection Happen? A Conversation Between Gary Habermas and Antony Flew*, ed. David Baggett (Downers Grove, IL: InterVarsity Press, 2009), 116.

[64]Licona, *The Resurrection of Jesus*, 597–98.

Interestingly, Ehrman does follow this historical procedure when it comes to other chief events in Jesus's life. Regarding his passion and death, for instance, Ehrman questions consistency between the Gospels on when Pilate had him scourged, whether Jesus carried his own cross, and the date and time of the crucifixion.[65] However, Ehrman definitively concludes: "One of the most certain facts of history is that Jesus was crucified on orders of the Roman prefect of Judea, Pontius Pilate."[66] While we cannot say for certain why Ehrman selectively applies this approach, his inconstancy as a scholar is plainly evident.

Reconciling the Differences

What is a contradiction? Strictly speaking, a contradiction occurs when two or more statements of fact yield mutually exclusive conclusions. Or, to paraphrase Aristotle, it is logically impossible to say something both *is* the case and *is not* the case at the same time. Regarding the Gospels, it would be a serious problem if, for example, one account said the women went to the tomb of Jesus on Sunday and saw him there, while another report *explicitly* said no women went to the tomb on that day and they never saw him. This would be an irreconcilable difference, a contradiction, and we find nothing so egregious in the resurrection narratives. Even if we did, however, it would not mean that both claims are necessarily false; one could be right and the other wrong. Yet Ehrman seems to think the fact that differences exist between the texts means none of them can be correct. Thus he not only confuses discrepancies with contradictions but also comes to an unreasonable conclusion.

---

[65]Bart D. Ehrman, *Jesus, Interrupted: Revealing the Hidden Contradictions in the Bible (and Why We Don't Know About Them)* (New York: HarperOne, 2009), 23–27, 44–45; idem, *Truth and History in the Da Vinci Code: A Historian Reveals What We Really Know about Jesus, Mary Magdalene, and Constantine* (Oxford: Oxford University Press, 2006), 116–17. These issues are handled well by Craig S. Keener, *The Gospel of John: A Commentary* (Peabody, MA: Hendrickson, 2003), 2:1070–72, 1100–03, 1120, 1129–31, 1133–34.

[66]Quoted in Licona, *The Resurrection of Jesus*, 600.

A brief illustration from Ehrman's own life story is relevant here. In one of his books, he talks about his strong beliefs all through graduate school, claiming he "started to lose his faith" sometime later. But elsewhere, he says it was precisely in graduate school that a "seismic shift" occurred, and he began to have serious doubts. Similarly, Ehrman clearly states that his faith had been "based completely on a certain view of the Bible," such that the more he studied it, the less he believed. Yet in other places, Ehrman claims, "But the problems of the Bible are not what led me to leave the faith." So which is it? Did Ehrman lose his faith during graduate school or afterward? Was it because his view of the Bible changed or not? If we follow his own line of reasoning, we should reject both accounts as unreliable.[67]

Regarding the alleged disparities between the Easter narratives, nothing like "interpretive gymnastics" is required to answer the above questions raised by Ehrman.

1. *Who went to the tomb first?* The names of the women given by Matthew, Mark, and Luke are not all the same, but Luke (24:10) also notes there was a group of women. Each author, then, simply chose to name some and not others. John only names Mary Magdalene, but her words indicate others were with her: "[W]e do not know where they laid him" (John 20:2).

2. *Was the stone rolled away when the women got there?* Mark, Luke, and John say the stone was rolled away by the time they arrived. Matthew, however, first writes that the women went to the tomb (28:1) and then says an angel descended and rolled it away (28:2). A careful reading of Matthew's wording, however, reveals that he does not claim the women were present for this occurrence; rather,

---

[67]Compare the wording of these remembrances in Bart D. Ehrman, *God's Problem: How the Bible Fails to Answer Our Most Important Question—Why We Suffer* (New York: HarperOne, 2008), 1–2; idem, *Misquoting Jesus: The Story Behind Who Changed the Bible and Why*, reprint (New York: HarperOne, 2007), 11–12.

Matthew is explaining what had already happened before
their arrival.

3. *Did they see one man, two men, one angel, or two angels?*
   This is answered in two points. First, angels were occasion-
   ally referred to as "men."[68] Second, if firsthand testimony
   was used, there is no reason to think all the eyewitnesses
   mentioned (or even saw) both angels.[69] Additionally, eyewitness reports are often shaped by the specific questions
   being asked, and the individual concerns of each Gospel
   writer may also account for why some omitted the second
   angel. But since none of them say there was *only* one angel,
   there is no contradiction.

4. *Did the women tell the disciples what happened or not?*
   Mark 16:8 says the women fled the tomb and "said nothing to no one," whereas in the other Gospels, they report
   what they saw and heard. This apparent disagreement has
   generated various explanations, but a fairly simple one is
   possible. The phrase "said nothing to no one" is similar to
   what Jesus says in Mark 1:44. After healing a leper, Jesus
   sternly warned: "See that you say nothing to no one. But
   go show yourself to the priest." The implication is that the
   healed man was to avoid telling others his good news first
   but instead go straight to the priest and tell him. Likewise,
   the women at the tomb were ordered by the angel to go
   inform the disciples of Jesus's resurrection. They therefore
   "said nothing to no one" along the way but rather shared
   the good news of Easter with the disciples first. While not

---

[68]See Tobit 5:5, 7, 10; Daniel 9:21; Acts 1:10. Luke uses these terms inter-
changeably on two occasions: Luke 24:3, 23; Acts 10:3, 30.

[69]J. Warner Wallace, *Cold-Case Christianity: A Homicide Detective
Investigates the Truth of the Gospels* (Colorado Springs, CO: David C. Cook,
2013), 77: "A lot depends on where a witness is located in relationship to
the action. We've also got to consider the personal experiences and interests
that cause some witnesses to focus on one aspect of the event and some to
focus on another."

conclusive, many scholars have found this interpretation persuasive.[70]

5. *Where did the disciples see Jesus—only in Galilee or only in Jerusalem?* The way Ehrman poses the question makes it easy to solve. To be sure, Matthew and Luke[71] only make mention of Jesus's appearances in Galilee and Jerusalem, respectively; yet nothing in their wording excludes the possibility that Jesus also appeared elsewhere (e.g., Emmaus). Again, the authors focused on select information for the sake of their particular narratives.

While not everyone will be satisfied with these proposed solutions, they are enough to show that the apparent conflicts are nowhere near as impossible to reconcile as Ehrman makes them seem. These are merely differences, not contradictions, each of which involves minor points of secondary importance.

Conclusion

A lot of territory has been covered in this chapter. We have seen how Jesus's fate on Good Friday is firmly established by the evidence despite challenges to the contrary. Robert Price's denial of Jesus's existence is a fringe theory largely based on a mishandling of the criterion of double dissimilarity. It results in rank skepticism not only toward Jesus but toward the entire field of history as well. For Louay Fatoohi, his ideology dictates how the facts are examined, causing him to conclude Jesus was never crucified. In essence, his position can be reduced to a single expression: "The Qur'an said it. I believe it. That settles it!" Since there is every reason to affirm that Jesus was nailed to a cross, there is likewise no reason to think he somehow survived this experience. Such a suggestion discounts

---

[70]See the discussion in Licona, *The Resurrection of Jesus*, 344–49.

[71]I. Howard Marshall, *The Gospel of Luke* (Grand Rapids, MI: Eerdmans, 1978), 970, notes Luke's use of narrative compression (or "telescoping," a practice that allowed historians to skip some details and condense others) with his Easter account.

the brutal nature of Roman scourging and crucifixion and ignores the medical evidence.

Bart Ehrman has disputed both Jesus's burial and resurrection on the grounds that the Gospels are deficient historical sources. We have seen, however, that his findings are highly questionable. When disputing the phrase "he was buried" in the earliest known creed, Ehrman relies on conjecture and the argument from silence. He selectively uses sources and omits archaeological evidence in his case against Joseph of Arimathea placing Jesus's body in a tomb. Ehrman also draws attention to differences in the Easter narratives, thinking they are telltale signs of the Gospels' defective character. In so doing, he not only mistakes them for outright contradictions; he also misconstrues problems with peripheral details as though they constitute grounds for dismissing the central event of Jesus's resurrection. Additionally, the discrepancies he names are not beyond reconciliation.

Where does this leave us? Historians are called to give the best explanation that takes into account all the available evidence. While our topics entail more issues than those covered here, we have encountered nothing that casts unanswerable historical doubt on the resurrection of Jesus. Therefore, regarding what really happened on that first Easter Sunday, we remain warranted in our belief and justified in our proclamation, "He is risen, indeed!"

Recommended Reading

Craig, William Lane. "Did Jesus Rise from the Dead?" In *Jesus Under Fire: Modern Scholarship Reinvents the Historical Jesus*. Edited by Michael J. Wilkens and J. P. Moreland, 141–76. Grand Rapids, MI: Zondervan, 1995.

Eddy, Paul Rhodes, and Gregory A. Boyd. *The Jesus Legend: A Case for the Historical Reliability of the Synoptic Jesus Tradition*. Grand Rapids, MI: Baker, 2007.

Evans, Craig A. "Getting the Burial Traditions and Evidence Right." In *How God Became Jesus: The Real Origins of Belief in Jesus' Divine Nature: A Response to Bart D. Ehrman*. Edited by Michael F. Bird, 71–93. Grand Rapids, MI: Zondervan, 2014.

Evans, Craig A., and N. T. Wright. *Jesus, the Final Days: What Really Happened*. Louisville, KY: Westminster John Knox, 2009.

Francisco, Adam S. "Defending the Deity of Jesus in the Face of Islam." In *Making the Case for Christianity: Responding to Modern Objections*. Edited by Adam S. Francisco and Korey D. Maas, 95–113. St. Louis, MO: Concordia, 2014.

Habermas, Gary R. "The Core Resurrection Data: The Minimal Facts Approach." In *Tough-Minded Christianity*. Edited by William Dembski and Thomas Schirrmacher, 387–405. Nashville, TN: B&H, 2008.

Habermas, Gary R., and Michael R. Licona. *The Case for the Resurrection of Jesus*. Grand Rapids, MI: Kregel, 2004.

Licona, Michael R. *Paul Meets Muhammad: A Christian-Muslim Debate on the Resurrection*. Grand Rapids, MI: Baker, 2006.

———. *The Resurrection of Jesus: A New Historiographical Approach*. Downers Grove, IL: InterVarsity Press, 2010.

Parton, Craig A. "Lawyers, Trials, and Evidence: Easter Triumph, Easter Legend, or Easter Fraud?" In *Making the Case for Christianity: Responding to Modern Objections*. Edited by Adam S. Francisco and Korey D. Maas, 69–92. St. Louis, MO: Concordia, 2014.

Wright, N. T. *The Resurrection of the Son of God*. Minneapolis, MN: Fortress Press, 2003.

2

Can a Historian Explain the Empty Tomb with the Resurrection of Jesus?

Adam S. Francisco

No historian doubts Julius Caesar was assassinated on the ides of March of 44 BC, and rarely do they question Jesus of Nazareth's crucifixion a little less than a century later. It is, as one skeptic put it, the one thing about Jesus that is "as sure as anything historical can be."[1] When it comes to Jesus's resurrection, though, there is little consensus. Few doubt he was buried and that the tomb was empty three days later. But for many, the general presumption is that historical approaches to the life of Jesus cannot explain the empty tomb by appealing to the resurrection.

Why? The evidence is the same for it as for the crucifixion. (It is even stronger than the evidence for Julius Caesar's assassination.) Yet while the death of Jesus on a cross is believable, the resurrection is not. This chapter explores the reasons a historian might make such a claim by exposing the philosophical assumptions behind what is often called the "historical problem of miracles." It then describes the assumptions of historical research and the implications they have on the empty tomb. The result will be a basic yet essential introduction to historical thinking and the resurrection.[2]

---

[1]John Dominic Crossan, *Jesus: A Revolutionary Biography* (New York: Harper Collins, 1991), 145.

[2]For a book-length treatment, see Michael Licona, *The Resurrection of Jesus: A New Historiographical Approach* (Downers Grove, IL: InterVarsity Press, 2010).

Hume, Historical Research, and Miracles

The origin of the discussion about historical research and what it is capable of describing relative to the case of miracles can be traced back to the eighteenth-century Scottish philosopher and historian named David Hume (1711–1776) and his celebrated work titled *An Enquiry Concerning Human Understanding*. Hume wrote the book to advance a robust empiricist epistemology and applied it to a variety of fields of research, including history and religion. He was no friend of the latter. "[O]ne of his most basic philosophical objectives," writes Paul Russell, was "to unmask and discredit the doctrines and dogmas of orthodox religious belief."[3] So, recognizing that the veracity of Christianity rested on the resurrection of Jesus, Hume went after it by attacking the legitimacy of claims that miracles of whatever sort have occurred and can be demonstrated by the historical method.

There are two parts to his argument. First, he reasoned philosophically: "A miracle is a violation of the laws of nature; and as a firm and unalterable experience has established these laws, the proof against a miracle, from the very nature of the fact, is as entire as any argument from experience can possibly be imagined."[4] That is, the normal everyday experience of human beings suggests that miracles are not part of the natural or normal order of things. The order that humans observe in nature is, he presumed, static and determined by natural, physical laws. These laws are fixed. They do not change, nor can they be suspended. Therefore the very concept of a miracle— defined by Hume as a "violation" of these laws—makes their occurrence unbelievable, if not virtually impossible.

Hume then applied his philosophy to claims that a miraculous event had actually occurred. He wrote, "The plain consequence is (and it is a general maxim worthy of our attention) that no testimony is sufficient to establish a miracle unless the testimony be of such a kind that its falsehood would be more miraculous than the fact which

---

[3]Paul Russell, "Hume on Religion," in *The Stanford Encyclopedia of Philosophy* (Winter 2014 edition), ed. Edward N. Zalta, http://plato.stanford .edu/archives/win2014/entries/hume-religion/.

[4]David Hume, *An Enquiry Concerning Human Understanding* (New York: The Liberal Arts Press, 1955), 122.

it endeavors to establish."[5] Because of the high (and almost certain) unlikelihood of a miracle ever occurring, no testimony—directly from eyewitnesses or from reports based on eyewitness testimony—can be sufficient enough to merit belief unless the reports become more incredible if the events they purport to describe were untrue. Or, in other words, the less incredible (or miraculous) explanation of an event is always to be preferred even if it contradicts good eyewitness testimony.

It was, in his mind, always more likely that eyewitnesses reporting miracles had lied or been mistaken. So in the case of a claim that a resurrection occurred, he suggested:

> I immediately consider with myself whether it be more probable that this person would either deceive or be deceived, or that the fact which he relates should really have happened. I weigh the one miracle against the other, and according to the superiority which I discover I pronounce my decision, and always reject the greater miracle. If the falsehood of his testimony would be more miraculous than the event which he relates, then, and not till then, can he pretend to command my belief or opinion.[6]

Hume's argument provoked a variety of responses from philosophers and Christian apologists alike almost immediately after its publication.[7] One of the most well known was the satirical *Historic Doubts Relative to Napoleon Bounaparte*, where Richard Whately (1787–1863) took Hume's principles, applied them to the extraordinary life of the then exiled emperor of the French, and found that the same line of reasoning forced one to doubt his existence.[8] The irony was that Napoleon was still living at the time. The same approach was also applied to the extraordinary life of Abraham Lincoln and incredible

---

[5]Ibid., 123.

[6]Ibid., 123–24.

[7]See James Fieser, ed., *Early Responses to Hume's Writings on Religion* (New York: Bloomsbury Publishing, 2005).

[8]See Craig Parton, *Richard Whately: A Man for All Seasons* (Edmonton, AB: Canadian Institute for Law, Theology, and Public Policy), 1997.

events at the Battle of Bunker Hill.[9] They all served to illustrate the philosophical and methodological weakness of Hume's maxim that no testimony—contemporary or historical—was sufficient enough to warrant acceptance of an incredible or miraculous event like a resurrection as a historical fact.

Despite the wide array of historical and contemporary criticism in works like C. S. Lewis's *Miracles* (1947/1960) and John Earman's *Hume's Abject Failure* (2000), the eighteenth-century skeptic's influence persists—even in the realm of theology. John Warwick Montgomery notes, "Hume's *Enquiry* can be said without exaggeration to mark the end of the era of classical Christian apologetics."[10] Jesus's miracles were a mainstay in the apologetic tradition until the eighteenth century, where especially the resurrection was marshaled as undeniable evidence for the deity of Jesus and therefore the compelling nature of his teachings. But after Hume, that ceased to be the case. His influence is still pervasive and remains especially strong in biblical scholarship, "endorsed, explicitly or implicitly, in many contemporary studies of the historical Jesus . . . and the New Testament."[11] A contemporary version of it is on display in what has been described as the standard text for introductory New Testament courses—Bart Ehrman's *New Testament: A Historical Introduction to the Early Christian Writings.*

Ehrman, Historical Research, and Miracles

Ehrman's *Introduction* treats the New Testament as the best available source for understanding the life of Jesus and the early Christian church worthy of the historian's attention. The miracles its authors

---

[9]See Oliver Price Buel, *The Abraham Lincoln Myth* (New York: The Mascot Publishing Co., 1894) and Charles Hudson, *Doubts Concerning the Battle of Bunker Hill* (Boston, MA: James Munroe and Co., 1857).

[10]John Warwick Montgomery, "Science, Theology, and the Miraculous," in *Faith Founded on Fact: Essays in Evidential Apologetics* (Edmonton, AB: Canadian Institute for Law, Theology, and Public Policy, 2001), 44.

[11]Timothy McGrew, "Miracles," in *The Stanford Encyclopedia of Philosophy* (Winter 2015 edition), ed. Edward N. Zalta, http://plato.stanford.edu/archives/win2015/entries/miracles/.

describe, however, are not. The reasons are set forth in the excursus titled "The Historian and the Problem of Miracle."[12]

Ehrman begins his case against historians being able to acknowledge miracles with the assertion: "Even if miracles *are* possible, there is no way for the historian who sticks strictly to the canons of historical evident [*sic*] to *show* that they have ever happened." The argument he advances to support this is what he calls "the 'historical' problem of miracle." This is an attempt to distinguish it from the fairly obvious presumptuousness of "the 'philosophical' problem of miracles." The latter assumes miracles do not occur, even that the very term is nonsensical, and thus rules out the miracles that Jesus performed.

This is very much the basis of Hume's first argument—namely, that miracles are a violation of the laws of nature. The laws of nature are, from the uniform experience of humans, firm and unalterable. Nothing—not even eyewitness testimony regardless of how good— would rise to the level (nowhere near it) of considering the claims that a miracle occurred.

Ehrman's argument is only slightly different. He begins by defining a miracle not as a violation of the laws of nature but an event "that contradict[s] the normal workings of nature in such a way as to be virtually beyond belief and to require an acknowledgment that supernatural forces have been at work." Immediately, he claims, this poses a "major stumbling block" for historians. They "have no access to supernatural forces but only to the public record, that is, to events that can be observed and interpreted by any reasonable person of any religious persuasion." And this precludes a supernatural explanation for extraordinary events.

Why? "If accepting the occurrence of a miracle requires belief in the supernatural realm, and historians by the very nature of their craft can speak only about events of the natural world (which are accessible to observers of every kind) how can they ever certify that an event *outside* the natural order—that is, a miracle—occurred?"

---

[12]Bart Ehrman, *The New Testament: A Historical Introduction to the Early Christian Writings*, 4th ed. (New York: Oxford University Press, 2008), 240–45. All subsequent quotations in this section, unless otherwise noted, come from this excursus.

Ehrman is cautious here not to appear presumptuous by ruling out the possibility of a miracle. He acknowledges, "I'm willing to grant that miracles . . . can and do happen." He just does not believe there can ever be sufficient evidence to establish that one has occurred and explains by comparing the historical discipline to the empirical sciences.

On the basis of and over the course of their experiments and empirical observations, scientists offer predictions of what will happen in the future. Historians work by describing singular, unrepeatable events of the past. Historical descriptions of what happened in the past are, by the unrepeatable and particular nature of their work, much less reliable than scientific descriptions of what will happen in the future. "Since historians cannot repeat the past in order to establish what has probably happened," he concludes, "there will always be less certainty in their conclusions . . . And the farther back you go in history, the harder it is to mount a convincing case."

This is especially the case with a miracle. Irrespective of when it allegedly happened, the evidence will always be so problematic and weak by comparison to what normally happens as to preclude the historian from affirming that such an event occurred. Miracles are unrepeatable events that defy what normally occurs in the natural world. They are thus extremely improbable. Yet the historian works in the realm of what is probable, argues Ehrman. Thus,

> Miracles create an inescapable dilemma for historians. Since historians can only establish what probably happened in the past, and the chances of a miracle happening, by definition, are infinitesimally remote, historians can never demonstrate that a miracle probably happened . . . Even if there are otherwise good sources for a miraculous event, the very nature of the historical discipline prevents the historian from arguing for its probability.

What this all means, then, is that the best explanation for the empty tomb on Easter morning is most probably not that Jesus rose from the dead.

The historian—if he is abiding by the canons of historical research and not imposing his or her faith on the evidence— has to remain neutral on the question of miracles, especially the resurrection. During a debate with apologist William Lane Craig in 2006, Ehrman put it this way:

> I'm not saying it didn't happen; but if it did happen, it would be a miracle. The resurrection claims that not only did Jesus's body come back alive; it came back alive never to die again. That's a violation of what naturally happens, every day, time after time, millions of times a year. What are the chances of that happening? Well, it'd be a miracle. In other words, it'd be so highly improbable that we can't account for it by natural means. A theologian may claim that it's true, and to argue with the theologian we'd have to argue on theological grounds because there are no historical grounds to argue on. Historians can only establish what probably happened in the past, and by definition a miracle is the least probable occurrence. And so, by the very nature of the canons of historical research, we can't claim historically that a miracle probably happened. By definition, it probably didn't. And history can only establish what probably did.[13]

There are, he contends, a number of other much more plausible explanations (because they are not supernatural) that have just as much going for them as the accounts found in the New Testament. For an example, he makes up the following story to explain the empty tomb:

> Jesus gets buried by Joseph of Arimathea. Two of Jesus' family members are upset that an unknown Jewish leader has buried the body. In the dead of night, these two family members raid the tomb, taking the body off to bury it for themselves. But Roman soldiers on the lookout see them carrying the shrouded corpse through the streets, they confront them, and they kill them on the spot. They throw all three bodies into a common burial plot, where within three days these bodies are decomposed beyond recognition. The tomb then is empty. People go to the tomb, they find it empty, they come to think that Jesus was

---

[13]Greg Koukl, "Is There Historical Evidence for the Resurrection of Jesus? William Lane Craig vs Bart Ehrman. A debate at College of the Holy Cross, Worcester, Massachusetts, United States, 28 March 2006," accessed 4 December 2016, http://www.reasonablefaith.org/is-there-historical -evidence-for-the-resurrection-of-jesus-the-craig-ehrman#ixzz40OiMyHUd.

raised from the dead, and they start thinking they've seen him because they know he's been raised because his tomb is empty.[14]

Ehrman does not believe this story is true, but he does claim that it is much more reasonable and therefore believable than the biblical one.

Ehrman's Philosophical Problem

There are a variety of problems associated with Ehrman's rejection of miracles as verifiable by the historian. They begin already with his definition of a miracle as an event "that contradict[s] the normal workings of nature in such a way as to be virtually beyond belief and to require an acknowledgment that supernatural forces have been at work." Why would such an event be, by definition, beyond belief? Ehrman notes in his excursus that there are many Christian historians who do believe miracles have occurred. "When they think or do this," he asserts, "they do so not in their capacity as historians but in their capacity as believers."[15] That is, their prior belief in miracles—and not the evidence—leads them to believe miracles such as the resurrection occurred.

This may be true of *some* Christian historians. But assuming for the moment that there is good historical evidence for a miracle such as the resurrection, is it not just as legitimate to assert that historians who deny the resurrection do so because it does not fit their assumptions about what normally occurs in nature, and they are therefore guilty of the same circular reasoning? While Ehrman does not overtly argue that proper historical research requires a commitment to a naturalist world view, he does require it follow a naturalist methodology, and in so doing is the implicit assumption of naturalism. The only reason an event that contradicts the normal workings of nature would be beyond belief is if one is not permitted to acknowledge that a supernatural force explains the event because of some prior commitment to naturalism.[16]

---

[14]Ibid., http://www.reasonablefaith.org/is-there-historical-evidence-for-the-resurrection-of-jesus-the-craig-ehrman#ixzz40Ok6EIDu.

[15]Ehrman, *The New Testament*, 244.

[16]For a rigorous exposure of the philosophical naturalism behind methodological naturalism, see Alvin Plantina's two-part essay "Methodological

Ehrman is right, though, in maintaining that what happened in the past can only be known to the historian by the evidence. Even here, however, his naturalist assumptions get in the way. This can be seen in his repeated use of terms that imply the probability of something. Miracles are "infinitesimally remote," he assumes, because they defy the way nature normally works. Therefore, even "otherwise good" or sound historical sources that contain regular, believable events are unreliable at the point they describe miraculous events. Because miracles are "infinitesimally remote," they are highly improbable. Historians work in the realm of probability when it comes to explaining the past. This, in Ehrman's presentation of the historical problem of miracles, prevents the historian from considering the evidence that a miracle happened, or at least places it in a realm of inquiry that is beyond the reach of the historian. In the end, Ehrman sums up his view of the possibility of miracles as events that, "[e]ven if they have happened, they are (in common parlance) *impossible*."[17] This is telling. It makes plain that his real problem with miracles is, in the final analysis, a philosophical one masquerading as a historical one. A case could even be made that he has elevated his philosophical assumptions to the level of an ideology such that facts that, under normal historical procedure, require a miraculous (or even anomalous) explanation are in a circular way interpreted by the initial assumptions. This is not the way historians approach evidence. It is, however, the way ideologues, propagandists, and conspiracy theorists do.

Historical Research and the Empty Tomb

So what do the "canons" of historical research tell us about miracles? When it comes to the basic assumptions historians make about the nature of historical research, the answer is nothing. Like other fields of knowledge, the historian assumes that a world exists outside of our minds and that it exists independent of our beliefs about it.

Naturalism?" in the online journal *Origins and Design* 18:1 & 2 (1997) at http://www.arn.org/odesign/odesign.htm.

[17]Ehrman, *The New Testament*, 240.

Yet particulars about it can be discovered and known by a careful and unbiased investigation of it.[18] What the historian tries to avoid is assuming what sort of interpretation of the evidence is most likely the case before examining it. The historian explains the past by determining what the most likely explanation is of a particular event in view of or from the evidence. The gold standard for assessing the veracity of a historian's description of the past, then, is not coherence with his or her other beliefs about the world. Rather, it is how well it corresponds to the evidence that is specific to the event under investigation.[19]

What, then, can the historian say concerning the end of Jesus's life? That he died by crucifixion is almost universally acknowledged.[20] With the exception of what amount to conspiracy theories, so too is his burial in a tomb that was discovered empty three days later.[21] The

---

[18]For a great defense of the historical method yielding justifiable knowledge and truth, see Richard J. Evans, *In Defense of History* (New York: W. W. Norton, 1999); and for an overview of how historians have approached their discipline from ancient to modern times, see Jeremy D. Popkin, *From Herodotus to H-Net: The Story of Historiography* (New York: Oxford University Press, 2016).

[19]See C. Behan McCullagh, *Justifying Historical Descriptions* (New York: Cambridge University Press, 1984).

[20]Historically, the Islamic tradition has, with few exceptions, denied the crucifixion of Jesus. This is not for historical reasons, though, but because the Qur'an implies as much. See Todd Lawson, *The Crucifixion and the Qur'an: A Study in the History of Muslim Thought* (Oxford: OneWorld Publications, 2009).

[21]This is not just what the Gospels and other New Testament documents say. The earliest attempts to discredit Christianity assume it to be the case as well. In the second and third century, Justin Martyr (*Dialogue with Trypho the Jew*, c. 108, trans. Marcus Dods and George Reith in *Ante-Nicene Fathers*, vol. 1, ed. Alexander Roberts, James Donaldson, and A. Cleveland Coxe [Buffalo, NY: Christian Literature Publishing Co., 1885], 295.) and Tertullian (*De Spectaculis*, c. 30, trans. S. Thelwall in *Ante-Nicene Fathers*, vol. 3, 47.) explain that the Jews were still circulating the story of the disciples stealing the body of Jesus just as they did in the days following the discovery of the empty tomb (see Matthew 28:11–15). Later Jewish polemics (fifth century at the earliest) likewise acknowledge Jesus's body "was not found in the grave where he had been buried," but rather than the disciples stealing the body, they alleged that a gardener removed it and buried it in the sand (see Morris Goldstein, *Jesus*

question we are left with is *why* the tomb was empty. The way a historian proceeds to answer it is by assessing the evidence and offering the most probable explanation as determined by the evidence and not *a priori* speculation about what is possible.

What evidence do we have that would explain the empty tomb? There is a surprising amount of relevant literary sources from biblical to non-Christian texts that need to be considered.[22] But the best evidence comes from the canonical Gospels. They are all—in their own unique ways—credible biographies of Jesus written by eyewitnesses or the companions of eyewitnesses.[23]

The authors provide the historian a tremendous amount of detail concerning Jesus's life, including accounts of Jesus appearing to his disciples three days after his death. They even include material that should have been omitted, especially if they were trying to persuade a first-century audience of something that did not happen.

For example, all four Gospels describe women as the first to visit the empty tomb and see the resurrected Jesus (Matthew 28:1–10; Mark 16:1–8 [9–11]; Luke 24:1–12; John 20:1–18). This is interesting since, in their context, a woman's testimony was regarded as irrelevant

---

in the Jewish Tradition [New York: MacMillan, 1950], 148–54). There is no evidence that suggests Jesus's body remained in the tomb. Had it been there, the Jewish or Roman officials would have exhumed and publicly displayed it to shut the mouths of the Christians who based their faith and their preaching on the resurrection. There have, of course, been some desperate attempts to explain away and deny the empty tomb by modern academics. But their wild conjecture and invalid historical inferences cannot compete with the evidence, all of which acknowledges that the tomb was empty (see, for example, Peter Kirby, "The Case against the Empty Tomb," in *The Empty Tomb: Jesus Beyond the Grave,* ed. Robert Price and Jeffrey Jaw Lowder [Amherst, MA: Prometheus Press, 2005], 233–60). For all the evidence supporting the empty tomb, see William Lane Craig, "The Historicity of the Empty Tomb of Jesus," *New Testament Studies* 31 (1985): 39–67.

[22]See Licona, *The Resurrection*, 199–276.

[23]See Richard Bauckham, *Jesus and the Eyewitnesses: The Gospels as Eyewitness Testimony* (Grand Rapids, MI: Eerdmans, 2008) and, among others, Mark D. Roberts, *Can We Trust the Gospels? Investigating the Reliability of Matthew, Mark, Luke, and John* (Wheaton, IL: Crossway Books, 2007).

and unreliable.[24] And yet they still included it. Why? The most likely—indeed, it is hard to conceive of any other—explanation is that it is what happened.[25]

The Gospel writers "could not afford to risk inaccuracies (not to speak of willful manipulation of the facts), which would at once be exposed by those who would be only too glad to do so."[26] The hostility Christianity faced almost immediately all but guarantees that they did not invent the story of Jesus rising from the dead. For both the Roman and Jewish officials in first-century Jerusalem had the means, motive, and every opportunity to debunk it.

They did try. Matthew 28:11–15 records that after the events of Easter morning—the stone being inexplicably rolled away and the tomb being empty—the guards that had been placed to keep it secure,

> went into the city and told the chief priests all that had taken place. And when they had assembled with the elders and taken counsel, they gave a sufficient sum of money to the soldiers and said, "Tell people, 'His disciples came by night and stole him away while we were asleep.' And if this comes to the governor's ears, we will satisfy him and keep you out of trouble." So they took the money and did as they were directed. And this story has been spread among the Jews to this day.[27]

This is the only other account of the empty tomb for which we have historical evidence. But Matthew tells us the story was contrived. While he might be considered partisan, it is still hard to imagine the

---

[24]See, for example, Josephus, *Antiquities*, 4.8.15.

[25]See Richard Bauckham, "The Women at the Tomb: The Credibility of Their Story," http://richardbauckham.co.uk/uploads/Accessible/The%20Women%20&%20the%20Resurrection.pdf.

[26]F. F. Bruce, *The New Testament Documents: Are They Reliable?* (Grand Rapids, MI: Eerdmans, 1960), 45.

[27]All biblical quotations come from *The Holy Bible, English Standard Version* (Wheaton, IL: Crossway, 2001). In the second and third century, Justin Martyr (*Dialogue with Trypho the Jew,* 108) and Tertullian (*De Spectaculis,* 30) explain that the Jews were still circulating the story of the disciples stealing the body of Jesus.

disciples doing what the Jews alleged. They would have had to do it when a security detail consisting of at least four guards was stationed in front of the tomb.[28] Additionally, had they stolen the body, there is no explanation for why they spent the rest of their lives promoting what they knew to be a lie and then, in the case of many of them, being tortured and executed for it without a single one of them exposing what would probably be the world's greatest conspiracy.

It would also be difficult for a historian to explain the growth or even the existence of the church if Jesus merely died and remained dead. It was, after all, the resurrection that convinced the disciples to believe Jesus's teachings and emboldened them to preach the Gospel of Christianity, with the resurrection itself constituting its earliest and most central proclamation regarding the crucified Christ Jesus.[29]

They also treated the resurrection as *the* event upon which Christianity stands or falls. In 1 Corinthians 15:14–17, for example, Paul wrote,

> And if Christ has not been raised, then our preaching is in vain and your faith is in vain. We are even found to be misrepresenting God, because we testified about God that he raised Christ, whom he did not raise if it is true that the dead are not raised. For if the dead are not raised, not even Christ has been raised. And if Christ has not been raised, your faith is futile and you are still in your sins.

Given that the crucifixion and resurrection were the heart and soul of the Christian message from the very beginning and that the church began its preaching in and around Jerusalem (Luke 24:33–35; Acts 2:24–25, 31–32; 3:15; 4:1–2, 10, 33), it is extraordinary that the numerous enemies of Christianity did not simply produce the body of Jesus to shut it down. Again, they had ample opportunity and the

---

[28]It is unclear from Matthew 27:65 whether the guards were Roman or a temple security detail. If the former, it would have consisted of at least four (see William Smith, *Dictionary of Greek and Roman Antiquities* [Boston, MA: Little, Brown, and Company, 1859], 250). If the latter, it would have been ten (see Alfred Edersheim, *The Temple: Its Ministry and Services As They Were at the Time of Jesus* [London: The Religious Tract, 1874], 119).

[29]See 1 Clement 42:3.

ability to do so, especially since on several occasions, the apostles were in their custody.

The Romans, who regarded Christianity as a pernicious superstition, and the Jews, who began killing Christians well before the Romans did (as in the stoning of Stephen, see Acts 7:54–60), could not discredit the message of Christianity even though it would have been easily discredited. This, however, has not stopped antagonists of Christianity from attempting to discredit on factual, historical grounds today. A wide variety of alternative explanations for the empty tomb apart from the resurrection have been proposed. Since the late eighteenth century, a number of "swoon theories" have posited that Jesus did not die on the cross.[30] Instead, he passed out and, appearing dead, was buried. Then, somehow, beset with multiple complex mortal wounds, he was revived and made his way out of a sealed tomb, eluding an armed sentry. Others have suggested that the witnesses of the empty tomb went to the wrong tomb or that Jesus's body was placed in the wrong tomb, and when his disciples visited the right grave, which was empty, they assumed he rose from the dead.[31] And another one claims that the eyewitnesses really did believe they saw Jesus alive after his death, but in reality, they were all hallucinating.[32] The foremost problem with all these explanations is that none of them correspond to the evidence in the historical record. They all basically amount to conspiracy theories.

Conclusion

The evidence from history is quite clear about certain facts pertaining to Jesus. He was crucified and died on a Roman cross.[33] He did not

---

[30]Perhaps the most famous book advocating the swoon hypothesis is Hugh Schonfield's *The Passover Plot: A New Interpretation of the Life and Death of Jesus* (New York: Bernard Geis Associates, 1964).

[31]See, for example, P. Gardner-Smith, *The Narratives of the Resurrection* (London: Methuen Press, 1926), 134–39.

[32]See, for example, Gerd Lüdemann, *The Resurrection of Jesus* (Minneapolis, MN: Fortress Press, 1994).

[33]See William D. Edwards, Wesley J. Gabel, and Floyd E. Hosmer, "On the Physical Death of Jesus Christ," *The Journal of the American Medical Association* 255 (1986): 1455–63.

swoon. The guarded tomb in which he was placed was empty three days later. The only historical rejection of the reports that he rose from the dead, by suggesting that the disciples stole the body, was merely an assertion contrived by the enemies of Jesus. The disciples did not have the means, motive, or the opportunity to steal the body. Concerning the eyewitness reports of the resurrection, the extant ones have been well preserved in the four canonical Gospels. All but one (John) of the twelve apostles (including Paul but precluding Judas) and eyewitnesses of the resurrected Jesus (e.g., Matthias and Mark), according to historical sources and tradition, went to their death standing firm on the claim that what they bore witness to was factual. Had they invented the story, one of them would have caved during their various trials and subsequent executions.

Any historical inquiry into the issue of Jesus's resurrection has all this (and even more) positive evidence to consider. There is no real substantial evidence to the contrary. The historical discipline requires that explanations of what happened in the past follow the trail of evidence and be fashioned around all the facts. As Philip Schaff put it, "The purpose of the historian is not to construct a history from preconceived notions and to adjust it to his own liking, but to reproduce it from the best evidence and to let it speak for itself."[34] We are left with no other explanation other than the fact that he rose from the dead. Alternative explanations are certainly possible, but if they are historical, they have to correspond to the evidence. The problem with the alternative explanations is that they are not drawn from and do not fit all or any of the evidence.

A historian who smuggles in an assumption about what can or cannot happen in the course of human events—either by restricting explanations methodologically or by philosophical presuppositions—is not operating as a historian. They are confusing philosophical speculation with historical explanation. Ehrman's excursus is an example of exactly this. He rules out the possibility of a miracle like the resurrection by defining it as the most improbable event and restricting historians to consider only what he deems probable *apart* from

---

[34]Philip Schaff, *History of the Christian Church*, vol. 1 (New York: Charles Scribner's Sons, 1910), 175.

consideration of the evidence. However, although a resurrection is not a normal human experience, the evidence is so compelling in the case of Jesus that the most probable explanation of the empty tomb is his resurrection. So not only can a historian explain the empty tomb by the resurrection, he or she is left with no real alternative but to assert what Christians confess: that Jesus was crucified under Pontius Pilate, died, was buried, and three days later, rose again from the dead.

Recommended Reading

Craig, William Lane. *The Son Rises: Historical Evidence for the Resurrection of Jesus.* Eugene, OR: Wipf & Stock, 2000.

Geivett, R. Douglas, and Gary R. Habermas, eds. *In Defense of Miracles: A Comprehensives Case for God's Action in History.* Downers Grove, IL: IVP, 1997.

Habermas, Gary R., and Michael Licona. *The Case for the Resurrection of Jesus.* Grand Rapids, MI: Kregel Publications, 2004.

Licona, Michael. *The Resurrection of Jesus: A New Historiographical Approach.* Downers Grove, IL: InterVarsity Press, 2010.

Montgomery, John Warwick. *History, Law, and Christianity,* 3rd ed. Corona, CA: New Reformation Press, 2015.

Swinburne, Richard. *The Resurrection of God Incarnate.* Oxford: Clarendon Press, 2003.

Wright, N. T. *The Resurrection of the Son of God.* Minneapolis, MN: Fortress Press, 2003.

3

John Dominic Crossan's Antichrist

John J. Bombaro

The lines of demarcation between those who affirm the resurrection of Jesus and those who repudiate it seem fixed and certain. Christians confess the resurrection. Non-Christians don't. At the scholarly level, things are no different.[1] On the believing side, we find N. T. Wright, Gary Habermas, and Michael Licona, to name but three. On the opposing side, there might be Barbara Thiering, Bart Ehrman, and Peter Atkins. Debates pit apologists against rationalists, theists versus atheists and agnostics, as they contest whether the bodily resurrection was a real historical event or the fruit of fertile imaginations. Yes, the debate over the bodily resurrection of Jesus seems very much a black-and-white, yes-or-no conversation. Except for the third way—the way of "progressive Christianity."[2]

---

[1] A unique exception is Pinchas Lapide, a Jewish theologian and Israeli historian, who affirms the bodily resurrection while denying the messiahship and deity of Jesus Christ in *The Resurrection of Jesus: A Jewish Perspective* (Eugene, OR: Wipf & Stock, 2002).

[2] For more on the phenomenon and characteristic holdings of progressive Christianity see, Bruce Mortan, *Progressive Christianity—What is It?* (Amazon Digital Services: Digital Bible Study Books, 2013); David Felton and Jeff Procter-Murphy, *Living the Questions: The Wisdom of Progressive Christianity* (San Francisco, CA: HarperOne, 2012); Robin Meyers, *The Underground Church: Reclaiming the Subversive Way of Jesus* (San Francisco, CA: Jossey-Bass, 2012).

There are scholars who *affirm* the resurrection of Jesus but *deny* its physicality. That is, there are those who admit that the disciples and apostles who testified to an encounter with the resurrected Christ experienced just that—seeing the once-crucified Jesus of Nazareth alive again. Christ is risen. However, there's a caveat: What such testators actually experienced was an autosuggested apparition or something similar or perhaps nothing at all. Apparitions, of course, are nonphysical images, but they are in some sense "experienced." They may also be mere literary fiction. The experience of Jesus's apparition seemed to have a human form, contend certain "progressive Christians," and so the resurrected Jesus the "witnesses" saw did not possess an actual body, transformed or otherwise, but rather his image, which appeared in bodily form. Risen, indeed.

This may sound like doublespeak or, perhaps, duplicity, but it remains a rhetorical tool for John Dominic Crossan, a winsome proponent of progressive Christianity.[3] For Crossan, the risen Christ is, optimistically, an ephemeral apparition, not a person possessing a transformed body. What's important for Crossan isn't substantiating the concrete physicality and historicity of Jesus's resurrection but coming to an understanding of how we may now positively construe the Gospel authors' articulation that Christ is "risen" through their parables about resurrection, which, like Jesus's original parables, carried metaphorical import. Understanding the resurrection as a meaning-laden parable enriched the early church through its implications, not the least of which was "Jesus is Lord." And so Crossan affirms the resurrection and the enduring lordship of Jesus understood not in categories of a concrete, literal-historical resurrection but in terms of a parabolic narrative (initiated by Jesus and advanced

---

[3]Crossan's best-selling works have been *The Historical Jesus: The Life of a Mediterranean Peasant Jew* (San Francisco, CA: HarperOne, 1993); *Jesus: A Revolutionary Biography* (San Francisco, CA: HarperOne, 2009); *The Birth of Christianity: Discovering What Happened in the Years Immediately after the Execution of Jesus* (San Francisco, CA: HarperOne, 1998); *Who Killed Jesus: Exposing the Roots of Anti-Semitism in the Gospel Story of the Death of Jesus* (San Francisco, CA: HarperOne, 1996); and a trilogy coauthored with Marcus J. Borg and published by HarperOne, San Francisco, CA (*The Last Week*; *The First Christmas*; and *The First Paul*).

by the apostles) striving to capture the pluriform meaning of God saying "yes" to Jesus's kingdom message after human authorities said "no." This, argues Crossan, is the original Christian way. But as we shall see, it is little more than a contemporary progressive way of addressing resurrection without having to subscribe to an antiquated and impossible world view replete with miracles, supernaturalism, and literalist commitments to Scripture. In short, it is the way of unbelief masquerading as "faith."

For those unacquainted with John Dominic Crossan, it would be a mistake to characterize him as an insignificant thinker marginally acquainted with Christianity. Quite the opposite. A once-devout Roman Catholic Irishman, he joined the Catholic monastic order of Servites and pursued holy orders at Stonebridge Priory in Illinois, being ordained in 1957. An able scholar, he returned to Ireland to earn a doctor of divinity degree (1959). His dissertation became the first of his now twenty-nine books, in addition to nearly one hundred and fifty other academic contributions.[4] Crossan has a world-class biblical, theological, and archeological pedigree. Over the last thirty years, he has been one of the most colorful, visible, and prolific contributors to both academic and popular conversations regarding the historical Jesus, appearing on radio, television, and newspapers hundreds of times. His mastery of the New Testament and Second Temple Judaism is widely recognized, offering many enduring insights to the life and times of Jesus. In debate, he is amicable, articulate, and congenial. Put simply, Crossan is a major contemporary scholar addressing the central figure and tenets of Christianity and doing so in a way that's neither pugnacious nor uninformed.

Yet he's not without controversy. Crossan has built a career on sometimes daring, other times provocative views on the Christian faith. In 1969, he voluntarily resigned his ordination within the Servite priesthood, citing a desire to express his speculative views within the realm of academia without ecclesiastical repercussions but also to marry Margaret Deganais, a professor at Loyola University

---

[4]John Dominic Crossan, "Professional Resume," accessed 16 January 2016, http://www.johndominiccrossan.com/Resume/Pages/Publications.htm.

Chicago[5]—a romantic relationship initiated and pursued while he was a priest. The same year, he joined the faculty at DePaul University in Chicago, where his challenges to orthodoxy fermented throughout a tenure of twenty-six years, only to rise to international fame as one of the cofounders (with Robert Funk) of the highly controversial Jesus Seminar in 1985. That seminar culminated in Crossan penning a new version of the Gospels, *The Five Gospels: The Search for the Authentic Words of Jesus: New Translation and Commentary* (1993), which presented what the seminar scholars believed were the most historically accurate statements in Matthew, Mark, Luke, John, and the Gospel of Thomas, through a disputed and now universally rejected methodology.

It can be reasonably argued that Crossan is the progenitor of the contentious third way of "progressive Christianity." The third way isn't a lonely way either. Crossan has company. Marcus Borg,[6] John Spong, David Jenkins, Elaine Pagels, Thomas H. West and Gerd Lüdemann[7] represent not the same position but their own "Christian" hues within a wide Crossanesque spectrum of affirming-while-denying approaches to the resurrection that are warmly embraced by ever-compromising mainline Christianity and sensational broadcasts.[8]

---

[5]Darrell J. Turner, editor, "John Dominic Crossan: Theologian." http://www.britannica.com/biography/John-Dominic-Crossan.

[6]Marcus J. Borg, a well-known and frequent coauthor with Crossan, may be said to share similar ideas about the resurrection and resurrection narratives. See, e.g., Marcus J. Borg and John Dominic Crossan, *The Last Week: What the Gospels Really Teach About Jesus' Final Days in Jerusalem* (San Francisco, CA: HarperOne, 2006), 190–216; N. T. Wright and Marcus J. Borg, *The Meaning of Jesus* (London: SPCK, 2001), 129–42; and Marcus J. Borg, *The Heart of Christianity: Rediscovering a Life of Faith* (San Francisco, CA: HarperOne, 1989), 48–57, 81–94.

[7]See chapter 8 in this volume for Carolyn Hansen's treatment of Lüdemann's vision hypothesis.

[8]Borg and Crossan have expressed their progressive views together and independently on A&E, History, Discovery, PBS, CNN, and the National Geographic Channel.

Crossan is not only a leader; he's also a follower and, specifically, a follower of Claude Lévi-Strauss (1908–2009), dubbed the "father of modern anthropology" due to his appropriation of *structuralism* to the study of humanity. Structuralism is a broad-ranging methodology asserting that all elements of human culture are only intelligible in terms of their relationship to a larger overarching structure, which itself consists of persistent laws of abstract culture.[9] In other words, any and all human beliefs (and resultant behaviors) must be interpreted in light of other antecedent governing beliefs. Lévi-Strauss applied structuralism to anthropology in a quest for the underlying patterns of thought in all forms of human activity. Crossan takes this interpretative paradigm and applies it to New Testament studies to understand why the earliest Christians would say the things they did about Jesus.

What he discerns are Hebrew cultural commitments to *myth*, which in turn condition Jewish understandings of parables in political and socioeconomic categories. Basic, however, is the human need for myth.[10] For Crossan, it is the antecedent, but one that's limited in terms of meaning and potential. Of greater potential are parables that reach beyond the limitations of myth to new possibilities of hope for justice and meaning because they utilize metaphors that facilitate strata of meanings. Jesus taught in such metaphoric parables, of course, and the *meaning* of the myth of "resurrection" to which Jesus refers on many occasions is to be interpreted parabolically. Indeed, Crossan even biographically depicts Jesus himself as a living parable,[11] whose life and kingdom vision are to be understood as a parabolic response to the limitation of myth for those first-century Palestinians languishing under Roman rule. The result is a peasant Jewish cynic upending the myth of Rome with parables

---

[9]Robert Audi, ed., *The Cambridge Dictionary of Philosophy* (Cambridge: Cambridge University Press, 1995), 770–71.

[10]John Dominic Crossan, *The Dark Interval: Towards a Theology of Story* (Allen, TX: Argus Communications, 1975), 60.

[11]Ibid., 123–28. For a detailed explanation of Crossan's methodology, see Richard Walsh, *Mapping Myths of Biblical Interpretation: Playing the Texts* (Edinburgh: T&T Clark, 2001), 124–31.

of God's kingdom.[12] Jesus is, for Crossan, a "rebel with a cause," a "peasant with an attitude," challenging the myth of the divine Caesar through a parabolic life.[13] Jesus was aware of the Hebrew myth but intellectually and ethically critiqued it, while at the same time deconstructing the imperial Roman cult myth by poetically creating an alternative narrative through parables and parabolic living, through which one can transcend *both* oppressive mythic institutions— Second Temple Judaism and the Caesar-dominated Roman world. And it is in this structuralist paradigm that Crossan comes to explain Jesus's resurrection allusions as powerful metaphors inspiring hope.

But what of the resurrection *event*? Here, we find another one of progressivism's ideological commitments: antisupernaturalism or, simply, naturalism. Crossan rejects the idea of the miraculous through a redefinition of *miracle* as "*a marvel that someone interprets as a transcendental action or manifestation.*"[14] Note that the onus falls on *interpretation* and that the miracle is not stated to be an act of God or theophany but only attributed to be so. Crossan says as much: "There must be . . . certain individuals or groups who interpret that marvel as an intervention by ancestors, spirits, divinities or God."[15] What was once a theological discussion has become an anthropological discussion for Crossan.

The same principle applies to the historical figure, Jesus of Nazareth. He cannot be in any way a supernatural figure. Consequently, Crossan operates by the presumptive interpretive paradigm that distinguishes the natural *historical Jesus* from the subsequently contrived, supernatural *Christ of faith*. The former is the object of research; the latter is the invention of fertile religious minds. For Crossan, however, the latter obfuscates the former, requiring modern principles of historical method to unearth the real Jesus, yet without stripping him of the romantic hope he

---

[12]In *The Historical Jesus*, Crossan describes Jesus as "[a] hippie in a world of Roman yuppies" (421–22).

[13]Crossan, *The Birth of Christianity*, xxx. Cf. Crossan, *The Historical Jesus*, 422–26.

[14]Crossan, *The Birth of Christianity*, 303. Italics in original.

[15]Ibid.

embodied in his teaching and engendered among his earliest followers. Jesus talked about resurrection and ascension, but these are metaphors of power, justice, and allegiance, not historical happenings. His first disciples understood this, claims Crossan, and furthered his parabolic message of hope and justice contra Rome and the high priesthood, but this message was given flesh and bones by later disciples who overutilized the metaphor and rendered it concrete to galvanize their ecclesiastical power. The original parables and their meanings must be mined behind or, better, *before* the New Testament authors' consciously invented—with ulterior motives—bodily resurrection narratives, dubbed "literary fiction" by Crossan:

> [T]hese are my conclusions: First, the Easter story is not about the events of a single day, but reflects the struggle of Jesus' followers to make sense of both his death and their continuing experience of empowerment by him. Second, stories of the resurrected Jesus appearing to various people are not really about "visions" at all, but are literary fiction prompted by struggles over leadership in the early Church.[16]

It is the contention of this essay that Dominic Crossan's occasional assertion of an apparitional Jesus (now a tenet of Christian progressivism) in contrast to a concrete bodily resurrection does four things, all of which undermine the reliability of the New Testament witnesses and betray the substance of the Gospel, as well as set forth a "Christ" that is other than Christ Jesus, the historical figure whom God raised from the dead (Acts 3:15). Such a "Christ," according to 2 John 7, is ἀντίχριστος, antichrist—"other than Christ." It also is the contention of this essay that Crossan's reconstructionist approach to early Christianity amounts to little more than a concerted effort to supplant Christian confidence in the once-crucified, now-risen Christ Jesus with a vacuous, politically correct religion.

---

[16]John Dominic Crossan and Richard G. Watts, *Who Is Jesus?: Answers to Your Questions about the Historical Jesus* (Louisville, KY: Westminster/John Knox Press, 1996), 121.

Crossan's Methodology

Notwithstanding its failure to persuade and its total loss of credibility, the Jesus Seminar provided a platform for Dominic Crossan to refine his methodological convictions that ultimately found expression in his most famous and tendentious work, *The Historical Jesus: The Life of a Mediterranean Jewish Peasant* (1991). In this creative work, Crossan interpreted the divinity and certain key events in Jesus's life metaphorically. That book and its 1994 successor, *Jesus: A Revolutionary Biography*, made Crossan (in the words of Darrell Turner) "one of the key figures in a new version of an old controversy concerning how best to distinguish the Jesus of history from the Jesus of the Gospels."[17]

While interested in what the first Christians *thought* happened to Jesus after his crucifixion, Crossan does not want to get bogged down in endless disputes about the facticity of an otherwise unverifiable literalist resurrection tradition:

> [F]ocusing on the factuality of these [miraculous resurrection] stories often misses their more-than-factual meanings. When treated as if they are primarily about an utterly unique spectacular event, we often do not get beyond the question, "Did they happen or not?" to the question, "What do they mean?"[18]

And so Crossan transcends what he considers the Gordian knot of whether or not a concrete resurrection actually occurred by instead focusing on an alternative interpretive paradigm that reads the resurrection in parabolic categories, placing the emphasis on the resurrection's *meaning*, not its historicity. "When we see these stories as *parable*," explains Crossan, "the 'model' for this understanding is the parables of Jesus. . . . The obvious insight is that parables can be true—truthful and truth-filled—independently of their factuality."[19] Progressive Christianity believes it can skirt the pitfall of establishing

---

[17]Darrell J. Turner, editor, "John Dominic Crossan: Theologian." http://www.britannica.com/biography/John-Dominic-Crossan.

[18]Borg and Crossan, *The Last Week*, 192.

[19]Ibid.

the historicity of the resurrection because *"the truth of a parable—of a parabolic narrative—is not dependent on its factuality."*[20] The upshot of seeing, particularly, the Easter stories as parabolic narratives permits a vast array of meaning unleashed from the narrowing parameters of historical reconstruction and associated prescientific dogmas that are, frankly, untenable in our post-Enlightenment age. The result is Christianity unshackled by Crossan: "Believe whatever you want about whether the stories happened this way—now let's talk about what they mean."[21] Thus, as to the event, one may be agnostic, indifferent, or skeptical. It doesn't matter. It's the meaning that matters. And the meaning Crossan finds makes no extravagant truth claim, no offensive proclamation, no endangering call of allegiance.

Challenge Points

The first point of challenge concerns Crossan's claim of resurrection appearances as apparitional occurrences because it calls into question the value of *any* meaning the earliest Christians tried to convey about or for it, metaphorically or otherwise. This would be due to the fact that such meaning was never actually retained in any known oral or written form, including the New Testament documents, since Crossan rejects both Paul as an early testator to a bodily resurrection and the Four Gospels as later, agenda-oriented compositions.[22] But without these texts, where does Crossan's parabolic interpretation of the resurrection originate? He needs a source.

Crossan forges another way by (1) positing apparitions of Jesus in order to affirm the idea and metaphorical implications of "resurrection" while (2) denying its epistolary significance and meaning stemming from its concreteness, such as we find in the New Testament Gospels and epistles. The key for him is to separate the "earliest" eyewitness testimony—the noncanonical *Gospel of Peter* and its original source, the "cross gospel"—from the later New

---

[20]Ibid.

[21]Ibid.

[22]Crossan, *The Birth of Christianity*, xxi-xxvii, 15.

Testament writings.[23] All the Gospels, he says, save for the *Gospel of Peter*, were written *after* 70 AD. Thus with the *Gospel of Peter* presenting the earliest written account of the resurrection in categories that accommodate his metaphor hypothesis,[24] Crossan can affirm that "Jesus lives" and "Jesus is Lord" are essential Christian confessions. However, it's exactly those affirmations that are undermined of New Covenant meaningfulness because they are inextricably and necessarily tethered to the concrete event of a bodily resurrection reported by what are in fact the earliest Christian documents—the writings of Paul and at least the Gospel of Mark. Crossan's privileging the "cross gospel" and *Gospel of Peter* alienates him from the only credible and plausible sources reporting the resurrection *and* its meaning.

But let us be plain. Just as "[b]odily resurrection has nothing to do with a resuscitating body coming out of its tomb," for Crossan, neither does an apparition have any external reality for the earliest Christians or New Testament writers: "Bodily resurrection means that the *embodied* life and death of the historical Jesus continues to be experienced, by believers, as powerfully efficacious and salvifically present in this world."[25] Resurrection, then, is *all* metaphor, simply metaphor, and really "one—but only one—of the metaphors used to express the sense of Jesus' continuing presence with his followers and

---

[23]Crossan, *The Historical Jesus*, Appendix A, 427–45. See also N. T. Wright's critique of Crossan's controversial dating of texts, in *Jesus and the Victory of God* (Minneapolis, MN: Fortress Press, 1996), 44–62. Gerd Theissen and Annette Merz write that "Crossan's extremely early dating of extra-canonical sources has not gained acceptance" (*The Historical Jesus: A Comprehensive Guide* [Minneapolis, MN: Fortress Press, 1998], 24 n. 13).

[24]St. Serapion (Patriarch of Antioch [191–211]) condemned the *Gospel of Peter* as docetic and a forgery (in Eusebius, *Historia ecclesiastica*, 4.12.2), and so the charge of docetism has persisted in, for example, F. F. Bruce, *Jesus and Christian Origins Outside the New Testament* [Grand Rapids, MI: Eerdmans, 1974], 93. However, recent scholarly work has shown this to be incorrect. See, P. M. Head, "On the Christology of the *Gospel of Peter*," *Vigiliae christianae* 46 (1992): 209–24. Note that the *Gospel of Peter* (consisting of one chapter) does not actually report an encounter with the resurrected Jesus.

[25]Crossan, *The Birth of Christianity*, xxxi.

friends," admits Crossan.[26] He is not talking mental states nor external ephemeral manifestations of the spirit-person Jesus. No, Jesus was crucified to death, and his discarded remains were consumed by wild dogs, says Crossan.[27] Instead, we are talking about the kingdom of God as an idea, a movement, and the legacy ("spirit") of Jesus lives in that. Crossan must be challenged on his dubious selection of texts.

Second, Crossan will be challenged for his departure from theological and soteriological expectations, guided by the Gospel narratives and explicitly articulated by St. Paul, that God redeems the totality of a human being according to a *Hebraic* (not Platonic) anthropology. The very basis for the redemption of not only our humanity but also the world itself is vacated of certainty and illustration, since nothing of this material world has been transformed and evidenced from *within this world*. Again, if human beings are saved, then Crossan's paragon for that redemption (social, economic, and political liberation) offers no expectation that it includes embodiment or even the salvation of human spirits. Crossan has drained the New Testament of eschatological hope. Misplaced then is the hope of the resurrection of the body when the object of assurance is at best an apparition, at worse a literary construct.

A third point of challenge confronts Crossan's mining for dynamic meanings latent within the metaphor of resurrection due to its shifting the focus from Jesus per se to messages latent within "parables of resurrection." Restated, Crossan makes the parable primary and the person and work of Jesus secondary. This distinction is akin to the difference in importance between Jesus *showing* the way and Jesus *being* the way.

The fourth point of challenge pertains to the loss of the simplicity and elegance of Paul's explication of the Gospel as a result of and consisting in no less than a concrete resurrection, due to Crossan's complex and sophisticated process of mining for the meaning of this parabolic, metaphorical "event." The concern here is the diminution of the Gospels as a unique literary genre that *does* something—namely, give testimony to, above all, the faithfulness of

---

[26]Crossan and Watts, *Who Is Jesus?*, 121.

[27]Crossan, *Jesus, A Revolutionary Biography*, 123–26.

God to redeem and recreate the world through the real-world death and concrete resurrection of his Messiah. *That*, Paul asserts, is the result of a concrete resurrection, not cleverly crafted parables.

When the resurrection is loosed from its concrete moorings by progressive Christianity and rendered metaphorical to mean almost anything and everything, it really ends up meaning nothing for certain, which is antithetical to the apostolic Gospel and creedal Christianity.

First Challenge Point: Crossan's Textual Foundation Not of the New Testament

But how does Crossan arrive at this conclusion, since there seems to be an admission on his part that *something* happened, that there were *some* original beliefs about resurrection among the earliest Christians? Certainly the Gospels and Paul are clear and emphatic that some occurrence gave rise to their proclamation and organization. Perhaps, says Crossan, but only subsequently so. The canonical Gospels, he says, are dependent upon (and depart from) an *earlier* Gospel, the nonextant "cross gospel," which was best preserved in the apocryphal but extant *Gospel of Peter*.[28] Paul, likewise, is to be rejected as an early source, since he represents second-generation Christianity.[29] And, his reasoning goes, second-generation Christianity represents a fundamental departure from the original sources, adding through redaction nonhistorical "nature miracles" (including a bodily resurrection) for reasons of appropriating ecclesiastical power: "[T]he nature miracles of Jesus are actually creedal statements about ecclesiastical authority, although they all have as their background Jesus' resurrectional victory over death, which is, of course, the supreme nature miracle."[30] Consequently, the New Testament writers are themselves fabricators of myth that results in further oppression: "[T]he *words and deeds* of Jesus were updated to speak to new situations and

---

[28]Crossan, *The Historical Jesus*, 427.

[29]Crossan, *The Birth of Christianity*, xxvii.

[30]Crossan, *The Historical Jesus*, 404.

problems, new communities and crises. They were adopted, they were adapted, they were invented, they were created."[31] In other words, setting the perverted New Testament aside for a moment, there are even earlier witnesses that give the true story from the 30s and 40s about a cynical peasant Jew and how he challenged the power brokers of his day with parabolic sayings and metaphorical actions, some of which were retained in form by the "cross gospel"/*Gospel of Peter* in the canonicals.

But are the "cross gospel" and the *Gospel of Peter* actually older than the canonical Gospels?

The Gospel of Peter

The so-called *Gospel of Peter* remained shrouded in mystery, being unknown other than by way of Eusebius's reference to Serapion's rejection of it (as well as his own)[32] and a solitary reference from Origen. In 1886–1887, however, during grave excavations in Akhmîm, Upper Egypt, a manuscript was found in the coffin of a monk, which is now known as the "Akhmîm fragment"—a small parchment book of thirty-three leaves written in Greek between the eighth to ninth centuries. The *Gospel of Peter* occupies part of that book with sixty verses, describing the events surrounding the end of Jesus's life, including his trial, crucifixion, burial, and resurrection. Because the final verse of the fragment identifies Simon Peter as the author, most scholars have concluded that this fragment is a portion of the lost *Gospel of Peter*.

Two additional fragments of this Gospel from the third century have been found among the Oxyrhynhus documents (P. Oxy. 2949), but their eighteen verses add little to the existing sixty and differ in several places.[33] Outside of these three fragments and third-century references, there are no other materials to assess. Consequently, scholars rightly place the *Gospel of Peter* as a mid- to late-second-century

---

[31]Crossan, *The Birth of Christianity*, 524. Italics in original.

[32]Eusebius, *Historia ecclesiastica*, 3.3.2; 3.25.6.

[33]Larry Hurtado, *Lord Jesus Christ: Devotion to Jesus in Earliest Christianity* (Grand Rapids, MI: Eerdmans, 2003), 442.

work. Indeed, outside of Dominic Crossan, one is hard pressed to find a single credible scholar who dates this Gospel before 150 AD because of (1) numerous historical errors, "including a preponderance of legendary embellishments and lack of first century historical knowledge"[34] and (2) the demonstrable dependence of the *Gospel of Peter* on, especially, Matthew but evidently all four Gospels.[35] Some of the embellishments and errors include the anachronistic guilt of the Jews, the culturally implausible high priest and scribes sleeping among the tombs of Golgotha, and talking crosses proclaiming the resurrection.[36]

Additionally, Crossan underestimates the role of oral tradition in the formulaic preservation of kerygma in Jewish culture such as we find codified in 1 Corinthians 15:3–7, as well as the significant and prolonged overlap of both oral and written traditions within first-century Christianity.[37] Together, these points have led scholars of all stripes to conclude that Crossan's appeal to the *Gospel of Peter* has no credibility. It is a mid- to late-second-century noncanonical document, repeatedly rejected by the Church fathers not only because

---

[34]Christian Apologetics and Research Ministry, "Does the Gospel of Peter Belong in the New Testament?" accessed 8 January 2016, https://carm.org/does-the-gospel-of-peter-belong-in-the-new-testament.

[35]Charles Quarles substantiates this point: "[A]n examination of the vocabulary, grammar, and style of the two documents strongly favors the dependence of the *Gospel of Peter* on Matthew. Robert Gundry, one of the most respected experts on issues related to Matthew's style, called the phrase a 'series of Mattheanisms' (Gundry, Matthew [Grand Rapids, MI: Eerdmans, 1994], 584). Similarly, John Meier noted 'when it comes to who is dependent on whom, all the signs point to Matthew's priority.' (Meier, *Marginal Jew*, 1:117)." Apologetics, accessed 16 January 2016, https://www.namb.net/apologetics/the-gospel-of-peter.

[36]Craig A. Evans, *Fabricating Jesus: How Modern Scholars Distort the Gospels* (Downers Grove, IL: InterVarsity Press, 2008), 84.

[37]See Richard Bauckham, *Jesus and the Eyewitnesses: The Gospels as Eyewitness Testimony* (Grand Rapids, MI: Eerdmans, 2006), chapter 9, "Models of Oral Tradition," and chapter 10, "Transmitting the Jesus Traditions."

its authorship could not be attributed to Peter but also because of its promotion of false doctrine and comparatively late composition.[38]

The "Cross Gospel"

When Crossan appeals to the "cross gospel" as the foundation for the *Gospel of Peter* and therefore the canonical Gospels,[39] he finds a similar result: total rejection by the scholarly community. Without so much as a single fragment to substantiate the existence of any so-called "cross gospel" nor any plausibility to his two-traditions model in which there allegedly exists a "male exegetical tradition [that used Hebrew Scriptures as a parabolic paradigm]" and a "female lament tradition" that turned the male tradition into a "passion-resurrection story," the academy has dismissed his methodology and conclusions regarding the origins of the Gospel narratives and resurrection proclamation as "eccentric and implausible."[40] Larry Hurtado calls the "cross gospel" postulation flatly unpersuasive.[41] William Lane Craig notes that Harvard University's Helmut Koester rejects Crossan's reasoning as "seriously flawed" and then cites N. T. Wright's appraisal in which he states that Crossan's antecedent Gospels to the canonical Gospels hypothesis "has not been accepted yet by any other serious scholar," and the dates and origins suggested by Crossan "are purely imaginary."[42]

---

[38]J. A. T. Robinson, *Redating the New Testament* (Philadelphia, PA: Westminster, 1976), 188; cf. Michael J. Krueger, *Canon Revisited: Establishing the Origins and Authority of the New Testament Books* (Wheaton, IL: Crossway, 2012), 117, 135. Eusebius condemned it as "altogether wicked and impious" (*Historia ecclesiastica*, 3.25.7.).

[39]"What we have there in my best reconstruction is but a single line of scribal tradition, from the *Cross Gospel* into and through the canonical gospels. . . ." Crossan, *The Birth of Christianity*, 573.

[40]Ben Meyer, critical notice of *The Historical Jesus*, by John Dominic Crossan, *Catholic Biblical Quarterly* 55 (1993): 575.

[41]Larry Hurtado, *Lord Jesus Christ*, 444 n. 51.

[42]Helmut Koestler, *Ancient Christian Gospels* (London: SCM, 1990), 220 and N. T. Wright, *Jesus and the Victory of God* (Minneapolis, MN: Fortress Press, 1996), 49, cited in William Lane Craig, "Presuppositions

There is no evidence for a "cross gospel," and no one but Crossan dates the *Gospel of Peter* to the first century, let alone the 30s or 40s. What is more, Paul's writings are actually the earliest known writings of Christianity, which renders Crossan's dismissal of Pauline testimony regarding the resurrection and its connection to the origins of Christianity inexcusable. It is actually Crossan, not the New Testament authors, who has been writing "literary fiction."

"Bracketing" Paul

In order to posit his "Gospels" as of primary importance in his account of the birth of Christianity, Crossan must make Paul's writings secondary. He therefore programmatically "brackets" out the Pauline epistles to focus on the Christianity of the 30s and 40s.[43] This approach to the historical research of the period, however, cannot be obtained for two simple reasons. First, explains Larry Hurtado, is the problem "of not having any direct source from Jewish Christian groups from these early decades on which to build a discussion."[44] Without any tangible or discernible evidence for the existence of a "cross gospel," the *Gospel of Peter* is our only consideration. But as has already been established, it not only is from a much later period,[45] but it also arises from *within* an established Christian community (likely Syria) with condemnatory statements about Judaism.[46] It is not of Jewish-Christian origins at all. Significantly, there is no going back further than Paul because Paul's letters are, indisputably, the earliest historical documentation of Christianity, with his first epistles

---

and Pretensions of the Jesus Seminar," accessed 16 January 2016, http://www.reasonablefaith.org/presuppositions-and-pretensions-of-the-jesus-seminar#text12. Even Bart Ehrman says that the *Gospel of Peter* is of little value for Jesus scholarship (*How Jesus Became God: The Exaltation of a Jewish Preacher from Galilee* [San Francisco, CA: HarperOne, 2014], 94).

[43]Crossan, *The Birth of Christianity*, xxvii and 15.

[44]Hurtado, *Lord Jesus Christ*, 82.

[45]For perspective, the mid- to late-second-century composition of the *Gospel of Peter* is as distant from the time of Jesus as the Civil War is from our time.

[46]Hurtado, *Lord Jesus Christ*, 443–47.

dating from ~48–50 AD,[47] and any source after 1 Thessalonians, 1 Corinthians, and Galatians must find continuity with *their* content, which is precisely what we find in the New Testament, especially the Gospel of Mark, Acts, and 1 Peter.[48]

The second problem with omitting Paul as part of Crossan's historical method, articulated by Larry Hurtado, is that "Paul was not simply a Christian figure of the 50s . . . the Christian Paul takes us back much earlier."[49] Crossan would have us believe Paul's conversion occurs deep into the Christian movement. It does not. If Jesus was crucified in the year 33 AD, then Saul of Tarsus was converted as early as 34 but no later than 35 AD. Paul enters at the ground floor, "within what in terms of social history must be regarded as the 'birth' of the Christian movement."[50] According to Paul Barnett, "Paul's letters can be dated with confidence as literature close in time to Jesus, written *by one who had been part of New Testament history almost from its inception,* whether as persecutor or as apostle."[51] Even earlier, Saul the zealous Pharisee is in Jerusalem persecuting the Way of Jesus (1 Corinthians 15:9; Philippians 3:6). Reflecting on that time that gave way to his dramatic conversion, Paul can say in Galatians 1:13, 21–23 that by 36/37 AD, the "churches of Christ" (in the plural!) were "glorifying God" that he "who used to persecute us is now preaching the faith he once tried to destroy" (Galatians 1:23).

So within a very compressed timescale, Jesus is being proclaimed as the once-crucified, now-risen Christ in Jerusalem, suffering persecution on account of it within its very same birth year, with established churches in cities as far away as Damascus (136 miles to the north), with Pharisee Saul of Tarsus overseeing persecutions, being converted, and testifying to extant churches within four years of the original crucifixion and resurrection events in regions as distant as

---

[47]Paul W. Barnett, *Jesus and the Logic of History,* ed. D. A. Carson (Downers Grove, IL: InterVarsity Press, 1997), 41.

[48]See Barnett, *Finding the Historical Christ* (Grand Rapids, MI: Eerdmans, 2009), chapter 8, "Christ in Paul's Letters."

[49]Hurtado, *Lord, Jesus Christ,* 82.

[50]Ibid.

[51]Barnett, *Jesus and the Logic of History,* 92. Emphasis added.

Syria and Cilicia (Galatians 1:21). Paul could hardly be closer to the origins of the Christian movement and, indeed, is so close that he can be numbered among the apostles and so with contemporary eye-witnesses to the resurrected Christ Jesus (1 Corinthians 15:8). And it is this same figure who writes to and about the churches of Christ, with which he has considerable history, knowledge, and intimacy, the Gospel that Christ Jesus himself delivered unto him (Galatians 1:12), confirmed by Ananias (Acts 9:17–19), and commended by Peter, James, and John in Jerusalem (Galatians 2:7–9). No source could be more fundamental in ascertaining the beliefs and practices of the early Christians than Paul.

In light of these facts, Crossan would have his readers still dismiss Paul by believing that the apostle was neither important nor influential to the early church and, while the earliest author and himself present at the inception of this movement, only became notable to the church at the end of the first century. Larry Hurtado responds by stating, conclusively:

> Whatever the validity of Crossan's judgment here, the extent of Paul's personal influence upon the theology of first-century Christianity is an irrelevant issue. Paul is important for historical analysis of the earliest Christian decades mainly because of his personal participation in Christian circles in these early years, his acquaintance with Christian traditions from the earliest years of Christianity, and the reflections in his letters of the beliefs and practices of Christian circles of the 50s and previous decades.[52]

The continuity between the proclamation of the earliest disciples before and after Easter does not depend on the narrative of Acts and certainly cannot be deduced from the *Gospel of Peter*. But it may be ascertained from scores of references in Paul's letters—the earliest Christian writings that are essentially germane to historical investigation. Paul's letters support the assertion of Peter in Acts that "God has made him both Lord and Christ, this Jesus whom you crucified"

---

[52]Hurtado, *Lord, Jesus Christ*, 84.

(Acts 2:36). Crossan doesn't have a valid source to make any possible claim about the earliest Christian beliefs whatsoever.

Second Challenge Point: Platonic St. Paul

The attempt to dismiss Paul receives justification by Crossan because of his alleged Platonic "dualism and inconsistency."[53] Here, Crossan speaks to the supposed 1 Corinthian 15 flesh *v.* spirit and natural *v.* spiritual juxtaposing, not realizing "that Paul simply reflects (and adapts in the life of his Christian beliefs) the dualistic categories that characterize ancient Jewish apocalyptic traditions."[54] Put differently, Paul is talking about what happens to human beings in the transformation occurrence through resurrection: the totality of their humanity—including their flesh—will be empowered by the Spirit of God; it will be rendered a "spiritual body."

Paul frames the introduction to 1 Corinthians 15:35–49 in a way that *confronts* Platonic dualism and the disdain for the body. He insists that the "resurrection of the dead" refers to the transformation into a new and glorious state—the future or eschatological state. Salvation, then, is an eschatological concept, not about returning but renewal. Salvation accordingly means the completion of that which was intended for the human being, including the body.

Although it is often assumed that Paul's distinction between flesh and spirit is the equivalent of the traditional philosophical distinction between body and spirit, as Crossan assumes, that's not the case. Paul's division is not ontological but eschatological: not about different kinds of being temporarily put together but between the fallen and the fully redeemed human person, in accordance with a Hebraic definition of human being given in, for example, Genesis 1:7, where physical matter plus "the Spirit of life" equals a human soul. In Jewish biblical thought, the picture is of a spiritual-physical unity, a psychophysical person whose very reality—the whole human person,

---

[53]Crossan, *The Birth of Christianity*, xxvii.

[54]Hurtado, *Lord Jesus Christ*, 90.

body included—depends at every turn on being upheld by the Spirit of God.[55]

The analogy of the seed in v. 36ff. allows Paul to assert both the radical *transformation* of the body in its resurrected state and yet its *organic continuity* with the mortal body that preceded it. This delicate balance between continuity and discontinuity characterizes the discussion as a whole. So while Paul agrees with the Corinthian deniers of the resurrection on the conviction that "flesh and blood cannot inherit the kingdom of God" (as he puts it in v. 50), he insists that our future life must nonetheless be *embodied*. That's the point of the resurrection: it transforms radically one body into a different kind of body. This is why he's at pains to argue that the concept of "body" is not univocal, where the meaning of "body" is the same even though the word is being applied to different orders of being. For instance, he says, there are many different kinds of bodies, including not only the endless diversity of animal bodies but also the various heavenly "bodies"—sun, moon, stars (vv. 39–41). A resurrected body uses up and alters beyond our understanding of physics human flesh as we know it.

Once this analogical use of the word "body" or "flesh" is established, we can more easily make the imaginative inference to a different kind of human body, a body raised up by God with a glory like that of the heavenly bodies—in short, what Paul calls (as he stretches the limits of human understanding and reaches for words that approach what he is talking about) "a spiritual body" (vv. 42–44). This sort of body is entirely outside our present experience (except insofar as we know something about it through the body of the risen Christ), but it is nonetheless a *body*.

All the analogies of vv. 36–41 lead up to the point of the argument in v. 42: "So it is with the resurrection of the dead." Binary contrasts follow to affirm the resurrection of the dead. Whereas our present bodies are "sown" in this life perishable, dishonorable, and weak, the resurrection body will be raised in the life-after-life-after-death imperishable, glorious, and powerful (vv. 42–43). "Human

---

[55]"Likewise, Paul's varied uses of the term 'flesh' (*sarx*) reflect recognizably biblical and Jewish traditions, not Platonism (not even a 'moderate' version)," writes Larry Hurtado, *Lord Jesus Christ*, 91.

beings are created to be perfected," writes Colin Gunton, "and so in a different way is the whole creation . . . There is therefore no creation 'in the beginning' without an eschatological orientation. From the beginning, it has a destiny, a purpose."[56] The claim of the New Testament is that in the true Israelite, Jesus of Nazareth, the promise is made concrete. Human failure and earthly corruption—the movement from creation to dissolution is reversed beginning with Jesus's bodily resurrection. *That's* the credible Gospel of Paul and the evangelists, and it is in keeping with the antecedent governing narrative of the Old Covenant.

Paul, then, does not articulate resurrection in a parabolic vacuum but inescapably relates the eschatological climax of redemption to a historical event: the concrete resurrection of Christ Jesus. When Paul speaks about the resurrection of Jesus, the miracles he refers to are not for the most part used as proof for things that would not otherwise be believed. They are part of a wider set of beliefs about the way God is and the way He publicly works in the world. This is why Paul, so far from retreating into a literary device (fiction), actually names witnesses of the resurrected Jesus (1 Corinthians 15:3–8) and challenges those with the means, motive, and ability to confirm or deny the Gospel message since "these things were not done in a corner" (Acts 26:26).

Third Challenge Point: Meaning over Matter

Because of a backlog of Jewish martyrs awaiting vindication,[57] the Judean societal need for hope, Jesus's desire to subvert the myth of Rome with his own parabolic and cynical take on death (viz. life!), and the notion of "resurrection" as the ultimate power play, Dominic Crossan metaphorically utilizes the concept of resurrection in order to articulate Jesus's and the earliest disciples' (whoever they may

---

[56]Colin Gunton, *The Christian Faith: An Introduction to Christian Doctrine* (Oxford: Blackwell, 2002), 19.

[57]See Crossan's argument in John Dominic Crossan and N. T. Wright, *The Resurrection of Jesus: John Dominic Crossan and N. T. Wright in Dialogue*, ed. Robert B. Stewart (Minneapolis, MN: Fortress Press, 2006), 25.

have been) kingdom message. That message is inherently malleable since it isn't fixed in any extant text and because the New Testament authors altered whatever resurrection parables they inherited for political purposes. In this way, Dominic Crossan doesn't actually report *on* Jesus as much as he ascribes whatever meaning he desires to this parabolic figure and the accounts about him, including the resurrection: Hence, "Emmaus never happened. Emmaus always happens."[58] In this way, Crossan shifts the focus of the Gospel from Jesus the Christ to messages latent within Christian parables.

Here, there are three responses. First, Jesus Christ is the message; he is *the* object of faith. Peter admonishes Christians to "grow in the grace and knowledge of our Lord and Savior Jesus Christ" (2 Peter 3:18). Likewise, Paul proclaimed "Jesus Christ and him crucified" (1 Corinthians 2:2) as his central message. Note that it is *Christ* crucified. For Paul, Jesus of Nazareth is the crucified Christ. Moreover, John concludes his Gospel with these words: "[B]ut these are written so that you may believe that Jesus is the Christ, the Son of God, and that by believing you may have life in his name" (20:31). These three testators would be in harmony with the recorded sayings of Christ himself:

> I am the bread of life. (John 6:35, 48)
> I am the light of the world. (John 8:12, 9:5)
> Before Abraham was, I am. (John 8:58)
> I am the door. (John 10:9)
> I am the good shepherd. (John 10:11)
> I am the resurrection and the life. (John 11:25)
> I am the way, the truth, and the life. (John 14:6)

Jesus shifts the focus from all known significant Jewish identity markers onto himself, claiming to fulfill their purpose and set himself as the new paragon of divine experience, life, salvation, righteousness, and knowledge.[59] Indeed, Simeon had it correct when holding the

---

[58]Crossan, *Jesus: A Revolutionary Biography*, 197.

[59]See N. T. Wright, *The Challenge of Jesus* (London: SPCK, 2000), *passim*.

infant Jesus and saying, "[M]y eyes have seen [YHWH's] salvation" (Luke 2:30), and it was Christ himself.

Second, N. T. Wright astutely notes, "The terms 'literal' and 'metaphorical' refer, properly, to *the ways words refer to things*, not to the things to which the words refer. For the latter task, the appropriate words might be 'concrete' and 'abstract.'"[60] And so Crossan has not actually dealt with the referent's terminus when it comes to the resurrection. Christians like Paul and Peter and John *did* develop metaphorical usages. However, they always referred to concrete states of affairs by their own admission and by intertestimonial confirmation[61] across the New Testament documents: "[T]he normal meaning of this [metaphorical] language was to refer, literally, to a concrete state of affairs."[62]

Lastly, the Gospels and Paul have a metaphor *for* resurrection with the concept of baptism (e.g., Romans 6:3–11). Here, again, the eschatological elements of redemption find their fruition not in a metaphor but in a concrete historical event—resurrection, which gives rise to an already meaning-laden metaphor in baptism. And yet even baptism isn't left in the dimension of literary fiction or theological placeholder. Baptism itself *is* a concrete event that brings to bear in the present the eschatological reality of resurrection through the revivification or regeneration of the human spirit (Titus 3:5). Resurrection, then, is not and cannot be reduced to a parabolic punch line for a paradigm of metaphoric meaning, since even baptism itself is event oriented, yielding the reality that it simultaneously *illustrates*. The resurrection is not the power of metaphor but another kind of power altogether, divine power eschatologically exercised, bringing into the present the promised redemption of all things,[63] beginning with the human body of Jesus Christ.

---

[60]N. T. Wright, *The Resurrection of the Son of God* (Minneapolis, MN: Fortress Press, 2003), xix.

[61]Barnett, *Finding the Historical Christ*, cc. 2, 4, 5, and 8.

[62]N. T. Wright, *The Resurrection of the Son of God*, xix.

[63]Gunton, *The Christian Faith*, 19.

Fourth Challenge Point: The Four Gospels

Earlier it was noted that the simplicity and elegance of Paul's explication of the Gospel as a result of and consisting in no less than
a concrete resurrection is lost amid Crossan's complex and sophisticated process of mining for the meaning of this parabolic metaphorical "event" through the foil of his imaginary "cross gospel." This is a
messy and unpredictable process, especially in light of what Crossan
says about the power-mongering evangelists redacting and confect-
ing swaths of the Gospels. But even this suggestion betrays everything we read about the disciples and apostles of early Christianity,
that they were honest to a fault, self-critical, and willing martyrs
who lost all for the sake of the Christ they vowed conquered physical
death through a bodily resurrection. Their eyewitness explanation
was more akin to Occam's razor (God raised Christ from the dead)
than Crossan's confusticated, baseless theories.

The four canonical Gospels are literarily unique in the ancient
world, being *sui generis*.[64] What distinguishes a Gospel from all other
literature is that it is the kerygmatic record of the words and deeds
of Jesus. The words and deeds of Jesus are not simply recounted, as
in Greco-Roman biography, in order to present the ethos of a person (approximating Crossan's view). Rather, the concern is to present Jesus as the Messiah and his death and resurrection as part of
his messianic calling and as essential to his accomplishment. This is
why a Gospel must be defined as the kerygmatic record of the words
and deeds of Jesus. The Gospels do something—namely, proclaim,
witness, and challenge. Kerygmatic is an adjective derived from the
noun kerygma, which is the Greek word meaning proclamation
or preaching. In the New Testament, it denotes the content of the
message that Jesus is the Messiah, the one anointed by God to bring
eschatological salvation to Israel, rejected, crucified, and vindicated
by being raised from the dead (Romans 16:25; 1 Corinthians 1:21; 2:4;
15:14; 2 Timothy 4:17; Titus 1:3). And the New Testament actually
becomes and does kerygmatic proclamation. In most cases, it seems

---

[64]Larry Hurtado, "Gospel (Genre)," *Dictionary of Jesus and the Gospels*, ed.
J. Green, S. McKnight, and I. H. Marshall (Downers Grove, IL: InterVarsity
Press, 1992), 276–82.

that the noun "kerygma" is the functional equivalent of Ευαγγέλιο—
Gospel. To say that the Gospel genre is the kerygmatic record of the
words and deeds of Jesus is to say that its ultimate purpose is to set
down in writing the originally oral proclamation of this kerygma of
the birth, life, death, resurrection, and ascension of God's Messiah,
Jesus of Nazareth.

As a genre of fulfillment, they bear profound continuity with
the Hebrew scriptures, yielding a story line that proclaims Jesus as
our righteousness and himself as our salvation, atonement, resurrection, and eternal life. The Gospel is simple and elegant, understood
by rural agrarians in the first century.

Crossan's Views from Crucifixion to Resurrection

Jesus of Nazareth was really crucified. There's no doubt in Crossan's
mind about this historical event: "[T]here is not the slightest doubt
about the *fact* of Jesus' crucifixion under Pontius Pilate."[65] It happened and we know this to be the case because of corroborating
extrabiblical testimony to the historicity of Jesus, such as we find in
Josephus.[66] To be sure, the entire passion narratives are parabolic
and derivative, but they are working from an actual event—the crucifixion of Jesus. Although, for Crossan, the *meaning* of crucifixion
supersedes all, there is the question of what actually happened to the
body of that executed Jesus, since it would not have been a constitu-
tive part of the parable of passion-resurrection.

Although Crossan truly believes it doesn't matter what happened, as a historian he resorts to what he understands to be the
burial practices for people in Jesus's circumstances—poor, crucified, and dead. As such, Crossan supposes that either (a) Jesus
wasn't removed from the cross but left as carrion for birds and dogs,
or (b) he was taken down by the authorities and thrown in a ditch,
covered with lime, and again left as carrion for birds and dogs.[67]

---

[65]Crossan, *The Historical Jesus*, 375. Italics in original.

[66]Josephus, *Antiquities of the Jews*, 20:9, 1.

[67]Crossan, *Jesus, A Revolutionary Biography*, 123–26. Crossan's hypothesis undergoes recycling in the work of Bart Ehrman, who likewise assumes

He concludes, "With regard to the body of Jesus, by Easter Sunday morning, those who care did not know where it was, and those who knew did not care."[68]

Each point may be contested. For starters, Jesus's poverty has never been established as fact. Arguments about wealth versus penury amount to equipollence. So, historically speaking, Crossan begins with presumption. More compelling, however, is Craig Evans's research regarding Jewish burial practices, which contra-indicate Crossan's dog-food theory.[69] Scholarly opinion agrees with Craig that the Jews of Jesus's day fastidiously observed Torah burial mandates regardless of the deceased's economic status and circumstances. And given that Crossan has no biblical support for his supposition, Evans finds ample verisimilitudes within the Gospels themselves. The likelihood of Joseph of Arimathea taking responsibility for Jesus's body and laying it to rest in his own family tomb comports with known *Jewish* sources, both biblical and extra-biblical. Furthermore, archeological findings have evidenced that even crucified Jews underwent prescribed burial customs.[70] Roman accommodation with these customs is also well known and amply recorded.

Still, buried or not, the empty tomb is irrelevant for Crossan.[71] And this may be the moment when the emperor is discovered to have

---

that Jesus's body "was left to decompose and serve as food for scavenging animals." (*How Jesus Became God: The Exaltation of a Jewish Preach from Galilee* [San Francisco, CA: HarperOne, 2014], 157).

[68]Crossan, *The Historical Jesus*, 125–27.

[69]Craig A. Evans, "The Silence of Burial," in *Jesus, the Final Days: What Really Happened*, ed. Troy A. Miller (Louisville, KY: Westminster John Knox Press, 2009), 39–73.

[70]Evans in Miller, *Jesus, the Final Days*, 53–55.

[71]Crossan has theological objections to defending the historical factuality of the empty tomb. Foremost is the undesirable effect it has on the meaning of Easter faith by dwelling on a past event as opposed to the continuing experience of the risen Christ. Additionally, the factuality of the empty tomb has a totalizing effect on other faiths, signaling the superiority of Christianity. Lastly, the miracle of the empty tomb bespeaks of an interventionist God, which he rejects.

no clothes. Whereas in the nineteenth and most of the twentieth centuries, skeptics took seriously and had to grapple with the fact of the empty tomb (and did so with accusations of apostolic thievery or swoon theory and the like), proponents of progressive Christianity dispense with any consideration of the tomb whatsoever. Jesus never makes it to a tomb. He's left to decompose in a shallow grave or consumed by birds or dogs. It becomes a clear signal that the shift in Crossan's mind from an acknowledgement of a historical trial and crucifixion to a parabolic resurrection and ascension is nothing other than his ideological commitment to antisupernaturalistic presuppositions. He omits the fact of the reported entombment of Jesus and its subsequent vacancy precisely because it has been predetermined in his naturalistic world view that God acting in human history through miraculous action is nonsense. And so, while Crossan may claim that it is the meaning that matters, that meaning has ceased to be exegetically derived and has become altogether eisegetical. There is no Christ risen from the dead, not really, not historically. What we are presented with, then, is a "Christ" unrelated to Jesus of Nazareth and, therefore, someone or something other than Jesus Christ—namely, antichrist. Thus Crossan, it turns out, is really that cynic he makes Jesus out to be.

Conclusion

John Dominic Crossan maintains the Gospels were never intended by their authors to be taken literally. But they were at the behest of the earliest named witnesses. He argues that the meaning of the story is the real issue, not whether a particular story about Jesus is history. Yet every bit of evidence from first-century Christians holds the two inseparably tethered, with the former argued and substantiated upon the latter. Crossan believes in a vision hypothesis of "resurrection" by faith but holds that bodily resuscitation was never contemplated by early Christians. However, there's no evidence for such an assertion, while orthodoxy has compelling testimony, founded upon established Jewish beliefs about corporeal resurrection. The fact is the rise and spread of earliest Christianity predicated upon the historical death and reported real-world bodily resurrection of Jesus Christ are demonstrably factual.

Crossan's methodology is predicated upon a late dating of the New Testament texts and an early dating of the *Gospel of Peter*. Yet again, Crossan's early dating of the *Gospel of Peter* stands contrary to all credible scholarship, and his postulation of a "cross gospel" is rejected in *toto*. Neither the imagined "cross gospel" nor the *Gospel of Peter* possess the possibility of meeting any criteria as the textual foundation for historical investigations into Jesus or the origins of Christianity.

In the final analysis, Dominic Crossan's metaphorical interpretations betray his presuppositional naturalism and commitment to structuralism. His facilitation of an apparitional Jesus is decidedly heretical because the "Christ" he posits is "other than" (ἀντίχριστος) the risen Jesus of Nazareth, the Christ of God. But he backs out of even this assertion by rendering any "vision" of a risen Jesus as "literary fiction."

For the earliest *known* Christians, such as Paul, the resurrection was seen to consist of passing through death and out the other side into a new sort of bodily life. As Romans 8 shows, Paul clearly believed that God would give new life to the mortal bodies of Christians and indeed to the entire created world: "If the Spirit of the God who raised Jesus from the dead dwells in you, he who raised the Messiah Jesus from the dead will give life to your mortal bodies also through his Spirit who lives in you" (Romans 8:11). This is a radical mutation from within Jewish belief and yet at the same time consistent with Jewish expectations concerning future embodied life. Crossan, on the other hand, focuses on the effect of "resurrection belief" rather than on the basis for belief in resurrection, which has always been *God raised Jesus from the dead* in the event proclaimed and celebrated as *the* resurrection.

The collapsed methodology and extravagant conclusions of John Dominic Crossan, while the stuff of unconventional reading and entertaining television programming, expose at a foundational level the radical departure of progressive Christianity from New Covenant faith and therefore from allegiance and devotion to Jesus Christ our Lord, who with the Father and the Spirit are one God, now and forever.

Recommended Reading

Barnett, Paul W. *Finding the Historical Christ.* Grand Rapids, MI: Eerdmans, 2009.

————. *Jesus and the Logic of History*, New Studies in Biblical Theology. Edited by D. A. Carson. Downers Grove, IL: InterVarsity Press, 1997.

Bauckham, Richard. *Jesus and the Eyewitnesses: The Gospels as Eyewitness Testimony.* Grand Rapids, MI: Eerdmans, 2006.

Copan, Paul, ed. *Will the Real Jesus Please Stand Up?: A Debate between William Lane Craig and John Dominic Crossan.* Grand Rapids, MI: Baker Academic, 1999.

Crossan, John Dominic, and N. T. Wright. *The Resurrection of Jesus: John Dominic Crossan and N. T. Wright in Dialogue.* Edited by Robert B. Stewart. Minneapolis, MN: Fortress Press, 2006.

Evans, Craig A., and N. T. Wright. *Fabricating Jesus: How Modern Scholars Distort the Gospels.* Downers Grove, IL: InterVarsity Press, 2008.

————. *Jesus, the Final Days: What Really Happened.* Edited by Troy A. Miller. Louisville, KY: Westminster John Knox Press, 2009.

Hurtado, Larry. *Lord Jesus Christ: Devotion to Jesus in Earliest Christianity.* Grand Rapids, MI: Eerdmans, 2003.

Walsh, Richard. *Mapping Myths of Biblical Interpretation: Playing the Texts.* Edinburgh: T&T Clark, 2001.

4

The Case against
The Case against Christianity:
When Jerusalem Came to Athens

Craig A. Parton

There is a marvelous scene in Woody Allen's Academy Award–winning film *Annie Hall*, where Allen is in line in New York City to buy a ticket to watch a film. In front of Allen is a very vocal and opinionated professional scholar who considers himself to be an authority on the life and work of Marshall McLuhan, the Canadian public intellectual and cultural commentator of a generation ago. After listening to this professor go on and on about how he teaches a class at NYU on the "real" Marshall McLuhan, an exasperated Allen pleads to the viewer: "Don't you wish you could bring Marshall McLuhan into this line right now and have him respond directly to these statements?" At which point the real and very living Marshall McLuhan steps before the camera and stands next to Allen and confronts the opinionated academic with the comment: "You understand nothing about my work. Your opinions are baseless and I think it a terrible crime that you even teach a class about me and my views." Allen looks at the camera and says: "Don't you wish life were like this *just once in a while*?"

Some of us, like Allen, wish life were indeed like that just "once in a while."

What follows is a fulfilling in part of that wish by bringing a critic face-to-face with those he criticizes.

Here we bring back persons who long ago left this world for the purpose of allowing them to "defend themselves" against a contemporary critic. In this case, we bring together a modern atheistic and avowedly anti-Christian philosopher (Michael Martin) with these historic figures who, as percipient witnesses of certain central events involving Jesus of Nazareth, respond directly to the contentions Martin has made in his various attacks on Christianity.

Moderator: Welcome to tonight's program, "Lawyers on Trial," a special PBS series that puts lawyers and judges on the witness stand and brings legal analysis and legal standards of proof to some of the most intractable and persistent questions of our day.

Through advanced fiber-genetic optics and the generous support of the Longevity Project at the Ponce de Leon Institute, and in partnership with the Biogenics Department of the Medical School of the University of California at San Francisco, we once again are presenting live testimony from historical persons who have been dead—in some cases for centuries. A patent application is pending, and this program may not be recorded for any purpose.

Tonight's program takes place at the University of California, Hastings College of the Law, just minutes away from the California Supreme Court building here in downtown San Francisco. We are meeting in the beautiful oak-paneled Wigmore Room, named in honor of the famous John Henry Wigmore, professor of evidence at Hastings almost a century ago.[1] Wigmore, along with such legal luminaries as William Prosser,[2] former United States Supreme Court Justice Arthur Goldberg, and Roger Traynor, former Chief Justice

---

[1] For the apologetical application of Wigmore's evidential methodology, see John Warwick Montgomery, *Christ as Centre and Circumference: Essays Theological, Cultural and Polemic* (Bonn, Germany: Culture & Science Publ., 2012), 182–93. The pertinent chapter is entitled "A New Approach to the Apologetic for Christ's Resurrection by Way of Wigmore's Juridical Analysis of Evidence."

[2] *Prosser on Torts* is the essential hornbook on the topic and is on its fifth edition and counting: William L. Prosser, *Handbook of the Law of Torts* (St. Paul, MN: West Publishing, 1941).

of the California Supreme Court, were members of the renowned "Over-65 Club" here at Hastings.

In attendance tonight are judicial officers from the state and federal benches both at the trial and appellate levels, as well as lawyers and first-year law students, or "1L's."[3] Questions from the audience are encouraged, and feel free to post them to our Twitter account so that they may be posed in real time. We also have a special interlocutor for tonight's panel: Professor Emeritus in Philosophy at Boston University, Dr. Michael Martin, author of *The Case against Christianity*,[4] whose position is that there is no credible, let alone legally compelling, evidence for the resurrection of Jesus of Nazareth.

We have a very distinguished and unusual group of witnesses for our discussion today. Our panelists are a group of prominent first-century judges and practicing lawyers[5] who all claim to have evidence going to the question we wish to address tonight: Did Jesus of Nazareth, who is called Christ, rise from the dead?

First, let's go around the table and hear a brief summary of your *bona fides* before we get to your own testimonies about the question before us.

Dr. Gamaliel: Chief Justice of the Jerusalem Supreme Court (known as the Sanhedrin[6]) in 33 AD, grandson of Hillel the Elder, one of

---

[3]For an account of the first year at the Harvard Law School, see Scott Turrow, *One L* (New York: Penguin Books, 2010). A number of former Harvard Law faculty have comprised the membership of the Hastings "Over-65 Club."

[4]Michael Martin, *The Case against Christianity* (Philadelphia, PA: Temple University Press, 1991).

[5]In point of fact, the functions of judge and lawyer, trier of fact and advocate, were not distinct in Jewish law in the first century. Thus Paul acted as both in his capacity as persecutor of Christians. Walter M. Chandler, *The Trial of Jesus from a Lawyer's Standpoint* (New York: Empire Publ. Co., 1908), 280; Acts 22:1–5. In the matter of the stoning of Stephen, members of the Sanhedrin acted as prosecutors, judges, and executioners (cf. Acts 7:57–8:1).

[6]The Sanhedrin was a collection of seventy-one scribes, elders (including Pharisees), and chief priests like Annas and Caiaphas (John 18:19–24), with

the great systematizers and teachers of Rabbinic law. I obtained a
Ph.D. in Mosaic Law[7] and was a professor of law in first-century
Palestine. Paul of Tarsus, Barnabas, Stephen, and other eventual
followers of Jesus Christ were some of my brightest students.[8] I
sat as a trial judge in literally hundreds of civil and criminal cases
and have listened to and weighed testimony from those in all walks
of life. The judges in my district relied on me for counsel in particularly difficult cases. For example, the Sanhedrin asked for my
advice when they were prosecuting John and Paul for sedition and
blasphemy.[9]

Very few of my decisions were ever overturned on appeal. I
have sentenced more than a few criminals to execution. Such capital
sentences, of course, are always subject to the confirmation of the
Roman governor, who alone has the authority to carry out a sentence for capital punishment.[10] So I know the importance of sifting
evidence carefully, especially in cases where the life of the defendant
is at issue. My activities in relation to Christianity in general and
Jesus of Nazareth in particular have been accurately recounted by a

---

ultimate authority in capital cases resting with the chief priests, who would then
confirm the death sentence with the Roman governor, who then would carry
out the punishment. The Great Sanhedrin has been compared with the Senate
of Rome, the Areopagus in Athens, and Parliament in England. Chandler,
The Trial of Jesus from a Lawyer's Standpoint, 176, 179. Jesus confronted and
rebuked its members on numerous occasions. See Matthew 21:31; 23:14–15,
27, 29–33; John 19:20–23.

[7] Acts 5:34.

[8] Ethelbert Callahan, *The Lawyers of the Bible* (Indianapolis, IN: Hollenbeck
Press, 1912), 60–61; Acts 22:3.

[9] Acts 5:38–39. In addition, the third-century Clementine literature known
as "The Recognitions of Clement" (traditionally attributed to Clement of
Rome) says in 1:65–67 that Gamaliel died a Christian. Both the Eastern and
Roman Catholic churches venerate him as a saint. The Greek learned Patriarch
Photius I of Constantinople, writing in the ninth century, says that Gamaliel
and Nicodemus were baptized together by Peter and John, though this claim
has not met with universal agreement. Callahan, *The Lawyers of the Bible*, 49.

[10] John 18:31.

professional physician named Luke, who interviewed me on more than one occasion.[11]

Justice Joseph of Arimathea: I too am a member of the Jerusalem Supreme Court. I provided my own tomb for Jesus and, along with trial lawyer Nicodemus, took the body of Jesus down from the cross on Golgotha, wrapped it in linens and spices,[12] and also personally oversaw placing the body in my tomb. I am accurately (and not flatteringly) referred to as a "secret follower" of Jesus by the chroniclers, but that pretty much came to an end when I asked Pilate for the body of Jesus so that I could give it a decent burial. After confirming with the centurion guard that Jesus was certifiably dead, Pilate granted my request.[13] My actions are discussed by Matthew, Mark, Luke, and John, and I was careful to verify each and every comment made about me.[14]

---

[11]As for Luke's careful confirmation of facts by personal interviewing, see Luke 1:1–4 where he confirms he worked with the eyewitness material and that he had "carefully investigated everything from the beginning"; see also F. F. Bruce, *The New Testament Documents: Are They Reliable?* (Grand Rapids, MI: Eerdmans, 1987), 90 ("Luke's record entitles him to be regarded as a writer of habitual accuracy"). J. A. Scott, professor of Greek at Northwestern University for forty years, calls Luke the Evangelist one of the most learned men of letters in the first century, who wrote "the clearest and best Greek written in that century." John A. Scott, *We Would See Jesus* (Chicago, IL: Abingdon Press, 1936), 134.

[12]For a detailed account of how involved this cement-like "mummy-gummy wrap" process was practiced in Judaism during the first century, see Merrill C. Tenney, *The Reality of the Resurrection* (Chicago, IL: Moody Press, 1963), 117. For the astounding condition in which the burial clothes were found, see John 20:6–7.

[13]Mark 15:44–45.

[14]Matthew 27:57–60; Mark 15:42–46; Luke 23:50–55; and John 19:38–42. Significantly, in addition to any personal sense of duty to Jesus that Joseph and Nicodemus may have had, the Sanhedrin would have been biblically, ceremonially, and legally obligated to ensure the burial of Jesus *before* sundown lest a curse be brought upon the land (according to Deuteronomy 21:22–33 and Josephus, *Jewish Wars*, 4.317: "Jews are so careful about funeral rites that even malefactors who have been sentenced to crucifixion are taken down

Nicodemus: I was also a member of the Sanhedrin, or the Supreme Judicial Council, and became close friends with Justice Arimathea. I was a professor of law, even called "Israel's teacher" by Jesus.[15] My activities are all documented in the Book of John.[16] I saw the dead body of Jesus and brought some embalming spices with me when I met Justice Arimathea at the cross. Like Justice Arimathea, I too was a "secret follower" of Jesus as Messiah until the falafel hit the fan after the crucifixion.

Paul of Tarsus: I am a lawyer by professional training, having sat at the feet of Gamaliel.[17] Most of my legal practice involved executing orders issued by the Supreme Court of my nation to seize the followers of Christ.[18] My legal career ended abruptly when I became a Christian, though I will say the training came in handy more than once when I knew Roman civil procedure well enough to appeal to Caesar and get myself to Rome for a formal trial under Roman law.[19] I was complicit in the execution of many Christians, including Stephen.[20]

---

and buried before sunset."), and, as Craig A. Evans has substantiated in his research, the Sanhedrin would have appointed certain members to ensure the proper disposal of remains of the crucified, suggesting further the plausibility of Nicodemus and Joseph for that task. Craig A. Evans, "The Silence of Burial," in Evans and N. T. Wright, *Jesus, The Final Days: What Really Happened*, ed. Troy A. Miller (Louisville, KY: Westminster John Knox Press, 2009), 39–73.

[15] John 3:10.

[16] John 3:1–21, which not insignificantly contains the "you must be born again" passage as well as John 3:16; John 7:50–51; and John 19:39–42.

[17] Acts 22:3.

[18] Acts 22:4–5; see Callahan, *The Lawyers of the Bible*, 56.

[19] Acts 22:29; Acts 25:10–12; see also A. N. Sherwin-White, *Roman Society and Roman Law in the New Testament* (Oxford: Clarendon Press, 1965) for an in depth look at the accuracy with which the book of Acts reflects Roman legal procedure and Roman society in the first century.

[20] Acts 7:57–8:1, 26:9–11 (which also suggests Paul employed torture as part of his bag of tricks to get confessions).

Moderator: A preliminary question: Why should we care about what role judges or lawyers play in the events we are going to discuss when as a class, they are portrayed so negatively in the Bible in the first place, right?

Dr. Gamaliel: That is not the whole or even predominant picture of the role of law and lawyers in the Bible. It is true that Jesus roundly chastises the legal professionals for their twisted interpretations of Mosaic law and wholesale amendments to the ten commandments. That said, the Law is introduced in the Bible early and often as a restraining force necessary after mankind's fall into sin in Genesis 3. From Moses as the first Law Giver, to judges like Deborah and Ezra, to practicing lawyers like Daniel and Jonathan who were trusted counselors to their clients, law and lawyers are often portrayed positively in the Old Testament.[21]

Paul: And of course in the New Testament, you have those of us at this table, along with lawyers like my colleague Zenas[22] and that fine advocate Apollos,[23] Barnabas and Stephen, and the whole legal system in place that functioned as the trial courts for the various trials of Jesus Christ.[24]

---

[21]Callahan, *The Lawyers of the Bible*, 28. Consider, for example, the important place given to Law and lawyers throughout the Bible but especially in the Old Testament. For how the tradition of lawyers interested in defending the central claims of Christianity has developed over the centuries, see Philip Johnson, "Juridical Apologetics 1600–2000 A.D.: A Bio-Bibliographical Essay," *Global Journal of Classical Theology* 3 (March 2002), 1–25. Johnson's list ranges from Hugo Grotius (the "father of international law") in the sixteenth century to such modern legal apologists as Sir Norman Anderson, Lord Hailsham, Jacques Ellul, and John Warwick Montgomery.

[22]Titus 3:13. Zenas and Apollos are already joined at the hip in the New Testament and clearly are of the learned class entrusted by Paul "with the parchments."

[23]Apollos was—at a minimum—a trained advocate and adept public communicator and later a well-qualified teacher of Christian doctrine. See Acts 18:24–26; 1 Corinthians 3:6.

[24]The subject of the trial of Christ and its conformance or deviation from Jewish legal procedure has been addressed by a number of lawyers. For

Moderator: As mentioned, Dr. Michael Martin has written a critique of Christianity and especially of the resurrection.[25] He raises a number of objections to Christianity, among them that the witnesses to the events around the resurrection were friendly, or at least predisposed, to the cause and told the story from a favorable viewpoint and glossed over unfavorable facts.[26]

Justice Arimathea: I benefitted so much from asking Pilate for the body of Christ? Really? I was ridiculed for that act, not extolled! They even thought I might have conspired with Nicodemus to hide the body and that with some persuasion, I would produce the corpse and end this pernicious lie being circulated about a risen Messiah. Remember, Luke even writes of me that I was a "secret follower" of Christ. And to my shame, I have to admit he was right. I was no zealot for the cause. I thought Jesus a great teacher deserving of a decent burial. Period. I bought the tomb for my family as a place for—read my lips—our family *bodies* to rest and decompose until our bones were collected for permanent placement in ossuaries.[27] Why would I risk the ridicule and persecution to be part of a conspiracy to hide

---

example, see as previously noted, Chandler, *The Trial of Jesus from a Lawyer's Standpoint*, as well as Irwin H. Linton's classic *The Sanhedrin Verdict* (New York: Loizeaux Bros., 1943). See also French Jurist Jean Imbert's *Le Proces de Jesus*, reviewed by John Warwick Montgomery in *Christ Our Advocate* (Bonn, Germany: Culture & Science Publ., 2002), 309–12.

[25]Shortly after the composition of this article, Michael Martin died (27 May 2015). Martin is the author of several influential books promoting atheism and its philosophical justification. See Michael Martin and Keith Augustine, *The Myth of an Afterlife: The Case against Life After Death* (Lanham, MD: Rowman & Littlefield, 2015); Michael Martin and Ricki Monnier, eds., *The Impossibility of God* (Amherst, NY: Prometheus Books, 2003); Michael Martin, *Atheism, Morality and Meaning* (Amherst, NY: Prometheus Books, 2002); Michael Martin, *The Case against Christianity* (Philadelphia, PA: Temple University, 1991); Michael Martin, *Atheism: A Philosophical Justification* (Philadelphia, PA: Temple University, 1989).

[26]Martin, *The Case against Christianity*, 77–78.

[27]For details on this aspect of first-century Jewish burial customs see, Evans and Wright, *Jesus, The Final Days*, 43–45.

the body and pull off a fraud? What was in it for me other than disbarment or worse?[28]

Paul: Well stated, Justice Arimathea, and I will let Nicodemus speak for himself, but I doubt bringing one hundred pounds of costly spices to the cross along with linens to bury Jesus did little to get him invited to all the right Sanhedrin cocktail parties.

As for Peter, John, and Thomas, they were back to their professions immediately after Jesus was crucified. Thomas, in particular, needed no more convincing that he had wasted three years of his life on a pipe dream and that the women's collective hysteria had resulted in them having visions of Jesus appearing and nothing more.

As for me, Dr. Martin, I was hardly "predisposed" to believe in the bodily resurrection of Jesus. My law practice was lucrative and fulfilling—prosecuting heretics was right down my alley. I loved being judge, jury, and executioner and certainly was not "looking to fill an empty void" in my heart when Jesus appeared to me on the Damascus road as Dr. Luke records in Acts 9. I in fact lost my law practice and my reputation for what I would later proclaim—the Gospel of Jesus Christ crucified and resurrected, not only for the Jew but also the gentile. I've given a written statement about this in my open letter to the Galatians.

Moderator: Dr. Martin just tweeted in a question from his seat here in the Wigmore Room: "Is it not possible that we will someday discover through scientific advancement how Jesus accomplished the resurrection? If the answer is 'yes,' then should we not suspend judgment on whether the resurrection actually and factually took place or not?"[29]

---

[28]One should read with some level of amusement the theory of Hugh Schoenfield presented in *The Passover Plot* (New York: Bantam Books, 1981). There, Schoenfield argues that Joseph of Arimathea and Lazarus were coconspirators who colluded with Jesus to orchestrate his own crucifixion, pass out on the cross—thus confounding the Roman guards, who assumed he was dead—and then to revive and fool the disciples into thinking he had been resurrected.

[29]Martin, *The Case against Christianity*, 74: "Jesus is supposed to have been restored to life without the benefit of modern medical technology. Still,

Dr. Gamaliel: First, there is no reason whatsoever that the facts as we know them don't give us a sufficient explanation for the empty tomb of Jesus. Dr. Martin may not *like* the explanation and may wish it were different, but one would think it a sign of maturity to accept the world the way it in fact operates and not live in a speculative hope that things will turn out differently if given enough time. To suspend the Christian proclamation of the empty tomb for an unnecessary hypothetical, if not counterfactual, is to ignore the facts as we have them.

Second, we are talking about a "resurrection" and not a "resuscitation." The eyewitnesses attest that Jesus was not just alive but that He was alive in a body with new and remarkable properties. So while advancements in medical science may result in some remarkable resuscitations in the future, there is little reason to believe those advances will result in a fully resurrected and transformed body that will never die.

Nicodemus: Perhaps an analogy might help: Suppose Dr. Martin was diagnosed with a medical condition, which while serious was not life-threatening as long as he had prompt but radically invasive surgery to address the problem. Now is it possible that the surgical remedy offered could be wrong and that a later discovery will conclusively show that surgery actually would not be necessary at all? Of course, it is *possible*; but in the meantime, Dr. Martin dies while waiting for his answer.

Justice Arimathea: In trials heard before the Sanhedrin, we talk about how necessary it is that witnesses are not allowed to "speculate" at what happened. Such guesswork or hypothesizing is inadmissible as legitimate testimony. The law and courts deal with actual evidence, and the actual evidence overwhelmingly affirms that this Jesus died and was buried, that His tomb was found empty three days later, and that no body was ever produced. Then, on ten separate

---

breakthroughs in medical knowledge could make it understandable how on rare occasions people can come back to life without such technology."

occasions,[30] He appeared to witnesses who attested to the fact of His bodily resurrection.

Moderator: We have a question from Justice Reinhardt of the Federal Court of Appeals for the Ninth Circuit, based here in San Francisco. He wants to know why Paul of Tarsus is even on the panel since he did not witness the resurrection and never mentions an empty tomb in his various New Testament epistles.

Paul: I beg your pardon, Your Honor, but who then appeared to me on the road to Damascus?[31] I was as terrified as anyone considering I was on my way to arrest and imprison Christians in Damascus as part of my business for the Supreme Court of my nation! I then spent a number of years with close followers of Jesus just to make sure I was not following some cleverly devised tale.[32] Considering the disciples and eyewitnesses welcomed me as an apostle—though technically speaking, I was not an eyewitness to the resurrected Lord until after His ascension—and considering I later endured some enhanced interrogation methods,[33] I had every motivation to disavow what I saw and had every reason to verify the facts.

As for me not mentioning the empty tomb in any of my epistles, it is obviously inferred by my repeated references to His bodily resurrection from the dead in all my letters.[34] If Dr. Martin were to simply say he "walked into this lecture hall tonight," would it be therefore an implicit *denial* that he did so "by using his legs"? No, the implication is that he did so with his legs, of course. The fact that Jesus was resurrected from the dead implies an empty tomb, for heaven's sake! Seeing Jesus outside the tomb means the tomb was vacant.

---

[30]These are systematically laid out in a variety of sources, but W. M. Smith does a superb job in his small volume, *The Supernaturalness of Christ* (Boston: W. A. Wilde & Co., 1940), 197–200.

[31]Acts 9:1–5.

[32]Galatians 1:11–2:10.

[33]1 Corinthians 11:16–29.

[34]1 Corinthians 15 is a dissertation on the centrality and nature of the resurrection.

Moderator: This is from a 1L at Hastings who asks what seems to me to be a very perceptive question: Do we have any witnesses to the moment of Jesus's resurrection itself (as opposed to the resurrected Jesus Himself), and if we do not, is this fatal to your case?

Nicodemus: None of us saw the molecules of His body reknit or His amino acids rekindle in the tomb, as one of your poets has said.[35] That would have been impossible in light of the fact that the tomb enclosure was blocked by a disc-shaped stone and was sealed to ensure it would not be moved.[36] I can tell you that Justice Arimathea and I took that body down from the cross, and there was no question that Jesus was dead. That much had been certified by the authorities twice over. Then, seventy-two hours later, there is solid eyewitness testimony (which spans six weeks or more, by the way) that He is alive and recognizable, and in fact was engaged while eating broiled fish, specifically refuting any suggestion that He was a mere ghost.

Dr. Gamaliel: You also have in the civil law the doctrine of *res ipsa loquiter*, or "the thing speaks for itself." It means that there is good and solid evidence that Jesus was dead at point A. There is good and solid evidence that He was found alive at point B. The obvious and legally supported inference is that the man has come back alive. The law does not require an eyewitness to the actual mechanism of *how* it occurred—it is inferred from the facts that are known.[37]

---

[35]"Seven Stanzas at Easter" from John Updike, *Telephone Poles and Other Poems* (New York: Random House, 1959). Updike reminds us that if He did not rise bodily, "[t]he Church must fall."

[36]The stone weighed not less than a ton. Tenney, *The Reality of the Resurrection*, 110–11.

[37]*Res ipsa loquiter* is chiefly used in tort actions (e.g., the patient wakes up after an operation and discovers that the surgeon has amputated the wrong limb). The patient sues and wins without the need to provide the evidence that the surgeon was negligent.

Res ipsa involves the following syllogism: (1) This kind of event does not normally occur in the absence of negligence; (2) The instrumentality in the instant case was under defendant's exclusive control; and (3) The plaintiff did not contribute to the injury. *Ergo*, Defendant is

Normally, of course, we have people alive at point A and dead at point B. But the point is that the evidence says the events got reversed in the case of Jesus of Nazareth. You are no more sophisticated today at determining if someone is dead or alive than we were in the first century.[38] Otherwise, we would have been busy about burying living people, which I must say there is no evidence we did!

Moderator: Dr. Martin is just itching to ask questions about what he says are all the contradictions in the accounts of the hours around finding the tomb empty. I am going to let him question you directly.
Dr. Martin, you have the floor for direct examination.

Dr. Martin: I would really like to examine your knowledge of how corrupted the texts are that contain the story of the resurrection of Jesus and how they provide no basis for knowing *anything* about a resurrection,[39] but that would take quite some time and likely be more than a bit embarrassing for you.

---

negligent—"the thing speaks for itself." Applied to the Resurrection of Christ: (1) Dead bodies do not leave tombs in the absence of some agency effecting their removal; (2) If the tomb was under anyone's exclusive control, it was God's, for it had been sealed, and Jesus, the sole occupant of it, was dead; (3) The Romans and the Jewish religious leaders did not contribute to the removal of the body (they had been responsible for sealing and guarding the tomb to prevent anyone from stealing the body), and the disciples would not have stolen it, then prevaricated, and finally died for what they knew to be untrue. Thus, only God was in a position to empty the tomb, which he did, by raising Jesus from the dead.

John Warwick Montgomery, *Tractatus Logico-Theologicus* (Bonn, Germany: Culture & Science Publ., 2002), propositions 3.6661–3.6662.

[38]For a discussion by a trial lawyer as to whether first-century writers were less capable of discerning whether someone was dead, see Thomas Sherlock's classic work, *The Tryal of the Witnesses of the Resurrection of Jesus* (London: J. Roberts, 1729), 60.

[39]Martin, *The Case against Christianity*, 88, citing "scholars" for the conclusion that any knowledge of what happened after the crucifixion is completely uncertain.

Paul: Hold it right there. Not embarrassing in the least, Dr. Martin. Matthew, Mark, Luke, and John are the best attested works of all antiquity in terms of their manuscript pedigree.[40] Perhaps as a philosopher and not a classical historian, you can't be expected to know how the Gospel accounts stack up against other works of antiquity, but I will save you the trouble: they are superbly attested and bibliographically solid. The existence of numerous and early copies have removed from serious debate the question of whether we have what the Gospel writers originally wrote down.

In addition, I find it curious that you admit that Jesus of Nazareth existed and that He died. The best sources for that information are the same sources that present Him alive again by "many infallible proofs."[41] You give no criteria, scholarly or otherwise, why the sources are to be trusted on the existence and death of Jesus but suddenly not to be trusted as to His resurrection and subsequent ten separate appearances to a wide diversity of people. This strikes me as entirely inconsistent.

Finally, I note that in your scholarship on this question of the transmission of the New Testament material down through the centuries, one could not find a single scholar cited by you that is not of the critical school of New Testament scholarship. *Not one.* You appear to have surrounded yourself only with those who write what you agree with[42] and ignore an entire body of scholarship that has

---

[40]Montgomery puts it nicely: "To express skepticism concerning the resultant text of the New Testament books . . . is to allow all of classical antiquity to slip into obscurity, for no documents of the ancient period are as well attested bibliographically as is the New Testament." J. W. Montgomery, *Where is History going? A Christian Response to Secular Philosophies of History* (Minneapolis, MN: Bethany Books, 1969), 46.

[41]Acts 1:3.

[42]Martin cites not *one* orthodox scholar in his attack on the reliability of the Bible or to support his conclusion that the "the quest for the historical Jesus is hopeless." Martin, *The Case against Christianity*, 88. Instead, we are treated with Jesus Seminar–level critic after critic and yet never so much as a citation to even one conservative New Testament studies scholar or any of the solidly Lutheran, Reformed, Anglican, or Roman Catholic biblical scholars of the last five hundred years.

concluded that the New Testament is in fine bibliographic shape and has come down to us as originally written. You don't have to agree with the other body of scholarship, but to neither acknowledge that it exists nor apparently even know it *does* exist makes me wonder if the fix was already in on your conclusion before you ever looked at the actual evidence.

The problem with your position on biblical reliability ends up being this, Dr. Martin: If you want to reject the reliability of the New Testament, you also are going to have to repudiate your knowledge of the classical world.[43]

Now show me a contradiction.

Dr. Martin: Gladly. Matthew says an angel was sitting on the rock outside the tomb (Matt. 28:2), while Mark says there was a "young man" sitting inside the tomb (Mark 16:5), and yet Luke says there were two men inside (Luke 24:4).[44]

Dr. Gamaliel: Are you asserting that because each writer selects what they record, necessarily leaving out certain details that others provide, that this means there is a *contradiction*?[45] A contradiction, Professor, is two things that cannot possibly both be true *at the same time*. Probably even the 1L or anyone with some training in logical fallacies could answer this objection.[46] It would only be a contradiction

---

[43]This is precisely where Dr. Avrum Stroll ended up in a fascinating debate with John Warwick Montgomery on the reliability of the New Testament. For the full story, see the foreword to Montgomery, *History, Law & Christianity* (Corona, CA: New Reformation Publications, 2015).

[44]Martin, *The Case against Christianity*, 78–80.

[45]That no one Gospel gives all the detail should be obvious. Only Luke covers the walk to Emmaus; only Matthew gives a record of the first appearance to the women; Matthew and Luke never mention the appearance to Mary Magdalene; only John tells of the second appearance to the eleven apostles with Thomas absent; none of the four give any detail about the appearance to James; and only Luke mentions Christ's private appearance to Peter on the day of the resurrection.

[46]A. J. Hoover, *Don't You Believe It!* (Chicago, IL: Moody Press, 1982), explains logical fallacies and in particular their application to theological argumentation.

if Matthew said "there was *only* one angel, and he was on the rock outside the tomb, and by the way, there were no angels inside the tomb." Mark would contradict Luke if Mark said, *q. d.,* "There was one and *only* one man inside the tomb."

Dr. Martin: Okay, but then you have contradictions about which women came to the tomb and what they reportedly saw. Matthew has Mary Magdalene and "the other Mary" going to the tomb (Matt. 28:1), while Mark has the two Marys and Salome bringing spices to anoint the body (Mark 16:1), while Luke has a whole cast of women including Joanna and others. So tell me, who was at the tomb?[47]

Justice Arimethea: The text provides the resolution to your question. You assume each woman went to the tomb only once, but the texts do not require this explanation and indeed suggest some went back more than once to confirm what their eyes could scarcely believe. Remember, some of the women were bringing spices to anoint the body—obviously they were expecting to find a dead body! I myself would have gone back several times to confirm the empty tomb if I had been there that Sunday morning!

It is also interesting that the Gospel writers have only women as the first witnesses to the empty tomb. Under Jewish law, the testimony of a woman was given less credibility.[48] If the writers were actually making this up on the fly, they would not have started the story with women coming to the tomb. The fact that they did gives added credibility to the accounts. In fact, Mark records that Mary Magdalene was the first to encounter the risen Christ and that the disciples frankly thought she was caught up in an emotional hangover from the crucifixion (Mark 16:9–20). Several of them ran to the tomb itself to empirically verify her testimony.

---

[47]Martin, *The Case against Christianity,* 78–80.

[48]Richard Bauckham, *Jesus and the Eyewitnesses: The Gospels as Eyewitness Testimony* (Grand Rapids, MI: Eerdmans, 2006), 48–51.

Dr. Martin: Well, then, you have the absolute chaos of Jesus's post-resurrection appearances, which are impossible to harmonize.[49] Some have him appearing first to Mary Magdalene,[50] others to the disciples in the upper room,[51] and some on the road to Emmaus,[52] and others still in Galilee.[53]

Nicodemus: I will say those appearances cut across time, races, gender, and vocations and have the ring of authenticity because you can't make up that kind of detail! As a lawyer that has appeared in cases for clients, I can tell you that one sign of a truthful witness is that they give detail—sometimes seemingly irrelevant and inconsistent detail. Liars, on the other hand, characteristically make up single-layered metanarratives that only offer a "big-picture" perspective. It is the difference between, say, "once upon a time in a kingdom far, far away" versus, "When Quirinius was Governor of Syria, a decree went out that all should be taxed."[54] Considering Jesus is the one who Himself rose from the dead, it leaves us in a poor position to criticize how and to whom he chose to announce that fact after His resurrection.

Paul: When I was in the legal profession before my disbarment by the Sanhedrin for failing to obey the command to arrest and prosecute Christians, I would salivate as a prosecutor for the kind of diverse testimony that is associated with Jesus's postresurrection appearances. Look at the different personality types involved: Mary Magdalene, Peter, James, John, and Thomas to start with! Then you

---

[49]Martin, *The Case against Christianity*, 80–81.

[50]Mark 16:9–20.

[51]John 20:19ff.

[52]Luke 24:13–53.

[53]Matthew 28:16–20.

[54]Luke the Physician, ever a stickler for detail, cites no less than seven more historical figures in three short verses, along with their precise official titles and in some cases, their familial connection to one another. See Luke 3:1–3, where Tiberius Caesar, Herod, Pontius Pilate, Philip, Lysanias, Annas, and Caiaphas are called out.

have the different vocations and emotional states of those to whom Jesus appeared—hardly a recipe for a joint hallucination:[55] You have Mary Magdalene standing outside the tomb weeping because the body is gone and she is clueless where it can be found;[56] the two disciples on the road to Emmaus are in a kind of confused depression over what had happened;[57] the apostles are huddled behind locked doors for fear of the Jews;[58] other disciples are gathered at Galilee in obedience to Christ's earlier command;[59] several of the disciples are already back fishing at the sea of Galilee;[60] five hundred see Him at one time in Galilee;[61] and Thomas, the hardboiled skeptic, is not buying any of it until he gets empirical verification by means of a personal visit from Jesus.[62]

And if mass and collective hysteria and hallucinations explain each of the appearances, why do the appearances suddenly stop after Christ's recorded ascension into heaven?[63]

---

[55]Martin's argument that a "mass hallucination" or "collective hysteria" explains the postresurrection appearances is found at page 92ff. Martin uses orthodox scholar Gary Habermas as a foil here, with dubious results. Though, we hasten to add that Habermas's "minimal facts" argument displays its various problems that are correctly noted by Martin. That argument has a number of fallacious premises and serious vulnerabilities in apologetical witness. As just one example of its tender underbelly, Habermas's minimal facts argument generally only uses facts about Jesus conceded by "practically all critical scholars" (Martin, *The Case against Christianity*, 88). That leaves the quantum of agreed-upon "facts" subject to the whims of the Jesus Seminar vote each new year, where we will soon find one day that the only fact all agree upon was that Jesus was, *maybe*, a Jew.

[56]John 20:11–18; Mark 16:9–11.

[57]Mark 16:12–13; Luke 24:13–35.

[58]Mark 16:14–18; Luke 24:36–40; John 20:19–23.

[59]Matthew 28:16–20.

[60]John 21:1–23.

[61]Matthew 28:16–20; 1 Corinthians 15:6.

[62]John 20:19–23.

[63]Hallucinations should have become chronic after five hundred had been brought under their sway. For a medical study of the phenomena of

Dr. Gamaliel: And something I think is often overlooked—namely, that the evidence for the empty tomb and resurrection was broadcast to the world on the very spot where, and at the very time when, the event was said to have happened, and yet no one was able to controvert it. It is not like the followers of Jesus are saying this all happened in Rome or in Athens or in Carthage and they should really check it out by sailing over there. There is no hint in the public proclamation of the resurrection that people should "take our word for it on faith."

That was the very moment when it was yet possible to test every assertion and to examine each witness and to expose the fraud or any misinformation that was circulating. Yet nobody could do it, though, if it was refutable. The Jewish leaders and the Romans certainly had the means, motive, and opportunity to find and produce the body.[64]

Dr. Martin: But my position is not only that the textual tradition behind this material is hopelessly corrupted and shrouded in mystery, that the material itself is contradictory and cannot be trusted on these grounds alone, and that natural explanations of the resurrection are more logical and scientific, *but also* that there are valid and reasonable alternative explanations for the resurrection.

Justice Arimathea: Such as?

Dr. Martin: Somebody (the disciples or the Jews or the Romans) stole the body.[65]

---

hallucinations, see Paul William Peru, *Outline of Psychiatric Case-Study* (New York: Paul Hoeger, Inc., 1939), 97–99.

[64]This point is made particularly clear by Harvard law professor Simon Greenleaf in his timeless classic, *The Testimony of the Evangelists: The Gospels Examined by the Rules of Evidence* (New York: J. C. & Co., 1874).

[65]This theory requires the perpetrators to also leave the burial clothes in a form to suggest a resurrection since that is exactly how Peter observed the clothes in the empty tomb. John 20:6–7. Unwrapping a corpse amidst one hundred pounds of spices and gummy ointment and then perfectly placing them to look like the body had passed through them, all the while avoiding the Roman guard, is simply ludicrous.

Dr. Gamaliel: That theory was trotted out by the end of that first Sunday. I investigated that and found it facially absurd. More important, there is not a shred of evidence for it! Some of my fellow judges at the Sanhedrin paid hush money to the Roman guards to present that position.[66]

The problem is, where does that line of reasoning take you? So the disciples proclaimed what they knew was a fraud, in direct contradiction to the teachings of Jesus about honesty, and for what purpose? To give false hope? Then they went out and died martyrs' deaths for that completely false message that they knew was false? None of the three interest groups had a motivation to hide the body of Jesus. The Jews and Romans certainly did not and were highly motivated to produce a body. The Romans set a guard on the tomb at the request of the Jewish authorities. Everyone knew where the tomb was[67] since Justice Arimathea's shocking request of Pilate to dispose of the body. The disciples would have had to deal with the Roman guards to pull off a body snatch.

Dr. Martin: What about the likelihood that these so-called appearances are actually episodes of collective mass hysteria brought on by group excitement that followed after some of the grieving women reported direct contact with Jesus?[68]

Paul: How does that apply to Thomas or to me for that matter? That was actually Thomas's main argument for *not* believing until

---

[66]See Matthew 28:11–15, where the powerful chief priests and elders assured the guards that they would cover their liability to Pilate.

[67]The well-known location of the tomb, its prominent owner, its Roman guard, and the fact that the women had been at the tomb a mere seventy-two hours before stamps "paid" on the argument that the women actually went to the wrong tomb. Moreover, if they did go to the wrong tomb, this does not explain the postresurrection appearances of Jesus since even Martin *apparently* concedes that Jesus died on the cross. We say *apparently* concedes because *The Case against Christianity* never attempts to directly refute the crucifixion material but only indirectly attacks it by challenging the entire historicity of Jesus.

[68]Martin, *The Case against Christianity*, 92ff.

he saw the resurrected Jesus and touched His wounds.[69] He did not trust the testimony of the witnesses and figured the women had hysterical tendencies. He was only forced to belief by seeing the resurrected Jesus Christ and touching his hands and side. In addition, as has been said, those appearances were over many weeks and to a variety of personality types.

Moderator: Let's move on to other issues.

Paul: May I ask Dr. Martin something?

Moderator: Please do.

Paul: Your claim about contradictions in the Gospel accounts and their failure to harmonize never mentions any of the historical and comprehensive scholarly efforts that have done so. Why not?

Dr. Martin: Because I do not consider them scholarly or successful in their effort—that's why!

Paul: Name the harmonization efforts you have read—*any* of them?

Dr. Martin: I read a lot of things, Sir, and I can't give you names off the top of my head.

Paul: Let's try it this way then. Are you familiar with Gleason Archer's extensive harmonization of the Greek texts of the Gospels as to the events surrounding the empty tomb?

Dr. Martin: That one does not ring a bell.

Paul: You should read it sometime because it gives textual explanation to every alleged "contradiction" you raise and answers them all.[70] Of course you are familiar with the works of William Arndt[71]

---

[69]John 20:19–23.

[70]Gleason Archer, *Encyclopedia of Bible Difficulties* (Grand Rapids, MI: Eerdmans, 1982), 347–56.

[71]W. F. Arndt, *Does the Bible Contradict Itself? A Discussion of Alleged Contradictions in the Bible* (St. Louis, MO: Concordia Publishing House, 1926).

and John Haley[72] dealing with the events surrounding the empty tomb, the resurrection, and postresurrection appearances, right? William Paley?[73] Edmund Bennett?[74] Andreas Althamer?[75] How about Augustine?[76] In your day, there is Dorothy Sayers?[77] Josh McDowell?[78] John Warwick Montgomery?[79]

Sayers was one of the first women to be awarded a degree from Oxford and was an astute literary critic. She puts it nicely when addressing alleged contradictions in the Bible:

> [One] is often surprised to find how many apparent contradictions turn out not to be contradictory at all, but merely supplementary. Take, for example, the various accounts of the Resurrection appearances at the Sepulchre. The divergences appear very great on first sight. . . . But the fact remains that *all* of them, without exception, can be made to fall into place in a single orderly and coherent narrative without the smallest

---

[72]John Haley, *An Examination of the Alleged Discrepancies in the Bible* (Grand Rapids, MI: Baker Books, 1977).

[73]William Paley, *A View of the Evidences of Christianity* (New York: James Miller Publishers, 1865).

[74]Edmund Bennett, *The Four Gospels from a Lawyer's Standpoint* (New York: Houghton, Mifflin & Co., 1899).

[75]Andreas Althamer, *Conciliationes Locorum Scripturae, qui specie tenus inter se pugnare videntur, Centuriae duae* (Wittenberg, Germany: Zacharias Lehman, 1582). This excellent volume (never translated into English) treats 160 discrepancies in the Bible and went through at least sixteen editions (1st ed., 1527). Cited to by John Warwick Montgomery, who possesses a personal copy, in *Crisis in Lutheran Theology* (Minneapolis, MN: Bethany Books, 1967), 20 note 12.

[76]See the excellent discussion of Augustine's apologetical acumen in Charles Joseph Costello, *St. Augustine's Doctrine on the Inspiration and Canonicity of Scripture* (Washington, DC: Catholic University Press, 1930), 30–37.

[77]Dorothy Sayers, *The Whimsical Christian* (New York: MacMillan, 1978).

[78]Josh McDowell, *Reasons Skeptics Should Consider Christianity* (San Bernardino, CA: Here's Life Publ., 1981). See also McDowell's *Answers to Tough Questions* by the same publisher.

[79]Montgomery, *Crisis in Lutheran Theology*, vols. 1 & 2. See esp. 1:15–44.

contradiction or difficulty and without any suppression, invention or manipulation, beyond a trifling effort to *imagine* the natural behavior of a bunch of startled people running about in the dawn-light between Jerusalem and the Garden.[80]

Dr. Martin: Everyone you just cited is a Christian believer though! See, there is the central problem with your reasoning, Paul. All those authors have drunk from the same rancid inebriant and assume the reliability of the text, which all competent scholars agree is full of corruption!

Paul: You don't get it. Set aside the issue of the "corruption of the text," which is, as we have noted already, a total canard. I am now only addressing your argument about contradictions in the text. That argument is wholly separate from whether the text has come to us as written. My point is simply that a boatload of careful work has been done over the past two thousand years to harmonize the events of the first Sunday morning, and your book shows you have ostensibly no familiarity with *any* of it!

I am afraid it appears that by your definition, one cannot be a scholar and hold to harmonization of alleged contradictions in the Bible. Nor can one be a scholar and hold to the reliability of the Bible. You appear to be on a rather insulated island where all you do is talk to like-minded critics.

How about a harmonization of postresurrection events that goes something like this: Mary Magdalene and Mary go to the tomb from Bethany, via John's house, picking up Salome from there (Matthew 28:1–15); Mary Magdalene rushes from the tomb to tell Peter and John (John 20:1); Joanna and Susanna arrive at the tomb, and the women go into the tomb (Matthew 28:5–7; Mark 16:5–7; Luke 24:3–8); the women tell the disciples and no one else (Matthew 28:8; Mark 16:8; Luke 24:9–11); Peter and John run to the tomb and return home (John 20; Luke 24:12); Mary Magdalene goes to the tomb again (John 20:11–18); Mary, wife of Clopas, and Salome set off to Bethany

---

[80]Dorothy Sayers, *The Man Born to be King* (New York: Harper & Bros., 1943), 19–20.

to tell the brethren and meet Jesus (Matthew 28:8–10); Clopas and another disciple go to Emmaus and later return and tell the others (Mark 16:11–12; Luke 24:13–35); Jesus appears to the disciples (Luke 24:36–43; John 20:19–23); Jesus appears again to the disciples, including Thomas this time (John 20:24–29); the Twelve return to Galilee and meet Jesus again there (John 21); and Jesus appears to James and finally appears one last time before the ascension (Mark 16:15–20).[81]

And I just did that on the fly, and by simply laying the texts side by side, and without employing your philosophical *a priori* that the writers *must* contradict one another since they tell different stories.

Moderator: Dr. Martin finishes his arguments against Christianity by contending that even if Jesus rose from the dead, it may not mean He was God and, by extension, the resurrection in this sense would not be necessarily incompatible with atheism because perhaps all it "proves" is that there are supernatural beings capable of performing resurrections.[82]

Dr. Gamaliel: Presumably an infinite number of possible interpretations of the meaning of Christ's resurrection exist. But does it not make sense to start the interpretive process by seeing if the person who actually rose from the dead expressed any opinion on what it means? Would not that opinion trump the speculations of anyone on this panel or in this room?

Nicodemus: Indeed! And it just so happens that the person in question told us exactly what His resurrection meant: It meant He was the Messiah, God the Son, Savior of the world,[83] whose perfect life

---

[81]Graeme Smith, *Was the Tomb Empty? A Lawyer Weighs the Evidence for the Resurrection* (Grand Rapids, MI: Monarch Books, 2014), 214–15.

[82]Martin, *The Case against Christianity*, 96–100.

[83]See N. T. Wright's monumental *The Resurrection of the Son of God: Christian Origins and the Question of God* (Minneapolis, MN: Fortress Press, 2003), vol. 3, 723–36. We note that the resurrection also established Jesus's claims to be the Messiah as prophesied in the Old Testament, since there are scholars who

and atoning death for the sins of the whole world was all sufficient to save even pathetic me.

Justice Arimathea: When I hear comments like those of Dr. Martin, that he has a better philosophy to offer than believing in Jesus, I am reminded of a comment made by Talleyrand to La Revelliere. La Revelliere, like you, Dr. Martin, bitterly hated the Christian religion and was attempting to introduce a new pseudophilosophical theory called "Theophilanthropy." After La Revelliere read a long paper about his philosophy and explained its principles, and after it got rave reviews from the attendees, Talleyrand remarked: "For my part I have only one observation to make. Jesus Christ, in order to found His religion, was crucified and rose again—you should have tried to do as much."[84]

And that is what I say to Dr. Martin tonight. Until you rise again on the third day, I will go with Jesus and the hard evidence for His death and resurrection establishing that He is God in the flesh, the Messiah promised in the Old Testament, and King of the universe and that there are good and sufficient grounds to put one's full trust in Him to get you over the river on that last day.

Paul: Another one of our company summed it up well:

> On the third day the friends of Christ coming at daybreak to the place found the grave empty and the stone rolled away. In varying ways they realized the new wonder: But even they hardly realized that the world had died in the night. What they were looking at was the first day of a new creation, with a new heaven and a new earth, and in a semblance of the gardener God walked again in the garden in the cool not of the evening but the dawn.[85]

---

accept the resurrection on the weight of the historical record alone but deny any connection of that fact with the possibility that Jesus was the Messiah. See Pinchas Lapide, *The Resurrection of Jesus: A Jewish Perspective* (Minneapolis, MN: Augsburg Publishing House, 1983).

[84]Duff Cooper, *Talleyrand* (London: Jonathan Cape Ltd., 1932), 96.

[85]G. K. Chesterton, *The Everlasting Man* (London: Dodd, Mead & Co., 1943), 261–62.

Dr. Martin: A garden of your own imagination, Paul. I still assert that the resurrection is not inconsistent with atheism.

Dr. Gamaliel: If you are right, the universe is indeed a cosmic madhouse.[86]

Moderator: Before we submit tonight's discussion to you, our audience, for your own private deliberation, I would like each side to provide a one-sentence summation of its position.

Dr. Martin: Christianity is based on corrupted ancient texts that ask one to suspend the laws of logic and reject the findings of modern science in order to believe that Jesus Christ (if he ever really existed) was resurrected from the dead—and even if he was resurrected, such a fact would not be inconsistent with atheism.

Nicodemus: The factual case for the life, death, and resurrection of Jesus of Nazareth would stand up in any court of law today and if true, means we either humbly meet the living Savior of the world to our eternal gain in this life and the life to come or meet him in the next life in judgment to our everlasting loss.

Moderator: We think it appropriate that we conclude this evening by hearing from a representative of a law school intimately connected to where this discussion has taken place tonight here at Hastings.

Hastings has sometimes been called "the Harvard of the West" due to the number of former Harvard Law School faculty who have taught at Hastings, especially as part of the Over-65 Club.

Simon Greenleaf was professor of evidence at the Harvard Law School in the nineteenth century and the author of the seminal three-volume treatise on evidence known to all scholars in the field (modestly titled, I might add, simply "Greenleaf on Evidence"). He

---

[86]Montgomery, *Tractatus Logico-Theologicus,* proposition 2.35233, citing Brightman's classic line that Roman Catholicism and Christian Science cannot both be true at the same time unless the universe is a "madhouse."

puts the issue cleanly about how we approach these questions in his classic work examining the New Testament pursuant to the rules of legal evidence:[87]

> All that [we] ask of men on this subject is that they would be consistent with themselves; that they would treat [Christianity's] evidences as they treat the evidence of other things; and that they would try and judge its actors and witnesses as they deal with their fellow men, when testifying to human affairs and actions, in human tribunals. Let the witnesses be compared with themselves, with each other, and with surrounding facts and circumstances; and let their testimony be sifted, as if it were given in a court of justice, on the side of the adverse party, the witnesses being subject to a rigorous cross-examination.

May we all reach our own personal determination based on the evidence presented—surely the potentially weighty consequences of the verdict we each reach on the topics discussed tonight demand nothing less.[88]

That concludes our program for the evening.

Recommended Reading
(All works by judges or lawyers)

Archer, Gleason. *Encyclopedia of Bible Difficulties.* Grand Rapids, MI: Eerdmans, 1982.

Callahan, Ethelbert. *The Lawyers of the Bible.* Indianapolis, IN: Hollenbeck Press, 1912.

Casteel, Herbert C. *Beyond a Reasonable Doubt: A Judge's Verdict on the Case for Christian Faith.* Joplin, MI: College Press Publishing, 1992 (rev. ed.).

Chandler, Walter M. *The Trial of Jesus from a Lawyer's Standpoint.* New York: Empire Publishing Co., 1908.

---

[87] Simon Greenleaf, *The Testimony of the Evangelists: The Gospels Examined by the Rules of Evidence* (Grand Rapids, MI: Kregel Classics, 1995), 41–42.

[88] We note that Professor Dr. Michael Martin died on 27 May 2015.

Ewen, Pamela B. *Faith on Trial: Analysis of the Evidence for the Death and Resurrection of Jesus.* Nashville, TN: B&H Publishing Group, 2013.

Gutteridge, Donald J. *The Defense Rests Its Case.* Nashville, TN: Broadman Press, 1975.

Hailsham, Lord (Quintin McGarel Hogg). *The Door Wherein I Went.* London: Collins, 1975.

Linton, Irwin H. *The Sanhedrin Verdict.* New York: Loizeaux Brothers Publishers, 1943.

Montgomery, John Warwick. *Christ as Centre and Circumference: Essays Theological, Cultural and Polemic.* Bonn, Germany: Culture & Science Publishers, 2012.

Smith, Graeme. *Was the Tomb Empty? A Lawyer Weighs the Evidence for the Resurrection.* Grand Rapids, MI: Monarch Books, 2014.

5

Justified Belief in the Resurrection

Angus Menuge

1. Introduction

By faith, Christians believe in the resurrection of Jesus Christ. But is there sufficient evidence to reasonably believe that this actually happened? Matthew McCormick thinks not: "[W]e have too little information of too poor quality to warrant our believing that Jesus returned from the dead."[1] McCormick is an atheist philosopher specializing in philosophy of religion, epistemology, and critical reasoning, and he thinks that if Christians employed the same epistemic standards to the resurrection that they apply to claims made outside their faith (including the claims of rival religions), they would reject it. The reason they do not, asserts McCormick, is that Christian faith means "believing despite insufficient or contrary evidence."[2] McCormick is a resolute disciple of William K. Clifford (1845–1879), an English mathematician and philosopher who argued that "it is wrong always, everywhere, and for any one, to believe anything upon insufficient evidence."[3] On this view, McCormick argues,

---

[1]Matthew S. McCormick, *Atheism and the Case against Christ* (Amherst, NY: Prometheus Books, 2012), 11.

[2]McCormick, 17.

[3]W. K. Clifford, "The Ethics of Belief," *Contemporary Review* 29 (Dec. 1876–May 1877), 289–309, 295. Available online at: http://www.uta.edu/philosophy/faculty/burgess-jackson/Clifford.pdf. The essay is also included in Clifford's

Christianity is irrational. He buttresses his case with a detailed skeptical examination of the sources of the New Testament and a philosophical critique of miracles.

McCormick is aware of Christian apologists like William Lane Craig, Gary Habermas, Michael Licona, and N. T. Wright, who have defended the historicity of the resurrection. But he maintains that such defenses fail because they rely on testimony from individuals who most likely were not eyewitnesses and were not "impartial, objective observers"[4] because they were influenced by "social conformity"[5] and believed what they "most want[ed] to be true."[6] And McCormick thinks that over time, the faithful would have scrubbed the record clean of any dissenters who offered contrary debunking accounts. By contrast, McCormick supposes that enlightened secularists like himself are better equipped to assess the data from an unbiased, neutral perspective.

There is no space to address each and every skeptical claim made by McCormick, but this chapter will focus on exposing the philosophical inadequacy of McCormick's method. We will see that McCormick profoundly misunderstands the relationship between faith and evidence (section 2) and that his own perspective is far from neutral (section 3). McCormick's biases are further shown by his tendentious handling of the evidence (section 4) and by his willingness to embrace a highly implausible naturalistic explanation of the resurrection appearances (section 5).

2. Faith and Evidence

In common with Richard Dawkins, Sam Harris, and many other new atheists, McCormick defines faith as believing "despite contrary or inadequate evidence."[7] Sadly enough, the view that faith is

---

The Ethics of Belief and Other Essays (Amherst, NY: Prometheus Books, 1999), 70–96.

[4]McCormick, *Atheism and the Case against Christ,* 147.

[5]Ibid., 148.

[6]Ibid., 232.

[7]Ibid., 215.

incompatible with good evidence describes the thinking of some Christians today, who have capitulated to a purely subjective and private understanding of their faith. But this does not reflect a biblical understanding, much less a proper definition, of faith. St. Paul is always clear that the Gospel he received is founded on the fact of the resurrection (1 Corinthians 15:20), and he invites skeptics to investigate the evidence by consulting living eyewitnesses (1 Corinthians 15:5–8) and the public record (Acts 26:26).

The Reformers explained that there are three dimensions of faith: *notitia*, *assensus*, and *fiducia*.[8] *Notitia* means the content of the faith (*what* is believed), *assenus* means intellectual assent to the content of the faith (*belief that* it is true), and *fiducia* means the personal trust and confidence in Christ and his promises (*belief in* Christ). *Notitia* and *assensus* can be supported by evidence and rational argument, but they are not saving faith (James 2:19; Hebrews 11:6). Saving faith requires *fiducia*, and that can only be produced by the Holy Spirit. As Luther insists in his commentary on the Third Article of the Creed, "I believe that I cannot by my own reason or strength believe in Jesus Christ, my Lord, or come to Him, but the Holy Spirit has called me by the Gospel, enlightened me with His gifts, sanctified and kept me in the true faith."[9] This is because we are spiritually dead enemies of God (Romans 8:6–7), who willfully suppress the natural knowledge of God (Romans 1:18) and cannot "accept the things of the Spirit of God . . . because they are spiritually discerned" (1 Corinthians 2:14). This does not mean, nor has it ever meant, that biblical faith is believing "despite contrary or inadequate evidence." Rather, faith always has *content*, and reasoned content at that.

McCormick seems to have partly grasped the idea of *fiducia* as a trust that is not created by reason. But he has erroneously concluded that the content of the faith (*notitia*) is not something the mind can assent to (*assensus*) on the basis of evidence. A famous analogy from C. S. Lewis illustrates the distinction:

---

[8]Philip Melanchthon, *Loci Communes* 1543, trans. J. A. O. Preus (St. Louis, MO: Concordia, 1992), 86–89.

[9]"The Small Catechism," in *Concordia: The Lutheran Confessions*, 2nd ed., ed. Paul McCain (St. Louis, MO: Concordia Publishing House, 2006), 330.

[M]y reason is perfectly convinced by good evidence that anaesthetics do not smother me and that properly trained surgeons do not start operating until I am unconscious. But that does not alter the fact that when they have me down on the table and clap their horrible mask over my face, a mere childish panic begins inside me. I think I am going to choke, and I am afraid they will start cutting me up before I am properly under. In other words, I lose my faith in anaesthetics. It is not reason that is taking away my faith: on the contrary, my faith is based on reason.[10]

Lewis notes that our difficulty in trusting the surgeon is not because there is insufficient evidence for the safety of the procedure: it is because we resist giving up autonomy and putting our life in someone else's hands. Similarly, the difficulty of the natural man's acceptance of Christ as the source of eternal life (*fiducia*) is not because the mind cannot rationally accept (*assensus*) that Christ overcame death in the resurrection (*notitia*). It is because the natural man would like to be lord of his own life and does not want to cede control to Christ. Human nature is not *disposed* toward the things of God: hence the divine gift of faith. McCormick's dichotomy between faith and justified belief is a false one, created by defining faith in terms of only one of its three dimensions. As such, the McCormick-defined faith is always a failing epistemological source.

Yet even when we consider *notitia* and *assensus*, McCormick's brand of evidentialism is inadequate. This is for three reasons. First, McCormick never explicitly defines "sufficient evidence" (and so it is an ever-moving target), and his implicit definition is unreasonably demanding. Many of the doubts McCormick raises about the New Testament record of the resurrection take the form of possibilities that the evidence does not exclude. For example, supposing the resurrection was a hoax, "Would we expect reports of information from the whistleblowers to have survived and made it into the body of evidence concerning Jesus's miracles or resurrection we have today?"[11] The trouble is, he provides no independent evidence that there was a hoax or a conspiracy of data scrubbing—it just seems likely to him.

---

[10]C. S. Lewis, *Mere Christianity* (New York: Macmillan, 1952), 107–8.

[11]McCormick, *Atheism and the Case against Christ*, 149.

In a court of law, any competent judge would dismiss his suggestion as speculation and turn us back to the evidence that we do have. Not only does this evidence support the historicity of the resurrection, it also undercuts McCormick's data scrubbing theory because when the resurrection was first proclaimed, it was not Christian believers but the Roman and Jewish authorities who controlled society's access to information—in effect, the media—and these authorities had the means and the motive to expose any deception. Had they been able to do so, the Christian message would quickly have been rejected, and most likely there would be no worldwide Christian church today. For the reasonable legal standard, "beyond a reasonable doubt," McCormick has substituted "beyond doubts rooted in unsubstantiated speculation." Using this standard, one could reject almost any murder conviction or historical event because of possible scenarios (involving aliens, etc.) that are compatible with the known evidence. Sound legal and historical interpretation must be rooted in the evidence that we actually have, not evidence we would like to have or might find in the future; otherwise we will be paralyzed by indecision, unable to draw any conclusion because it *might* be false.

Second, it simply is not true that anyone has, or can have, "sufficient evidence" for everything that they believe. There are a few reasons why this is so. We cannot demand a sufficient reason for every belief for the same reason we cannot demand a sufficient reason for each premise in an argument: it generates an infinite regress, as each reason is simply another premise requiring another reason, *ad infinitum*. Following this method, no premise would ever be established, and so we could never come to know any new conclusions. Further, one cannot really prove the first principles of rational inquiry (e.g., the law of noncontradiction or the inductive method), since any argument for these principles *already assumes them*.[12]

---

[12]For example, suppose one comes to doubt sense perception as a reliable source of knowledge. It may show one is unlikely to be deceived if a variety of senses (sight, sound, touch, etc.) agree or if many people report the same experience, but any such argument still relies on sense perception. Likewise, any logical argument that I give for the law of noncontradiction will already assume that principle, and the argument that scientists should use the inductive method because it has worked so well in the past itself relies on that method.

In other words, there's an inherent circularity for epistemologies of both rationalism and empiricism. (This is universally admitted but too frequently omitted in philosophical discourse.) In effect, such arguments would offer a proof of proofs, which, again, is circular. And what evidence could one give in favor of evidentialism? Giving evidence for evidentialism already assumes a key claim of evidentialism—that it is reasonable to base our beliefs on evidence.

Third, in matters of belief, McCormick completely ignores the fact that it makes a huge difference whether what we are asked to consider is a proposition like "X = 86" or "Caesar crossed the Rubicon"—whose truth or falsity may have no impact on our life—or a proposition like "Jesus is Lord," which, if true, should fundamentally reorient all that we do. Where a belief also involves a commitment to act—to a certain way of life—it is not rational *only* to consider evidence: one will also consider what is at stake and the potential losses and gains entailed. A patient who tries an experimental drug despite having only weak evidence for its efficacy rationally affirms that *a* chance of life is better than none, even if there is also some chance the drug will hasten his death. This is because he considers not only evidence but also the value of life. Likewise, William James argued, "If religion be true and the evidence for it be still insufficient, I do not wish . . . to forfeit my sole chance in life of getting upon the winning side."[13]

In his *Pensées*, Blaise Pascal argued that even if the evidence for and against Christianity is evenly balanced, still one should wager in favor of it because there is an infinite gain if it is true and little to lose if it is false, whereas if one wagers against it, there is an infinite loss if it is true and little to gain if it is false. Critics of "the wager" point out that one cannot create faith (*fiducia*) by reason and that it falsely assumes that there is only one religion to consider. But Pascal is clear that the point of his wager is not to manufacture faith but to shock the unbeliever out of diversionary trivial pursuits so that he attends church and listens to God's Word if only because it might be true. Exposed to the means of grace, the

---

[13]William James, "The Will to Believe," in his *The Will to Believe Other Essays in Popular Philosophy* (New York: Dover, 1956), 27.

Holy Spirit may then call that person to faith. And one can also argue, independently of evidential considerations, that Christianity is more worthy of our consideration than other religions.

Christianity should get our attention because it is the only religion that *if true* would do anything to solve the human predicament. As Pascal noticed, man is aware of an abyss between what he should be and what he really is. He is wretched because he cannot attain this perfect standard and yet great because this reveals his need for God: "Man's greatness comes from knowing he is wretched. . . . It is the wretchedness of a great lord, of a dispossessed king."[14] If true, could any religion heal this tragic condition so that we can attain the wholeness and holiness for which we long?

Philosopher John Hare calls this the "moral gap" between God and man.[15] He argues that most religions attempt to handle the gap by either "lowering the bar"—so that God does not require perfection[16]—or "inflating the capacity" so that man can eventually approach God on his own steam. Two examples of religions that lower the bar are the Judaism of the Pharisees, which focused on external compliance with God's Law, and Islam, which requires not perfection but only a greater balance of good over evil deeds. But external compliance with the Law does not heal or redirect our sinful heart, and we know God wants us—not just our outer behavior—to be holy. And a God who does not demand moral perfection is not a Holy God—such a being stoops to bargaining and accepts a compromise.

On the other hand, Eastern religions like Buddhism and Hinduism inflate the capacity, suggesting that over many cycles of reincarnation, we can reduce bad karma and increase good karma. But future good actions do nothing to cancel out past bad actions. And it is illogical to think that one can become perfect by building up

---

[14]Blaise Pascal, *Pensées*, trans. A. J. Krailsheimer (New York: Penguin Books, 1966), #114 and #116.

[15]John Hare, *The Moral Gap* (New York: Oxford University Press, 1997).

[16]Jesus himself refused to lower the bar of divine moral expectation in Matthew 5:48: "You therefore must be perfect, as your Heavenly Father is perfect" (ESV).

good karma. If we start with a finite stock of good karma, any finite addition yields another finite amount. We can never approach perfection from imperfection; we can never fulfill an infinite demand with finite contributions.

Is there a solution that lets God be God—perfectly holy and just—and yet tells the truth about man—a being unable to live up to the perfect standards he knows are intended for him? Here, Christianity is unique. In Christ, God Himself bridges the gap between God and man but without compromising his holiness. Christ keeps the moral demand perfectly (his active obedience), and he pays the price for all our failure to do so (his passive obedience), so God's demand for justice is satisfied. But when Christ's payment in full is accepted by God, he offers his availing righteousness to us. We are made right with God, not by our righteousness—which is like filthy rags (Isaiah 64:6)—but by the righteousness of Christ.

Thus even apart from evidence, Christianity has a claim to be taken seriously, because it is the only religion that, if true, offers a credible solution to the human predicament. But the fact that something would help *if* it is true does not show that it *is* true, and we cannot base our belief *solely* on the potential benefit of believing, since then we would also have to believe in magic and various mythical creatures that might make life better. So McCormick is right that the evidence matters. Yet here it is significant that unlike most religions, which focus exclusively on rituals and rules for living, Christianity concerns God's actions in history and invites investigation of the data.

3. A Mythical Neutrality

To make this investigation reasonable, however, we must consider the best way to handle the problem of human bias. McCormick is right that investigators can be biased by expectations, peer pressure, and the desire to confirm what they already believe. But is this an especially acute problem for the earliest disciples and apostles of Jesus as McCormick believes? And is his own mode of investigation as free from bias as he seems to assume?

McCormick argues that the biblical reports of the resurrection are not credible because they reflected believers' "enthusiasm, desire,

[and] ideological commitments"[17] and because their "low levels of scientific knowledge, education, and literacy" would have given them "a low level of skepticism for what we would identify as supernatural, miraculous, or paranormal claims."[18] However, both of these charges commit a genetic fallacy (and hint of red herrings, too) and reveal a serious modernist bias in McCormick's own approach.

The fact that believers were enthusiastic about spreading the good news does not discredit their testimony. These are the accounts of converted unbelievers who certainly did not expect or desire a resurrection at that time in history. There was no antecedent ideological commitment to a resurrected Messiah in the midst of human history. Indeed, as N. T. Wright has convincingly established in his massive scholarly contribution to the subject, it was entirely out of keeping with their pluriform Jewish world views and eschatologies.[19] They were mainly Jews, and we know that the Pharisees, for example, accepted the notion of a resurrection only at the End Times, not one within history, while the Sadducees rejected the idea of a resurrection altogether. For a first-century Jew, the whole idea of God becoming man would have seemed pagan (the sort of thing a god of Greco-Roman mythology might do) and directly contrary to the *Shema* (central creed) of Israel: "Hear, O Israel: The LORD our God, the LORD is one" (Deuteronomy 6:4). The Messiah's crucifixion was equally alien to Jewish thought because "a hanged man is cursed by God" (Deuteronomy 21:23), and the idea that the same one cursed by God would also be glorified by a resurrection was repugnant. Thus first-century Jews were strongly predisposed to *disbelieve* any report of a resurrection like Jesus's, and only highly compelling evidence could be expected to overcome their biases. And *that* is the point—namely, that these commonplace and conventional Jews became enthusiastic about proclaiming the risen Lord and his kingdom only *after* experiencing compelling evidence. They had standards for truth,

---

[17]McCormick, *Atheism and the Case against Christ*, 80.

[18]Ibid., 81.

[19]N. T. Wright, *The Resurrection of the Son of God* (Minneapolis, MN: Fortress Press, 2003).

and the resurrection claim met those standards, which, contrary to McCormick's caricatures of the times and people of the New Testament, were very much like our own standards.

Western secularists like McCormick simply have different biases than those they tend to criticize or caricature—they are biased against the miraculous in general—and unless one begs the question by assuming that there are no miracles, this does not show that their view is more objective. As C. S. Lewis pointed out, "[O]ur preconceptions would prevent us from apprehending miracles if they really occurred."[20]

McCormick thus overstates his case against the scientific understanding of first-century Jews. He cites with approval Bart Ehrman's claim that such people did not understand the idea of "inviolable 'laws' of nature."[21] Of course, if "inviolable" just means there can be no miracles, this begs the question against them in advance of investigating the facts (another McCormick-cum-Ehrman fallacy). As David Hume (1711–1776) taught us, empirical observation may reveal that certain events are regularly conjoined, but it does not follow that the connection is necessary.[22] In modern thought, that idea comes from the controversial philosophical assumption that nature is an autonomous, closed system; but this simply assumes there can be no miracles. But in any case, it is obvious that first-century people did have a basic understanding of laws of nature, since that understanding is required to detect a miracle in the first place. As C. S. Lewis pointed out,

If a man had no conception of a regular order in Nature, then of course he could not notice departures from that order. . . . Complete ignorance of the laws of nature would preclude the perception of

---

[20]C. S. Lewis, "Miracles," in his *God in the Dock: Essays on Theology and Ethics*, ed. Walter Hooper (Grand Rapids, MI: Eerdmans, 1970), 25–37, 26.

[21]Bart Ehrman, *The New Testament: A Historical Introduction to the Early Christian Writings* (New York: Oxford University Press, 2004), 226, quoted in McCormick, *Atheism and the Case against Christ*, 82.

[22]David Hume, *An Enquiry Concerning Human Understanding* (New York: Oxford University Press, 2008), section 7, "Of the Idea of necessary connexion."

the miraculous just as rigidly as complete disbelief in the supernatural precludes it, perhaps even more so.[23]

The bias in McCormick's own approach becomes clearer in his sweeping remark that *"Religiousness, superstition, and supernaturalism are positively correlated with ignorance; when people have more education, they are less likely to believe."*[24] McCormick is here simply assuming that a highly secularized modern education conceals no biases of its own.[25] If "education" means acceptance of scientism, according to which materialistic science is the only reliable source of knowledge, it is trivially true that being educated excludes rationally justified belief in the supernatural. But if the question is whether there is evidence that a supernatural event has occurred, assuming scientism begs the question. And taken literally, McCormick would have to say that some of the greatest thinkers of history—Augustine, Aquinas, Luther, Kepler, Copernicus, Boyle, Leibniz, and Newton—as well as more recent luminaries—C. S. Lewis, John Warwick Montgomery, William Lane Craig, Gary Habermas, Robert Larmer, John Lennox, John Polkinghorne, Craig Keener, Alvin Plantinga, and J. P. Moreland—are uneducated because they believe in miracles.

A more fundamental problem is McCormick's naïve dichotomy between "religiousness" and his own perspective. This makes the erroneous suggestion that being religious is avoidable—that it is an option for some people. But as Roy Clouser argues, "A religious belief is a belief in something as . . . having unconditionally non-dependent reality."[26] In other words, religion centers on what one takes to be the ground of all being. In that sense, McCormick's belief that all events have a materialistic explanation is just as religious as the theist's. And so where theism and materialism are the

---

[23]Lewis, "Miracles," 26.

[24]McCormick, *Atheism and the Case against Christ*, 81. Italics in original.

[25]See Michael Polanyi's arguments to the contrary in *Science, Faith, and Society* (Chicago: University of Chicago, 1958, 1964).

[26]Roy Clouser, *The Myth of Religious Neutrality: An Essay on the Hidden Role of Religious Belief in Theories*, Revised Edition (Notre Dame: University of Notre Dame Press, 2005), 23.

world views in competition, McCormick's presumption in favor of materialistic science reflects his own religious bias.

McCormick also expands his bias to Christian theology, broadly speaking, and how he thinks God should behave. He complains that even if some miracle reports are reliable, there are just too few miracles, and this is unjust because it means that even if a few people are miraculously healed, the majority are not.[27] But if there were a miracle in every case, those miracles would necessarily be undetectable; indeed, we would think they occurred according to the laws of nature. So the miracles could not play their important pedagogical role as signs—revealing to a fallen world something of God's character and His plan to rescue and heal us.[28]

And in fact, we find that McCormick's real complaint is that God should not need to do any miracles, for if God is perfect, "That being's actions will perfectly and completely achieve that agent's purposes."[29] In other words, McCormick thinks God would have made the world so that no miracles were necessary. However, this is a deistic conception of God that does not take seriously the biblical idea that God wants people to love Him and their neighbors and that love by its nature cannot be coerced. McCormick actually suggests that "it would have been a simple matter to directly implant belief into all people's minds."[30] Not only would this produce automata, not the loving sons and daughters that God wants; it would also violate one of McCormick's own core principles—rational autonomy—which argues that people should make up their own minds solely based on the evidence. God cannot both brainwash people into believing in Him and grant them rational autonomy.

It is also worth noting that McCormick never seriously considers the implications of *other* Christian beliefs in evaluating miracles. Thus he complains that even if miracles occurred, this does not

---

[27]McCormick, *Atheism and the Case against Christ*, 179–80.

[28]That is, biblical miracles are meaning laden due to their contextualization within an established and ongoing narrative-history. There is nothing random or arbitrary about biblical miracles.

[29]McCormick, *Atheism and the Case against Christ*, 186.

[30]Ibid., 187–88.

necessarily point to God (an omnipotent, omniscient, holy being) because a lesser power might have done it.[31] But there is no discussion of the difference it makes if the precise circumstances of the miracle are foretold in advance (itself requiring a miracle, since ordinary humans have a miserable track record of predicting future events in any detail) together with an explanation of its meaning.

In the Old Testament, we find prophecies including unusual and specific details about Christ's crucifixion (Psalm 22; Isaiah 53:1–9) and resurrection (Psalm 16; Isaiah 53:10–12).[32] As Lydia McGrew has argued,[33] the predictions of Christ's death also provide evidence that Jesus is the prophesied Messiah, which gives independent support for the resurrection, because the Old Testament claims, paradoxically, that this same Messiah will have dominion over all other kings (Psalm 72) and have an eternal reign (Daniel 7:13–14). The messianic context tells us that Christ's death and resurrection are God at work in man: for unlike sinful humans, the "son of man" can directly approach God the Father, "the Ancient of Days" (Daniel 7:13) and has an "everlasting dominion" (Daniel 7:14). Isaiah 53 explains that Christ as Messiah was crucified for our "transgressions" and "iniquities" so that we are "accounted righteous" before God, and He is then blessed with new life ("he shall prolong his days"):

> Surely he has borne our griefs
>   and carried our sorrows;
> yet we esteemed him stricken,
>   smitten by God, and afflicted.
> But he was pierced for our transgressions;

---

[31]Ibid., 176–83.

[32]In *Science Speaks: An Evaluation of Certain Christian Evidences* (Chicago, IL: Moody, 1958), Peter W. Stoner uses probability theory to adjudicate the likelihood that just eight of the more than three hundred prophecies commonly associated with the messiahship of Jesus could happen by chance. His results (verified by the American Scientific Affiliation) show that the chance any man might have lived from when the prophecy was assumed to have been made to the present time and fulfilled all eight is just 1 in 10^{16}.

[33]Lydia McGrew, "Probabilistic Issues Concerning Jesus of Nazareth and Messianic Death Prophecies," *Philosophia Christi* 15:2 (2013), 311–28.

he was crushed for our iniquities;
upon him was the chastisement that brought us peace,
    and with his wounds we are healed.
...
Yet it was the will of the LORD to crush him;
    he has put him to grief;
when his soul makes an offering for guilt,
    he shall see his offspring; he shall prolong his days;
the will of the LORD shall prosper in his hand.
Out of the anguish of his soul he shall see and be satisfied;
by his knowledge shall the righteous one, my servant,
    make many to be accounted righteous,
    and he shall bear their iniquities. (Isaiah 53:4–5, 10–11)

Now if we have evidence that God has acted in Christ to overcome the human predicament (the moral gap discussed earlier), it is of little consequence whether the miracle by itself proves each and every attribute of God. For one thing, there are *other* arguments for God's attributes (many theists favor a cumulative-case approach to establishing God's attributes[34]). And what the resurrection does clearly show is that we have a God worthy of worship who has acted to rescue mankind in a decisive way regarding the greatest concern among human beings—namely, death itself.

In common with many of the New Atheists, McCormick assumes that his own position is neutral and unbiased. But it patently is not, since he clearly assumes that science is committed to methodological naturalism, which says that scientists may only infer natural causes. He thinks each person should ask, "Are my reasons for [believing the] resurrection better than all of the reasons we have for thinking that the entire scientific enterprise's naturalistic worldview is correct?"[35] Interestingly, McCormick's methodological naturalism directly conflicts with his evidentialism: the decision to allow only natural causes is made *before* investigating the evidence and so cannot be justified by that evidence. Thus he does not see any

---

[34]See, for example, Richard Swinburne, *The Existence of God*, 2nd ed. (New York: Oxford University Press, 2004).

[35]McCormick, *Atheism and the Case against Christ*, 64.

pressure to advance a serious alternative account of the resurrection: "[W]e don't need to have a fully articulated naturalistic explanation in place with the supporting evidence to believe reasonably that there is such an explanation."[36] A presumption of methodological naturalism thus allows McCormick to issue a promissory note—saying that there must be a naturalistic explanation—without shouldering the burden of actually providing one.

Detractors like McCormick might reply that there is inductive evidence for methodological naturalism—the evidence for physical laws that connect physical causes to physical effects. But to use inductive evidence to exclude taking miracle reports seriously would simply be to repeat Hume's erroneous reasoning about miracles and belies, again, skeptical bias while feigning neutrality. Hume argued that we can never reasonably believe a person reporting a miracle because it would "violate" the laws of nature, and "firm and unalterable experience has established these laws."[37] Now if the idea of "firm and unalterable experience" means that no one ever has experienced a miracle (the experience is "firm") and no one ever could (it is "unalterable"), this clearly begs the question, since this is the very point at issue. But in any case, the frequency of nonmiraculous events has nothing to do with the likelihood that a particular historical event is a miracle. Historians do not use *induction* (which applies to generalizations of repeatable effects) but *abduction*, an inference to the best explanation of a singular event. According to the logic of abduction, given the available data, we are to select the best of competing explanations. Unless it is excluded at the outset, there is no reason that a supernatural explanation should not be more probable than its naturalistic competitors. And naturalistic promissory notes have no weight, since they do not offer an actual explanation for the competition.

That Hume is mistaken in applying the probability of frequency to historical cases is clearly shown by Bayesian probability theory.[38] According to Bayes's theorem (Figure 1), even if an event initially

---

[36]Ibid., 67.

[37]David Hume, "Of Miracles," in John Earman, *Hume's Abject Failure: The Argument against Miracles* (New York: Oxford University Press, 2000), 143.

[38]See Ibid., Part I.

seems unlikely,[39] new evidence can rationally convince us that the event occurred. By following Hume down this path, McCormick likewise pursues a line of reasoning that simply does not obtain and frankly betrays his modernist bias against premodern testimony, among other things.

Figure 1: Bayes's theorem applied to miracles

Posterior Probability		Prior Probability		Relative Likelihood
$\dfrac{\Pr(M / E\&B)}{\Pr(\text{Not-}M / E\&B)}$	$=$	$\dfrac{\Pr(M / B)}{\Pr(\text{Not-}M / B)}$	$\times$	$\dfrac{\Pr(E / M\&B)}{\Pr(E / \text{Not-}M\&B)}$

Key:

M = a miracle

E = new evidence

B = background knowledge

Pr (A / B) = the probability of A given B

As applied to miracles, Bayes's theorem shows that even if the prior probability of a miracle (M) is low based on our background knowledge (B), there may be evidence (E) that is very unlikely if no miracle occurred (Not-M) but very likely if there was a miracle (M). This is the relative likelihood. When multiplied by the prior probability, this is sufficient to give a high posterior probability for M.

This result applies not only to miracles but also to unexpected natural events. Using Hume's logic, no one should have accepted Sir Arthur Eddington's report that during a total eclipse in 1919, the light of distant stars bent around the sun, since the report conflicted with all prior observations. To the contrary, Eddington's report was recognized as an important confirmation of Einstein's theory of general relativity. Richard Whately (1787–1863) effectively satirized Hume's argument: if correct, we should deny the reports of

---

[39]Unless of course its probability is zero. But in a contingent universe, there is no *a priori* justification for assigning any logically and metaphysically possible event a probability of zero. As an evidentialist, McCormick should agree that the evidence must decide.

Napoleon's existence, for "In vain will [we] seek in history for something similar to this wonderful Buonaparte."[40]

Nor is it relevant to object that too many reports of miracles are unreliable (like most of those claimed at Lourdes) or too biased. As C. S. Lewis points out,

> No doubt most stories of miracles are unreliable; but then, as anyone can see by reading the papers, so are most stories of all events. Each story must be taken on its merits: what one must not do is to rule out the supernatural as the one impossible explanation.[41]

Bias indeed should be taken seriously but not by pretending that methodological naturalism is unbiased. Instead, the best approach for investigating historical events, one that fully takes bias into account and has effective mechanisms to counteract its influence, is modeled on a courtroom. In a court of law, it is assumed that witnesses may be biased for or against a particular verdict. But testimony still has strength if it derives from multiple, independent eyewitnesses and if it can survive hostile cross-examination. In a way, McCormick seems to concede this, because the bulk of his book is an attempt to show we do not have such evidence for the resurrection, but as we have just seen, not only does modal logic acknowledge the plausibility (if not probability) of a miracle like the resurrection, but the content of varied attestations provide what amounts to be jurisprudence-quality evidence.

4. Handling the Evidence

Eyewitness Testimony?

McCormick asserts that the problem with the Gospel accounts of the resurrection is that

---

[40]Richard Whately, "Historic Doubts Relative to Napoleon Buonaparte," in *Richard Whately: A Man For All Seasons*, ed. Craig Parton (Edmonton, AB: Canadian Institute for Law, Theology & Public Policy, 1997), 71.

[41]Lewis, "Miracles," 27.

none of the authors were eyewitnesses to the events themselves. They heard the stories from others and recorded them many years after the alleged events transpired. The number of people through whom the stories passed before they were written down in the Gospels is unknown.[42]

But his claim is both controversial and highly misleading. It is controversial because John's Gospel explicitly presents itself as eyewitness testimony (John 21:24–25), and this claim was not questioned until the rise of modern biblical criticism.[43]

But the real issue is not whether the individual writing an account was an eyewitness, but whether what they were recording was eyewitness testimony. Thus, although the author of Mark was not an eyewitness,

> the Gospel of Mark itself, by means of the literary device of the *inclusio* of eyewitness testimony, indicates that Peter was the principal eyewitness source of this Gospel and that the authors of the Gospels of Luke and John both understood Mark to be making this claim.[44]

In fact, "three of the four Gospels [Mark, Luke and John] use the literary device of the *inclusio* of eyewitness testimony."[45] And because it is the content of the writing, and not the author, that is critical, it is not only the Gospels, but Paul's letters and Acts that are relevant. Thus Gary Habermas points out,

> The strength of the testimony for Jesus' death and resurrection comes from several facets of the evidence. First, the material . . . was quite *early*. These early Christian traditions predate the writing of the

---

[42]McCormick, *Atheism and the Case against Christ*, 38.

[43]This is to say nothing of Paul's written testimony of his own personal encounter with the risen Christ Jesus (Galatians 1:12; 1 Corinthians 15:8; cf. Acts 9:3–6).

[44]Richard Bauckham, *Jesus and the Eyewitnesses*, 204. Peter is the first disciple mentioned (Mark 3:16) and the last one mentioned (Mark 16:7).

[45]Bauckham, *Jesus and the Eyewitnesses*, 131.

New Testament. . . . In the case of 1 Corinthians 15:3ff. and the Acts creeds . . . this material dates within a few years of the actual events. This is not disputed by the critical community. Second, these creeds present *eyewitness* testimony for the facts that they report.[46]

A second way in which McCormick's claim is misleading is that he suggests that a long chain of hearsay communication preceded the recording of the events. But he neglects to mention two critically important factors. First, as Richard Bauckham argues,

> the period between the "historical" Jesus and the Gospels was actually spanned, not by anonymous community transmission, but by the continuing presence and testimony of the eyewitnesses, who remained the authoritative sources of their traditions until their deaths.[47]

In particular, in his list of eyewitnesses of the resurrection (1 Corinthians 15:5–8),

> Paul takes it for granted that most of the people were still alive when he was writing, but makes the point explicit in his remarkable reference to the (otherwise unknown) appearance [of the risen Christ] to more than five hundred believers. . . . The explicitness of this detail . . . shows that he intends it to be a kind of authentication: if anyone wishes to check this tradition, a very large number of the eyewitnesses are still alive and can be seen and heard. Paul thus takes for granted the *continuing accessibility and role* of the eyewitnesses. . . .[48]

This ongoing presence of eyewitnesses would serve as a powerful corrective to distortions of the events due to the foibles of memory, editorial modification, or propagandistic motivations.

---

[46]Gary Habermas, *The Historical Jesus: Ancient Evidence for the Life of Christ* (Joplin, MO: College Press Publishing Company, 1997), 169–70.

[47]Bauckham, *Jesus and the Eyewitnesses*, 8.

[48]Ibid., 308.

Second, as F. F. Bruce pointed out, those accounts also withstood the equivalent of cross-examination:

> [I]t can have been by no means so easy as some writers seem to think to invent words and deeds of Jesus in those early years, when so many of His disciples were about. . . . And it was not only friendly eyewitnesses that the early preachers had to reckon with; there were others less well disposed who were also conversant with the main facts of the ministry and death of Jesus. The disciples could not afford to risk inaccuracies (not to speak of willful manipulation of the facts), which would at once be exposed by those who would be only too glad to do so. . . . Had there been any tendency to depart from the facts in any material respect, the possible presence of hostile witnesses in the audience would have served as a further corrective.[49]

Textual Criticism

McCormick thinks we do not really have the wealth of independent sources for the resurrection we seem to have (the over five thousand Greek manuscripts of the New Testament plus over nineteen thousand in translation), because "any connection to the originals is built upon the slender bottleneck of just a few of the earlier manuscript fragments."[50] But McCormick fails to acknowledge that the case for the reliable transmission of the New Testament is far stronger than it is for comparable works of antiquity. Both in terms of the time gap between the original autographs and the earliest extant copies and in terms of the number of copies, the New Testament is unparalleled. To get an idea of the significance of the New Testament manuscript evidence, compare the record for nonbiblical texts. These are secular texts from antiquity that have been reconstructed with a high degree of certainty based on the available textual evidence: Josephus Flavius's monumental first-century history, *The Jewish War*, survives in only nine complete manuscripts dating

---

[49]F. F. Bruce, *The New Testament Documents: Are They Reliable?* (Downers Grove, IL: InterVarsity Press, 1981), 43.

[50]McCormick, *Atheism and the Case against Christ*, 40.

from the fifth century—four centuries after their composition.[51] Tacitus's *Annals of Imperial Rome*, a seminal historical resource for the ancient Roman world, survives in partial form in only two manuscripts dating from the Middle Ages.[52] Thucydides's *History* survives in eight copies. There are a mere eight copies of Caesar's *Gallic Wars*, eight copies of Herodotus's *History*, and seven copies of Plato's works, all dated over a millennium from the original. Bruce Metzger states that Homer's *Iliad* has the most impressive manuscript evidence for any secular work with 647 existing copies.[53]

Apologist Greg Koukl cites F. F. Bruce, who puts the discussion into perspective: "No classical scholar would listen to an argument that the authenticity of Herodotus or Thucydides is in doubt because the earliest manuscripts of their works which are of any use to us are over 1300 years later than the originals."[54]

Sir Frederick Kenyon (1863–1952), the director and principal librarian of the British Museum, argued that after the discovery of the Chester Beatty Papyri in the 1930s (dated to c. 200 AD and containing large portions of the New Testament),

The net result . . . is in fact to reduce the gap between the earlier manuscripts and the traditional dates of the New Testament books so far that it becomes negligible in any discussion of their authenticity. No other ancient book has anything like such early and plentiful testimony to its text, and no unbiased scholar would deny that the text that has come down to us is substantially sound.[55]

---

[51]Paul Barnett, *Is the New Testament History?* (Ann Arbor MI: Vine Books, 1986), 45.

[52]Norman L. Geisler and William E. Nix, *A General Introduction to the Bible* (Chicago, IL: Moody Press, 1986), 405.

[53]Bruce M. Metzger, *The Text of the New Testament* (New York: Oxford University Press, 1968), 34.

[54]Bruce, *The New Testament Documents*, 16–17 cited in Greg Koukl, "Is The New Testament Text Reliable?," 4 February 2013, accessed 4 October 2015, http://www.str.org/articles/is-the-new-testament-text-reliable#.VsS0mpMrL64.

[55]Sir Frederic G. Kenyon, *The Bible and Modern Scholarship* (London: John Murray, 1948), 20.

As F. F. Bruce explains, the sheer number of manuscripts makes a difference because of lower textual criticism, a science dedicated to providing an accurate reconstruction of the original text. While Bart Ehrman, whom McCormick cites with approval,[56] has complained about the many—perhaps four hundred thousand—variants in New Testament manuscripts, Bruce explains:

> When we have documents like our New Testament writings copied and recopied thousands of time, the scope for copyists' errors is so enormously increased that it is surprising that there are no more than there actually are. Fortunately, if the greater number of MSS increases the number of scribal errors, it increases proportionately the means of correcting such errors . . . The variant readings about which any doubt remains among textual critics of the New Testament affect no material question of historic fact or of Christian faith and practice.[57]

And more recently, Timothy Paul Jones provides a more detailed and direct response to Ehrman:

> Ehrman's estimate of the 400,000 variants among the New Testament manuscripts may be numerically correct—but what Ehrman doesn't clearly communicate to his readers is *the insignificance of the vast majority of these variants.* Most of these 400,000 variations stem from differences in spelling, word order, or the relationships between nouns and definite articles—variants that are easily recognizable, and, in most cases, virtually unnoticeable in translations! . . . In the end, more than 99 percent of the 400,000 differences fall into this category of virtually unnoticeable variants! Of the remaining 1 percent or so

---

[56]See especially, McCormick, *Atheism and the Case against Christ,* 39–40 and 112–13.

[57]Bruce, *The New Testament Documents: Are They Reliable?,* 14–15. Indeed, New Testament scholar Craig Evans further contextualizes the deceptiveness of the Ehrman charge by explaining that given the millions of manuscripts and manuscript fragments of the New Testament, variants appear on the average of one every five or six pages. Craig Evans, "Jesus and Modern Scholarship," *White Horse Inn,* #1002, 20 June 2010, https://www.whitehorseinn.org/show/jesus-in-modern-scholarship/.

of variants, . . . none of the differences affects any central element of the Christian faith.[58]

McCormick also claims that we have no reason to trust the process that resulted in the New Testament canon recognized by Athanasius in 367 AD, because, "for more than three hundred years after Jesus, a multitude of alternate Christian sources containing different accounts and doctrines circulated until one group of them was carved out of the noise and sanctioned."[59] This is really just a restatement of Elaine Pagels's earlier conspiratorial view, according to which the triumph of "orthodoxy" over Gnostic competitors was simply an exercise of sociopolitical power.[60] The problem with this thesis is that it overlooks strong evidence that a protocanon consisting of core Christian documents was decided very early.

As Gary Habermas notes, early sources such as Clement of Rome's *Epistle to the Corinthians* (c. 95 AD), Polycarp's *Epistle to the Philippians* (c. 115 AD), and the *Didache* (a manual of Christian teaching from the late first or early second century AD) all cite the words of Jesus as recorded in the synoptic Gospels.[61] Habermas argues persuasively that

> the canonical Gospels were widely recognized as being authoritative well before the late second century. . . . Therefore, when the earliest Gnostic Gospels were being written in the mid to late second century AD, at least the teachings of Jesus as presented in the canonical Gospels had already circulated for quite awhile and had been well established as Scripture. The same might be said for the Pauline corpus.[62]

---

[58]Timothy Paul Jones, *Misquoting Truth: A Guide to the Fallacies of Bart Ehrman's "Misquoting Jesus"* (Downers Grove, IL: InterVarsity Press, 2007), 43–44.

[59]McCormick, *Atheism and the Case against Christ*, 42.

[60]Elaine Pagels, *The Gnostic Gospels* (New York: Random House, 1979).

[61]Habermas, *The Historical Jesus*, 111.

[62]Ibid., 113–14.

So precisely, those New Testament writings that contain eyewitness accounts of the resurrection were already accepted as scripture before the Gnostic Gospels came on the scene.

Further, anyone who examines the texts of the Gnostic Gospels can see why they were excluded from the developing canon. In general, these documents are *pseudepigrapha*—assigned to famous individuals like Thomas, Peter, or Judas, who were not their authors, do not have apostolic approval (the apostles being long since dead), and contain obviously alien and contradictory teachings about Jesus and salvation. For example, in the Gospel of Judas, Judas is the hero who will "sacrifice the man that clothes"[63] Jesus, a clear expression of the Gnostic teaching that the body is a prison house, in direct opposition to the Christian teaching of a bodily resurrection.[64] Christians who had already accepted the Gospel accounts of Jesus's life and teaching had every reason to reject these Gnostic documents long before Athanasius's official identification of the twenty-seven books of the New Testament canon.[65]

Thus what we have in the New Testament is a reliable text including eyewitness testimony to the resurrection. And, employing his famous "minimal facts" approach, Habermas shows that even highly critical scholars, including members of the Jesus Seminar, grant a number of facts best explained by the historical fact of the resurrection.[66] These are that (1) Jesus died by Roman crucifixion;

---

[63]See The National Geographic Society, "The Gospel of Judas," 7, available at http://www.nationalgeographic.com/lostgospel/_pdf/GospelofJudas.pdf.

[64]For more detailed critique of "The Gospel of Judas," see Erwin Lutzer, "The Gospel of Judas: A Cheerfully Told Lie," in *Tough-Minded Christianity*, eds. William Dembski and Thomas Schirrmacher (Nashville, TN: B&H Academic, 2008), 337–49. For a more general critique of the claim that the Gnostic Gospels were wrongly excluded from Scripture, see Douglas Groothuis, "The Gnostic Gospels: Are They Authentic?," available at http://www.equip.org/article/the-gnostic-gospels-are-they-authentic/#christian-books-3.

[65]For more details, see Michael J. Kruger, *Canon Revisited: Reestablishing the Origins and Authority of the New Testament Books* (Wheaton, IL: Crossway, 2012).

[66]See Gary Habermas, "The Core Resurrection Data: The Minimal Facts Approach," in *Tough-Minded Christianity*, 387–405.

(2) Paul, a persecutor of the church, became a believer because he believed he saw the risen Christ; (3) the disciples had already had experiences that they thought were the risen Christ; (4) "The resurrection appearances were proclaimed *immediately*"[67] after Jesus's death; (5) James, the brother of Jesus, who had been a skeptic, was converted after an experience he took to be of the risen Christ; and (6) the disciples were transformed by their experience and were willing to die in bold proclamation of the resurrection. These minimal facts are clearly inconsistent with McCormick's speculations about data scrubbing and canon manipulation.

5. Mass Hallucinations and Other Evasions

Like Ehrman, McCormick suggests that the resurrection appearances can be accounted for as bereavement hallucinations.[68] It is a fairly common phenomenon for seniors to think they see a spouse or other loved one again for a short time after they have died. But there are multiple problems with the hallucination theory. First, in 1 Corinthians 15:5–8, there are many appearances on different occasions, including large and different groups of people. Even for one group of people, it is very unlikely that they would all experience the same hallucination in all the same modalities (auditory and tactile as well as visual) at the very same time. But it is even less likely that *every* member of *several* different groups on *several* different occasions would share that hallucination.[69] In addition, hallucinations are derived from the content of past experience and expectation. But Paul had never previously seen Jesus before and did not expect to do so. Likewise, first-century Jews, and especially Jesus's skeptical brother James, certainly did not expect to see Jesus again.[70]

---

[67]Ibid., 394.

[68]McCormick, *Atheism and the Case against Christ*, 85.

[69]Gary Habermas, "Jesus Did Rise from the Dead," in *Debating Christian Theism*, ed. J. P. Moreland, Chad Meister, and Khaldoun Sweis (New York: Oxford University Press, 2013), 471–83, 474.

[70]Peter S. Williams, *Understanding Jesus: Five Ways to Spiritual Enlightenment* (Milton Keynes, UK: Paternoster Press, 2011), 191.

And there are still more problems when we look into the particular appearances in more detail. In the case of bereavement hallucinations, people recognize the person for whom they are grieving. But, as C. S. Lewis pointed out, "any theory of hallucination breaks down on the fact . . . that on three separate occasions this hallucination was not recognized as Jesus [Luke 24:13–21; John 20:15; John 21:4],"[71] giving further evidence that he was not expected. But Jesus also did things like having conversations, breaking bread (Luke 24:30), and eating fish (Luke 24:42) that a hallucination cannot do, and he frequently invited the disciples to touch him (Luke 24:30; John 20:27). So one would have to claim simultaneous multimodal hallucinations that conveyed the experience of talking and eating with a person one could touch as well as see! And Mike Licona cites the authority of Gary Sibcy, a licensed clinical psychologist with a doctorate in clinical psychology, who reports:

> I have surveyed the professional literature (peer-reviewed journal articles and books) written by psychologists, psychiatrists, and other relevant healthcare professionals during the past two decades and have yet to find a single documented case of a group hallucination. . . .[72]

And even if such a thing did occur, it is incredibly unlikely that all the details, including experience in multiple modalities, would be sufficiently consistent that the many eyewitnesses would accept the reports written down in their own lifetimes.

McCormick does have a few other arguments he can use to reject the resurrection. But the problem is that they prove too much: if accepted, they would show it is unreasonable to believe things that many sensible people believe, including McCormick.

---

[71]C. S. Lewis, *Miracles: A Preliminary Study*, 2nd ed. (New York: Macmillan, 1978), 147.

[72]Gary Sibcy, personal correspondence, cited in Mike Licona, *Evidence for God*, ed. William A. Dembski and Michael Licona (Grand Rapids, MI: Baker Books, 2010), 178.

For example, McCormick mounts a corrosive attack on the reliability of memory. He cites psychological studies to show that "we forget the sources of claims we hear, true or false . . . we are demonstrably bad at remembering events . . . [and] the degree of confidence about our ability to remember important events is often grossly out of synch with the facts."[73] He even says that we make up a lot of what we call memory: "[T]he narrative of events that you construct is heavily influenced by your expectations, your desires, your biases."[74] No doubt there is some truth in all this, but it overlooks the fact that "ancient Mediterranean culture valued, hence emphasized, memory to a degree Western readers consider extraordinary."[75] And if the possibility of unreliable memory is a reason to reject the reliably preserved, multiply attested reports of nonhallucinating eyewitnesses to the resurrection, that would mean that we ought to reject vast amounts of history. Would anyone seriously argue that Caesar's crossing of the Rubicon was the embellishment of an overactive memory, a projection of Suetonius's desperate need to believe in Julius Caesar?

McCormick also does not consider the fact that the modern scientific method itself depends on both testimony and memory. Scientists rely on other scientists' reports of their observations and experiments, and they are not always in a position to recreate them (consider a total eclipse, the return of a comet, or a laboratory experiment one lacks the equipment to repeat). So if McCormick goes too far in discrediting the ideas of testimony and memory, it would require him to lose confidence in the modern science that he thinks discredits a supernatural world view. If we accept the reasonable view that memory and testimony can be trusted so long as there are sufficient checks and balances, we can trust modern science; but then we must also face the powerful evidence for the resurrection.

---

[73]McCormick, *Atheism and the Case against Christ*, 92.

[74]Ibid., 93.

[75]Craig S. Keener, "Gospel Truth," in *Come Let Us Reason: New Essays in Christian Apologetics*, ed. Paul Copan and William Lane Craig (Nashville, TN: B&H Academic, 2012), 99–112, 106. See also Bruce J. Malina, *The New Testament World: Insights from Cultural Anthropology*, 2nd ed. (Louisville: Westminster/John Knox Press, 1993).

A second example of this strategy is McCormick's claim that because the resurrection is an extraordinary claim—on a par with claims to witnessing witchcraft or an alien abduction—we should require extraordinarily good evidence to accept it.[76] Part of this reflects McCormick's antisupernatural bias, as we saw earlier. But he is also mistaken that the confirmation of a resurrection requires extraordinary evidence. Thomas Sherlock (1678–1671) made the point beautifully:

> Suppose you saw a Man publickly executed, his Body afterwards wounded by the Executioner, and carry'd and laid in the Grave; that after this you should be told that the Man was come to Life again; what would you suspect in this Case? not that the Man had never been dead, for that you saw your self; but you would suspect whether he was now alive: But would you say the Case excluded all human Testimony. . . . ? A Man rising from the Grave is an Object of Sense, and can give the same Evidence of his being alive as any other Man in the World can give. So that a Resurrection consider'd only as a Fact to be prov'd by Evidence is a plain Case; it requires no greater Ability in the Witnesses than that they be able to distinguish between a Man dead and a Man alive; a Point in which I believe every Man living thinks himself a Judge.[77]

The important point is that establishing *that* a resurrection occurs does not require any unfamiliar, special test. We do not have to confirm some bizarre theory of *how* a resurrection happens but simply apply the normal tests for telling if someone is alive or dead. The only difference in the case of the resurrection is that the tests are applied in reverse of the normal order (death preceding life instead of life preceding death).

But we have overwhelming evidence that Jesus died on the cross: it is confirmed not only by the biblical account but by many external

---

[76]McCormick, *Atheism and the Case against Christ,* 144–45.

[77]Thomas Sherlock, "The Tryal of the Witnesses of the Resurrection of Jesus," in Earman, *Hume's Abject Failure,* 125–32, 129.

sources (such as works of Cornelius Tacitus, Lucian of Samosata, and Seutonius[78]) and by medical analysis. As Habermas explains,

> Crucifixion is essentially death by asphyxiation, as the intercostals and pectoral muscles around the lungs halt normal breathing while the body hangs in the "down" position. Therefore, faking death on the cross still would not permit one to breathe; one cannot fake the inability to breathe for any length of time.[79]

And the flow of blood and water after the spear wound (John 19:34) indicates that Jesus was already dead of congestive heart failure.[80] Now that various swoon and other conspiracy theories have been thoroughly discredited,[81] we are left with overwhelming evidence that Jesus died on the cross but was then seen alive again. That is all we need to show that a resurrection occurred, and this combined with the fact that the specific manner of death and the resurrection were foretold as signs of the Messiah should lead our minds to accept (*assensus*) the historical fact of the resurrection (*notitia*).

6. Conclusion

McCormick tries to bury the resurrection account in a miasma of corrosive skepticism. But his arguments misunderstand the relation between faith and evidence and depend on naturalistic assumptions that are heavily biased against accepting any testimony for a miracle. They also mislead the reader by denying clear evidence that the New Testament accounts of the resurrection derive from eyewitnesses. The attempts to discredit this possibility

---

[78]See Josh McDowell, *New Evidence that Demands a Verdict* (Nashville, TN: Thomas Nelson, 1999), 120–21.

[79]Habermas, *The Historical Jesus*, 73–74.

[80]William D. Edwards, MD; Wesley J. Gabel, MDiv; Floyd E Hosmer, MS, AMI, "On the Physical Death of Jesus Christ," *Journal of the American Medical Association*, 21 March 1986, Volume 256, available online at http://brainshavings .com/on-the-physical-death-of-jesus-christ.html.

[81]Habermas, *The Historical Jesus*, 72–99.

by appeal to bereavement hallucinations and the need for extraordinary evidence for an extraordinary event also fail. The historical fact of the resurrection rises unscathed from McCormick's miasma, showing that Christians are justified in believing that God raised Jesus from the dead.

6

Un-Inevitable Easter Faith: Historical Contingency, Theological Consistency, and the Resurrection of Jesus Christ

Jonathan Mumme

Orientation

Learning to drive before satellite navigations systems aided the task, north, south, east, and west were realities of import. Fortunately for me, the roads of south-central Minnesota had been laid as a grid, aligned with these cardinal directions. Without a printed map, orientation ran by landmark. Daydreaming with cheap fuel in the tank, I more than once experienced a mental turn or cognitive about-face without so much as turning the steering wheel. "Hmm, I must be going north," I may have thought to myself, forming a picture-map in my mind's eye, only to have my orientation disturbed by a landmark: "Wait a minute—isn't that the old Schwartz farm, from the *west*? I must be going *east!*" And then, without so much as a twist of the wheel or a change of gear, in my mind's eye the whole grid shifted around me, and I was driving in a "different" direction.

From the days of the early church to the early modern period, Christians believed in a bodily resurrection from the dead, in which a material continuity between deceased and resurrected persons was maintained, be it in the prototypical case of Jesus or in the future case of believers. This was, one might say, taken to be "true north." True north was the resurrection fact. But moving along a trajectory set in the eighteenth century by H. S. Reimarus, who eschewed conceiving the resurrection of Jesus as that of a body from a tomb, a largely German exegetical tradition including such scholars as D. F. Strauss and R. Bultmann came to question all miracles as myth and relegated the resurrection to this ahistorical category.[1] Thus today, be they German-or English-speaking, it is commonplace that avid skeptics help set the grid for how Jesus and early-Christian claims about his resurrection are to be understood, received, and believed or, as is often the case, left behind.[2] Without the bodily resurrection of Jesus, "true north" has not only shifted—it has disappeared. Those who would explore the terrain of the Christian faith are left to cruise rather aimlessly, with little more than conflicting guesses at who Jesus is and what he did to guide them.

In such a landscape, it is not inevitable that self-professing Christians accept the bodily resurrection of Jesus; between "evangelistic skeptic[s]" and "gung-ho apologist[s],"[3] the cardinal direc-

---

[1]See Rowan Williams, "Resurrection," in *The Oxford Companion to Christian Thought*, ed. Adrian Hastings (Oxford: Oxford University Press, 2000), 616–18. Cf. Hans Urs von Balthasar, *Mysterium Paschale: The Mystery of Easter*, trans. Aidan Nichols, O.P. (Edinburgh: T&T Clark, 1990), 191–93 on the related role of F. D. E. Schleiermacher in this process.

[2]Göttingen exegete and scholar of early Christianity, Gerd Lüdemann, for example, understanding only about 5 percent of the words attributed to Jesus in New Testament as having any historical connection to him, views the bodily resurrection of Jesus as a deliberate falsification of the early church; *The Resurrection of Jesus: History, Experience, Theology*, trans. John Bowden (London: SCM Press, 1994); *The Great Deception: And What Jesus Really Said and Did*, trans. John Bowden (London: SCM Press, 1998). John Dominic Crossan, of the "ultra-radical" (Williams, "Resurrection," 617) Jesus Seminar, holds that Jesus's body was not even buried, much less resurrected; *Jesus: A Revolutionary Biography* (San Francisco, CA: HarperSanFrancisco, 1994); *The Birth of Christianity: Discovering What Happened in the Years Immediately After the Execution of Jesus* (San Francisco, CA: HarperSanFrancisco, 1998).

[3]Dale C. Allison Jr., "Resurrecting Jesus," in *Resurrecting Jesus: The Earliest Christian Tradition and Its Interpreters* (New York/London: T&T Clark, 2005), 198–375, quotations 339.

tions of whose compass(es) often point in opposite directions, it may appear that perhaps the best one can do is point to a given landmark and suggest some direction by way of it. A recent example of such scholarly effort is the work of Dale Allison, whose impressive investigation of modern research on apparitions of the recently deceased he brings to bear on his own field of New Testament studies.[4] Allison suggests that since the percipients of such encounters can attest to sensations of touch and a certain solidity of the apparitions, one need not take postcrucifixion appearances of Jesus that bear similar characteristics as necessarily implying the resurrection of his body from the tomb.[5] Apparitions furnish an alternative interpretive direction. Or do they? Although Allison stimulates an interesting point for heuristic comparison, we shall see that this modern phenomenology of apparitions fails to dislodge the cardinal direction indicated by the work of N. T. Wright. Wright has substantiated that the referent of the word "resurrection" and its cognates in early Christianity (as specified by the Jewish and Greco-Roman contexts in which Christian faith arose) points to a bodily resurrection of Jesus of the sort that would necessitate an empty tomb.[6] A transformed body, not an apparitional form, is precisely what the New Testament authors claimed to have witnessed.

---

[4] Ibid., esp. 269–99.

[5] See note 4 above; although Allison also addresses the New Testament resurrection formulae and confessions (229–39), and offers direct analysis of its appearance stories (239–69) as well as takes up the question of the tomb and the body (299–337; cf. 352–63, arguing against J. D. Crossan for the burial of Jesus by Joseph of Arimathea), that which he rather uniquely adds to contemporary scholarship is his research on apparitions and the conclusions that he in part draws from it (see 337–52). Allison describes himself as a "mainstream Protestant" (344) while admitting that he is also "reluctantly a cryptic Deist" (215) to whom the resurrection is attractive as a denial of a "Kafkaesque universe" (219). But whether the "God of Western theism" actually aligns with "the God of Israel" (343) is something I mean to question in this essay.

[6] N. T. Wright, *The Resurrection of the Son of God*, Christian Origins and the Question of God, vol. 3 (Minneapolis, MN: Fortress Press, 2003); the point is established largely in cc. 2–4 (pp. 32–206).

This essay will argue, first, that a bodily[7] resurrection of Jesus is the most historically plausible explanation for the rise of early Christianity precisely because such claim by the early Christians was anything but inevitable. Second, this essay means to highlight how the bodily resurrection of Jesus is theologically consistent with the overarching story of the Christian Scriptures in a way that a non-bodily postmortem existence of Christ is not, such that the former embraces and interweaves with the overarching story, while the latter surrenders it. There follows then a brief conclusion that contemplates the metanoetic and metamorphic potential[8] of the resurrection of Jesus as a landmark cropping up in the landscape of human history.

Dale Allison: Jesus's Resurrection Appearances as One Landmark among Others

Engaging in historical investigation while recognizing certain limits of such inquiry, Dale Allison takes up the question: "What might it mean to say that Jesus rose from the dead?"[9] Presenting seven main "elucidations of belief in Jesus' resurrection,"[10] this historian tentatively supports what he would describe as genuine visions on the part of Jesus's followers combined with a misinterpretation of a tomb that was most likely empty by rather mundane means.[11] At least so far as Allison's own faith is concerned, Jesus is one who triumphed over death and is vindicated as an object of faith. As he

---

[7]By "bodily," I mean a sort of resurrection that would necessitate an empty tomb and not simply some perceived solidity in the postmortem appearances of Jesus; cf. Allison's position below.

[8]From μετανοέω, which indicates a change of mind and heart, and μεταμορφόω, which indicates transformation.

[9]Allison, "Resurrecting Jesus," 198.

[10]Ibid., 201; these are orthodox belief, misinterpretation, hallucinations, deliberate deception, genuine visions, belief in God's vindication, and rapid disintegration of the body plus visions.

[11]Thus the emptiness of Jesus's tomb was not necessary for the kind of resurrection he underwent, for his body remained a corpse but just happened to be elsewhere.

deliberates the genuineness or veracity of accounts of Jesus's post-mortem appearances, his study of modern research into apparitions and bereavement processes plays a significant role. Even if Jesus did not rise from the dead in such a way that would necessitate his tomb being empty, postmortem perceptions of him might still be real and perhaps even "solid," presenting him as a proper object of faith.

Allison's approach constructively raises at least two relevant questions. First, what can be ascertained about the appearances of a postmortem Jesus by entertaining the findings of modern investigations into encounters with and apparitions of deceased persons? Second, what can be learned from the bereavement processes of their percipients? Based on research begun in the 1880s and accelerating since the 1970s, Allison argues that the postmortem appearances of Jesus are unique neither in being shared experiences of multiple persons and groups nor in extending over a period of time.[12] In the data that he is surveying,[13] such appearances and apparitions are rather common, and this data can be read as shielding the Christophanies (i.e., the appearances of the Christ after his death) of the New Testament Gospels from generalizing dismissal[14] and preserving them as accounts reflecting authentic experiences not simply to be equated with hallucination.[15] As he takes findings from the fields of psychical research, parapsychology, anomalistic psychology, psychiatry, palliative medicine, geropsychology, and geriatrics into consideration, Allison also finds evidence of encounters wherein the deceased person was experienced as "overwhelmingly real and indeed seemingly solid."[16] The fact that apparitions today are not only perceived but are sometimes perceived as solid allows him to conclude that even such appearances of Jesus as are recorded in Luke 24:36–43, John 20:24–29, and John 21:9–14, which are often presumed to be later anti-Docetist additions (given their emphasis

---

[12]Allison, "Resurrecting Jesus," 269f.

[13]See note 4 above; the literature from the various fields (mentioned in the next sentence) surveyed in the footnotes of these pages is vast and various.

[14]As for example by J. D. Crossan; Allison, "Resurrecting Jesus," 285.

[15]Ibid., 286–88.

[16]Ibid., 281.

on Jesus's tangibility and physicality), may actually preserve a primitive conviction about the risen Jesus.[17] Thus, in the grand scheme
of things, some of Allison's conclusions appear rather conservative;
apparitions of deceased persons are not simply hallucinations and
may even entail a certain solidity. In a grid set in part by radical
skepticism, these conclusions can, on the one hand, plead for a given
veracity of the New Testament's appearance stories. On the other
hand, the whole of this data draws on examples of deceased persons
naturally understood to be still in their graves, cremated, or otherwise in a state not entailing a return to bodily life. As Allison applies
modern examples of apparitions to the postmortem appearances of
Jesus as recorded in the New Testament, he reasons that if Jesus was
buried, which he believes to be the case,[18] real and even seemingly
"solid" appearances of Jesus need not entail an empty tomb. After all,
many people today enjoy very real experiences in which deceased
friends or family members appear to them without their coffins
being empty. The modern apparitional research is certainly interesting in its own right, but Allison's use of it to interpret the accounts of
Jesus's resurrection exhibits a number of fallacies.

Without denying that these data are in some way heuristically
valuable, transference to the case of Jesus that means to show that the
brains of his followers did not "need external stimuli in order to create" a body that was "physical or material" and that they could experience him "in bodily form as eating, speaking, and walking" without
any "physical, material body"[19] is either dubious on the part of Allison
or logically illegitimate. Beyond Allison's claim that the data presented
reflect results from "different times and places" that demonstrate "a
cross-cultural phenomenon"[20] from "different regions of the globe,"[21]
it is not readily apparent how the field of data substantially extends

---

[17]Ibid., 289–92.

[18]Ibid., 299–337; he favors a mundane explanation for its emptiness, 335f.

[19]Ibid., 281, note 327, citing Pieter F. Craffert, "'Seeing a Body into Being':
Reflections on Scholarly Interpretations of the Nature and Reality of Jesus'
Resurrected Body," *Religion and Theology* 9 (2002): 101.

[20]Allison, "Resurrecting Jesus," 271, note 297.

[21]Ibid., 273.

beyond North America and Western Europe,[22] and so beyond examples from Western societies shaped, at least in part, in their perceptions of death and the dead by a Christian tradition that espoused physically tangible encounters with the risen Jesus as a central tenet of its faith. This is significant because it can hardly be legitimate to substantiate a "resurrection" of Jesus needing no empty tomb based on examples taken from societies and cultures whose very thinking about the dead has been shaped precisely by categories provided by such a bodily resurrection of Christ in the Christian tradition. One of Allison's own examples, that of a widow speaking of encounters with her deceased husband, confirms the point:

> He looked real, alive. . . . I put my arms around him, it felt just like you or I, just real. You know like, the Lord appeared, you know when he died, and he was alive and he asked the man to feel the nail hole in his side. My husband was just as real as if he was here with me now.[23]

Observation about occurrences described in categories provided by "the Lord" can hardly be used to draw conclusions about this self-same Lord. Put simply, the woman cited is perceiving the appearance of her husband in categories provided her by St. John's account of Jesus's resurrection, and it is logically illegitimate to draw conclusions about Jesus's resurrection from it. Could or would she even talk about what she "felt" in such an encounter had the Christian resurrection narratives not provided the categories? Clearly one can't know, and that is the point, as it would be for many percipients in the West. And not only does Allison point to little non-Western evidence; he points to very little of it prior to 1882.[24] There is some

---

[22]Ibid., 274, note 306 does mention a study of Hopi Indian women; regarding whether or not the encountered Jesus had feet, he mentions "worldwide folklore," 278.

[23]Ibid., 291, quoting Eda Devers, "Experiencing the Deceased: Reconciling the Extraordinary" (Ph.D. diss., University of Florida, 1994), 55.

[24]In his related excursus on bereavement, Allison ("Resurrecting Jesus," 365) admits, "[M]y points of comparison are inevitably based upon data gathered from the contemporary world."

generalization about ancients having contact with the dead, but such encounters are no demonstration of belief that the dead actually returned to life.[25] Examples such as those drawn from the works of Bede, Uranius the Presbyter, and Bonaventure,[26] or those having to do with Thomas Beckett, John of the Cross, and Teresa of Avila,[27] are data legitimate for substantiating a resurrection of Christ neutral to the state of his tomb only insofar as these (pre-Enlightenment) authors and the (pre-Enlightenment) percipients present and understand them as such. It seems, however, highly doubtful that this is the case. If one could ask Bede, Uranius, Bonaventure, Thomas Beckett, John of the Cross, and Teresa of Avila if Jesus had risen from the dead and if his tomb must thus have been empty, there could hardly be any doubt of their answer. Indeed, there never was a doubt until modern skeptics offered an alternative psychologized (hagiographical) reading of the medieval theologians of the church. In truth, such a bodily resurrection of Jesus was "true north" even for the mystics of the pre-Enlightenment Christian tradition, and they were known for their orthodox confession and subscription to creedal Christianity.[28]

Shortly, it may be that grieving modern Westerners can perceive a given solidity in appearances of deceased loved ones whose bodies still remain corpses. But as Western categories of postmortem experiences have been shaped by the Christian tradition itself, this data can hardly be used to measure that tradition's origin. Allison's approach is simply anachronistic. And, as the next section will show, no one at the time of the onset of Christianity would have equated such experiences with "resurrection" anyway. It may today be inevitable that a subset of mourners experience very real and even "solid"

---

[25]Ibid., 274, note 307 cites Pliny (first century) as recognizing that the bereaved have contact with the dead, but as Wright shows, Pliny specifically denied the notion that the dead could return to life: *The Resurrection of the Son of God*, 33 note 9, 65 note 193.

[26]Allison, "Resurrecting Jesus," 280, note 322.

[27]Ibid., 279, note 320; 281, note 326.

[28]On the limits of the possibilities for this data in Allison's own mind, see ibid., 284f. Skepticism is a position that "runs both ways" (ibid., 298); when not out to set the grid, one may simply point to features in the landscape and suggest that they might be valuable.

encounters with deceased loved ones; it is anything but inevitable that the grieving followers of Jesus would or could have spoken of such encounters (if theirs were of such a sort) as "resurrection."

N. T. Wright:
Jesus's Resurrection as a Shift of the Landscape

One might well expect that what differentiates historians from one another is their handling of history. One might not expect that the difference between two historians could be seen in the tense of a single verb. The tense of a single verb is, however, the key difference between the historical investigations of Dale Allison and N. T. Wright into the resurrection of Jesus. Whereas Allison begins his inquiry by asking what "Jesus rose from the dead" *means*, Wright begins by asking what this *meant*, or, more specifically, to what such a claim referred.[29] When "resurrection" and its cognate verbs were applied to Jesus by early Christians, to what were they referring? What was the referent of such words? Wright's seminal work, *The Resurrection of the Son of God*, begins with a thoroughgoing investigation of "resurrection" in ancient pagan[30] and Jewish usage in and around the first century of the Common Era.[31] The importance of this historical contextualization of early Christian resurrection language can hardly be overestimated, leading Wright, as it does, to significant conclusions regarding the resurrection of Jesus and the emergence of Christian faith. Though the following paragraphs will illustrate Wright's findings about pagan, Jewish, and early Christian use of "resurrection"

---

[29]On the difference between "meaning" and "referent," see Wright, *The Resurrection of the Son of God*, 719–23; cf. xviiif. Cf. Gerald O'Collins, S. J., "The Resurrection," in *Christology: A Biblical, Historical, and Systematic Study of Jesus* 82–113 (Oxford: Oxford University Press, 1995), 83–90.

[30]For Wright, "pagan" refers to non-Jewish and non-Christian (itself in its early form understood as a development of Second Temple Judaism) religion. In the main, Wright takes stock of Greco-Roman writers, but some ancient Egyptian sources play a passing tertiary role too (see, for example, *The Resurrection of the Son of God*, pp. 46f, 80f).

[31]The period that Wright takes into consideration is roughly two to three hundred years both before and after Jesus; see ibid., 38f.

in greater detail, a succinct initial summary is in order. Whether by pagans, who held it to be impossible, or by Jews, who in the main had come to hope for it at the end of time, "resurrection" always referred to a return to embodied existence after an interim period of being in a state of death; "resurrection" is not synonymous with life after physical death and so a new construal of death but is rather death's reversal, entailing a state of embodied living after the state of death. Simply put, for Jews committed to resurrection beliefs as part of their scripture-tradition and for all known Christians, "resurrection" was *always* about physical bodies and *never* about apparitions.

The pagan world of the day took its cues for thinking about existence after death and the possibility and/or impossibility of resurrection in the main from Homer and Plato.[32] The former held that the dead were but subhuman shades or phantoms in the gloomy domain of Hades. Whether they thereby fared better than the dead in the thought of the Epicureans, who denied them any existence whatsoever, would have been debatable. If any path did follow death, the one leading into Hades was not matched by a path out; there was no return. Plato, in identifying the self with the soul as opposed to with the physical body, succeeded in renovating Hades into a jollier place of certain pleasures. Transmigration, in which the soul of a deceased person would pass into a different body, was also a possibility, but the greater hope was a complete break with any cycle of physical existence, wherein the soul is still confined to the prison house of a body. Emperors could await, or arrange, divinization, and philosophers and virtuous persons might attain to an "astral immortality." The ancient pagan world thus evidenced a rather broad spectrum of thought on life after death, but one unifying factor was that the dead were not restored to bodily life. "Resurrection" was, quite simply, not possible, and for a good Platonist, it wasn't even desirable.[33]

---

[32]One might say that the visceral, fearful face of death can be sensed in Homer, whereas the philosophical ideal of how one might face death nobly is embodied in Plato's Socrates.

[33]Wright, *The Resurrection of the Son of God*, 32–84.

In the Hebrew Old Testament, Wright finds an unfolding of hope in resurrection across three stages.[34] In the earliest stage of this hope's emergence, the dead are understood to be asleep with ancestors in Sheol, in which they are without a future and from which no return is expected. Hope at this point centered on the land, the family, the nation, and the temple; their prosperity was the substance of hope in YHWH's faithfulness to his people and to creation. This faithfulness was, however, also experienced personally, and out of such experience then seems to have grown a conviction that his faithfulness would also be known beyond the grave. Finally, in a motion that takes up both the communal/national nature of the hope and the element of YHWH's faithfulness even beyond the grave, texts such as Daniel 12:2–3, Isaiah 52–53, Hosea 13:14, and Ezekiel 37 evince a confidence that YHWH would finally restore Israel's fortunes, remove her oppression, and grant her peace, "even if it took a great act of new creation to accomplish it."[35] "Resurrection" as spoken of here is neither synonymous with Sheol, nor is it a new spin on life after death. Rather, resurrection is what happens after life-after-death—that is, after the present state of *being* dead. Resurrection *awaits* those presently dead and will mean for them a restoration of bodily life that decisively reverses their current state. The Hebrew Old Testament's unfolding hope of resurrection is born of convictions about YHWH, convictions about his justice and his faithfulness to the land, the people, and to creation. Therefrom emerged the belief that "the relationship with YHWH would be unbreakable even by death, and the eventual belief that YHWH would raise the dead."[36] Resurrection, then, is a hope that unfolds in the history of Israel and through the Hebrew Scriptures.[37]

---

[34]Wright makes no claim that they move in an absolutely linear fashion but that one gives way to the next, which itself does not replace but reaffirms the hope that preceded it.

[35]Ibid., 121.

[36]Ibid., 85–128; quotation, 127.

[37]Skeptics who deny a Jewish Scripture tradition of resurrection beliefs and interpretation would do well to consider the research of eminent Harvard University Professor of Jewish Studies and Hebrew Bible, Jon D. Levenson, particularly his works, *Resurrection and the Restoration of Israel: The Ultimate*

The generalization that Greeks believed in immortality, whereas Jews believed in resurrection is, in relation to Second Temple Judaism, an oversimplification. The Jewish faith, after the exile, had interacted with Hellenistic culture and housed a spectrum of beliefs that often evidenced rather robust appropriation of Greek thinking. Jewish belief about life after death and resurrection was no exception.[38] Though texts in the Hebrew Old Testament understood as pointing to resurrection may have been sparse, the strand of expectation that stood as the majority opinion in Second Temple Judaism had come to await some form of resurrection. This distinctly Jewish hope, indeed represented only among the Jews, was counterbalanced by more Hellenized forms of that faith. The minority opinion of the biblically conservative Sadducees,[39] whose political conservatism wished no disruption of the comfortable status quo they enjoyed under foreign rule, was that there was no future life at all, neither a resurrection nor an intermediate state that might have preceded it. The majority belief in resurrection, though not restricted to Pharisaic Judaism, was typified by the teaching of the Pharisees and is attested even in prayers at the very heart of the liturgy at that time. As the weight of Jewish Bible reading shifted from Hebrew to the Greek of the Septuagint, passages that spoke of resurrection now came through as loud and clear witnesses, while further passages, not previously so forthright, were magnified in this direction, including bits of the Torah. A major component of the Pharisaical/Sadducaical divide[40] was the revolutionary potential of resurrection hope. The previous hope for resurrection grew to potent expression in 2 Maccabees, where a powerful act of new creation guaranteed a resurrected life with new bodies to

---

Victory of the God of Life (New Haven, CT: Yale University Press, 2008) and *The Death and Resurrection of the Beloved Son: The Transformation of Child Sacrifice in Judaism and Christianity* (New Haven, CT: Yale University Press, 1995). But also, see Kevin J. Madrigal and Jon D. Levenson, *Resurrection: The Power of God for Christians and Jews* (New Haven, CT: Yale University Press, 2009).

[38]Wright, *The Resurrection of the Son of God,* 129–206.

[39]Sadducees accepted only the Torah as codified divine revelation.

[40]See Matthew 22:23–34 and parallels, Acts 23:5–10.

martyrs killed under tyrannical foreign rule.[41] A very this-worldly resurrection hope, entailing the judgment of enemies, vindication, and renewed bodily life, could act as gasoline on sparks of revolt. Politically, the Sadducees' fear was justified; in 70 AD, one such revolution ended the Sadducaical strand of Judaism. Apocalyptic texts of the period, along with Josephus, Pseudo-Philo, certain Qumran texts, and other sources, each in their own way either directly express hope in "resurrection" or indirectly show an expectation of the same by way of a two-stage eschatology that would include a future embodied existence for those who have died. Philo, on the other hand, provides a thoroughly Hellenized point of view: with typical Platonic dualism, the souls of those who have died enjoy a blessed, disembodied existence. This, their immortality, neither needs nor awaits an overturning, and this immortality is not termed "resurrection." On the whole, a majority of Jews around the time of Jesus believed in and hoped for an End Times, bodily resurrection; those who did not could recognize the revolutionary potential of this hope.

Of the broad spectrum of beliefs about life after death that characterized Second Temple Judaism, Wright makes several overarching observations important for contextualizing early Christian claims about the "resurrection" of Jesus.[42] First, "resurrection" could either metaphorically refer to the restoration of Israel or literally to the restoration of the bodies and bodily life of those who had died, but both types of reference are concrete, pointing to events, and are not abstract. Second, referring to persons, immortality of souls and resurrection are never synonymous, but they are also not mutually exclusive categories, for Jews who espoused belief in resurrection held that the dead were currently in YHWH's hand, paradise, and/or Sheol; souls

---

[41]2 Maccabees 7:9–11 (ESV): "'[T]he King of the universe will raise us up to an everlasting renewal of life, . . .' After him, the third was the victim of their sport. When it was demanded, he quickly put out his tongue and courageously stretched forth his hands and said nobly, 'I got these from heaven, and because of his laws I disdain them, and from him I hope to get them back again.'" The hope is, by the confession of the sons' mother, of a peace with God creating from nothing; see 7:27–29.

[42]Wright, *The Resurrection of the Son of God,* esp. 129–31, 200–206 (numbering of the following summary by J. M.).

were held in an intermediate state not by any inherent power of their own, but by the power of YHWH, the creator. Third, where life after death was hoped for in a way not thoroughly Hellenized (à la Philo), the hope was two stage, entailing not only hope for life after death but also for embodied life after an intermediate life-after-death, the event of which would mark the turn from the current to the coming age. Fourth, the hope of resurrection intertwined with national hopes and a wish for vindication in the judgment of YHWH in a way that embraced creation and the creator's faithfulness to it. Fifth, and most importantly for these considerations, whether one affirmed or denied the prospect, "resurrection" was never a description of the state of those who had died; instead, in referring to the dead, "resurrection" meant the undoing and defeat of death and a return to bodily life, a life that followed any existence the dead currently had. Finally, messianic expectations and the hope for resurrection were not directly associated: "There are no traditions about a Messiah being raised to life; most Jews of this period hoped for resurrection, many Jews of this period hoped for a Messiah, but nobody put those two hopes together until the early Christians did so."[43] And it should be added that they did so as the continuation of Jesus's own teaching about the necessity of Messiah dying and being raised on the third day (e.g., Mark 8:31; 9:9–10, 31; 10:33–34; 12:24–27).

It was in a pagan and Second Temple Jewish milieu that Christian faith emerged with its fundamental belief about resurrection and Jesus of Nazareth. The early Christian claim that Jesus had been raised from the dead directly challenged the belief systems of the pagans and, as a morphology[44] of a given strand of hope within Judaism, posed to Jews an essential challenge to find the fulfillment of their people's hopes in this Jesus, whose claim to being YHWH's Messiah had come to be vindicated in this utterly surprising fashion. Perhaps Wright's most important contribution in writing on the resurrection of Jesus actually comes in his investigation of what comes *before* Jesus, thereby setting a historical context for the referent of resurrection language so central to the claims of the early Christians.

---

[43]Ibid., 205.

[44]Ibid., 9, 28 speaks of "mutation."

Their claims, he rightly contends, must be understood "within the worldview and language of second-Temple Judaism,"[45] itself located in the Hellenistic pagan culture of the Roman Empire. "When the New Testament writers spoke of resurrection, both their own and that of Jesus, this is the grid of language-use within which they must have assumed their words made sense."[46] To understand "resurrection" in such a way—to assign it (a) meaning(s) not evidenced in the historical context in which Christianity arose—is not simply to mistake northwest for north and so sidewind a bit through the proper countryside, but to be off the grid altogether. Off the grid for "resurrection" are referents such as a heavenly, exalted status; the passage of the human Jesus into divine power; or some sort of felt presence that remained among his followers. Like it (as did some Jews in the form of an apocalyptic or eschatological hope) or lump it (as did the pagans),[47] "resurrection" referred to something bodily and entailed for the dead a return to embodied life.

Thus that to which "resurrection" refers, at least historically, is in no doubt. The *plausibility*, on the other hand, of a given person rising from the dead was just as controverted in the first century as in the twenty-first, for "nowhere within Judaism, let alone paganism, is a sustained claim advanced that resurrection has actually happened to a particular individual."[48] Far from being an inevitable, or for that matter even plausible, option for postmortem existence in a pre-Enlightenment world view, the claim that a man—Jesus of Nazareth—had been raised from the dead very much took its world, Jewish and pagan, by surprise.[49] Based on the expectations of the first century, the claim that a man, even a Jew claiming to be the Messiah, had been raised from the dead was decidedly uninevitable even though

---

[45]Ibid., 28.

[46]Ibid., 200.

[47]See, for example, Paul's exchange at the Athenian Areopagus (Acts 17:19–32): "Now when they heard of the resurrection of the dead, some [Greeks] mocked" (v. 32).

[48]Wright, *The Resurrection of the Son of God,* 28.

[49]See, for example, ibid., 315. Surprised too were his disciples; cf. von Balthasar, *Mysterium Paschale,* 200.

the Jewish Scripture traditions provided something of a conceptual antecedent in their hope of an End-Time resurrection. And precisely given the pronounced uninevitability of this claim, the plausibility that a momentous event stands behind its emergence is strengthened. The most plausible reason that early Christians claimed that Jesus had been raised from the dead is that Jesus was raised from the dead. Only contingent on such an event having actually taken place can one adequately explain the rise of the Easter faith and the claim of the early Christians that Jesus had been raised from the dead.[50]

Wright's examination of the New Testament documents shows that the referent of "resurrection" language remained the same as before and thus intelligible though fundamentally shocking to those encountered by the Christians' message. Given the broad spectrum of Second Temple Jewish belief about life after death, the resurrection faith of the early Christians appears highly uniform and universal. Resurrection moved from being a distant hope, somewhat on the periphery of Jewish thinking, to a central tenet of and indeed foundational event for the Christian faith—a reality for Jesus now, who by his resurrection had ushered in the new age, and reality for those "in Christ Jesus"[51] when this age would be fully unveiled and the current age brought to a close. The earliest Christians claimed something unprecedented, unexpected, and thus even for Jews, uninevitable: Jesus *had been* raised from the dead. And with this landmark event, the whole grid of the landscape had shifted, and that shift constituted the Gospel as the earliest proclamation among Christians.

Intermediary Conclusion

Although Dale Allison rejects Wright's studiously argued opinion that the empty tomb and the postmortem appearances of Jesus

---

[50]Wright, *The Resurrection of the Son of God,* esp. 686–97. What the resurrection is historically for the church, it is theologically for Christology: "In the New Testament the fact of the resurrection of Jesus Christ from the dead constitutes the starting point of Christology." Joseph Ratzinger, *Jesus von Nazareth: Beiträge zur Christologie, zweiter Teilband,* Gesammelte Schriften, ed. Gerhard Ludwig Müller (Freiburg: Herder, 2013), 6/2:668–71, 668.

[51]See, for example, Romans 8:1.

constitute both sufficient and necessary conditions for explaining the emergence of the Christian faith, he does not do so in either a convincing or logical manner.

Allison's *Resurrecting Jesus*, though published after Wright's *The Resurrection of the Son of God*, does not dislodge a (and perhaps *the* most important) contention of Wright's research: in and around the time of Jesus, "resurrection" was always concrete (referencing an event), and when it was predicated of a person who had died, it referred to a return to bodily life. In fact, Allison does not even substantially address the uniform referent of "resurrection" in the pagan and Second Temple Jewish contexts that Wright extensively elucidates. One may, of course, point to modern landmarks that are of some heuristic value in this or that direction, but directly or indirectly assigning meanings to "resurrection" in the New Testament writings, for which "bodily" need not require a tomb vacated by Jesus, is simply to be off the grid of what can be called historic Christianity as measured by and accountable to early Christianity, including the historical context of its "resurrection" vocabulary. To put it another way, Wright's work is a map of the landscape and of the use of "resurrection" in the ancient world, giving a solid indication of true north in what early Christians claimed by saying that Jesus had been raised from the dead. What Allison, on the basis of modern research into the phenomenology of apparitions of the dead, suggests as a possible explanation for the perceived bodiliness of Jesus's resurrection would be no "resurrection" at all by the standards of the ancient usage of the term, if the tomb could still have been occupied, which is, of course, the case with the graves and tombs of those perceived in these modern apparitions. And, as Allison admits, the flesh-and-bones bodiliness of Jesus's resurrection is a matter indifferent to his hope.[52] True north, as measured by the compass of the earliest Christianity, can hardly be a matter indifferent to the direction in which Christians hope, think, and speak, if their confessed hope has to do with that Jesus who "suffered under Pontius Pilate." Allison remains virtually silent, offering no rejoinders to Wright, regarding the most important research that fundamentally negates his foundational thesis. The reasons are

---

[52]Allison, "Resurrecting Jesus," 344.

clear enough: he is entirely without historical context and meaning on his side.

Further, Allison's objection that the most tangible of the appearances of the postmortem Jesus (Luke 24:36–43 [with the exception of v. 39], John 20:24–29 and 21:9–14) show him to be no more than angelic fails not in relation to the appearances themselves but certainly in their appropriation by early Christians and (more significantly) by their opponents. It is indeed true that Second Temple Jews had in the angels a category of beings that could exhibit features of physicality or "transphysicality"[53] while lacking flesh and blood and understood as incorporeal.[54] Angels could appear to be human, allow themselves to be touched, and even eat and drink.[55] If, however, the postmortem appearances of Jesus as reported by the early Christians readily would have been and indeed could have been appropriated under this category, what need would there have been for avid persecution of the early Christians by the Jewish leaders and a Pharisee like Saul? Why speak with "resurrection" language if Jesus were understood to be angelic? The Pharisees themselves could understand the intermediate state of those who had died as an angelic existence.[56] Clearly the early Christians claimed something different, something more for Jesus than an angelic postmortem existence—indeed, something akin to a new creative act of God upon the human person (Romans 8:29; 1 Corinthians 15; Galatians 1:1; Colossians 1:18; 1 Thessalonians 4:13–17).

In summary, the main contribution of Allison's work comes in offering data with perhaps some heuristic bearing on what "resurrection" might *mean* today while bypassing what Wright shows it to have *meant* in and around the first century of the Common Era. Taking Allison and Wright as a model comparison, one might also conclude that, at least so far as the resurrection of Jesus is concerned,

---

[53] Wright's preferred term for talking about the physicality of the resurrected Jesus; Wright, *The Resurrection of the Son of God*, 477, 606f., 612.

[54] For their incorporeality see Allison, "Resurrecting Jesus," 290 note 358.

[55] See Genesis 18–19 and Judges 6:11–24; cf. Hebrews 13:2 and Mark 16:5. Further sources by ibid., 289 notes 355–57.

[56] Act 23:8; cf. Wright, *The Resurrection of the Son of God*, 131–34.

the difference in conclusions drawn by historians of early Christianity lies finally not only in what they make of given historical data but in whether or not they are open to the possibility of bumping into God in human history.[57] This bids us to ponder history and the greater Christian story.

Creation, Hi-Story, and Physicality: The Consistency of the Grid with the Bodily Resurrection as True North

History is a bounded exercise, with bounds lying behind and before the present, in which historical inquiry and its bounded investigations take place. In one direction, history is a question of origins, in the other of ends, and between origins and ends, causalities and consequences are of interest. Of cause and consequence, origin and end, there are accounts; stories and story are both the stuff and the bounds of hi-story.[58]

Early Christians, as the people of Israel before them and the Christian church after them, knew the bounds of history in creation and new creation. The present is related to and bounded by the

---

[57]Both Wright and Allison acknowledge that proofs of history are never mathematical; they have to do with probabilities (Allison, "Resurrecting Jesus," 337–40; Wright, *The Resurrection of the Son of God,* 706). In this particular comparison, it is the theologian-historian who wills to let historical investigation lead where it may that comes out with a strong argument for the bodily resurrection of Jesus being as probable as Augustus's death in 14 or the fall of Jerusalem in 70 AD; "It is important to see that we have got this far by following the historical argument, not by invoking any external or a priori beliefs" (Wright, 710). On the other hand, Allison, 347 states that Wright's argument "puts more faith in historical reason than I can summon." Admittedly, and actively evidenced in his own argumentation, some explanations are, a priori, ruled out or deemed less likely than others; see, for example Allison, 335f: "So, given that the return to life of a man truly dead must also be deemed, *in the abstract*, even more unlikely than Joseph moving Jesus' body, it is not immediately apparent why the traditional Christian interpretation should be, as it is for so many, instinctively deemed more plausible than a conjecture involving wholly mundane postulates." (italics JM).

[58]The fluidity is more clearly sensed with the German *Geschichte*, translatable as both "story" and "history."

past and the future in such a way that origin and end are the same, with both being markedly distinct from the present. Any history that fails the origin and end of creation and new creation fails the Christian story, the Christian faith's great account of history. Though theological consistency might be measured in other ways, it must be measured against "In the beginning God created"—against that Beginning and End who also makes all things new.[59] Appropriation of the "resurrection" of Jesus Christ that falls short of a bodily resurrection entailing emptiness of tomb—claim what perceived reality and solidity it may!—fails theological consistency measured against the θεός (God) who created and creates anew. It fails the Christian story. The bodily resurrection of Jesus Christ, on the other hand, is theologically consistent with origin and end and so with the greater story of God, the creator, who will be who he will be, having, finally, his creation as he created it to be. Unless one wishes to adopt a rather dualist anthropology, the end of Jesus as Jesus has to do with what happened to his body, and a climax to his story, such as offered by Allison, is incommensurate with the governing narrative of Scripture precisely because the bodily and tangible is surrendered rather than esteemed and elevated.[60]

"In the beginning," God was who he was not in separation from the cosmos but in communion with it; immanence and transcendence are not categories in the intent of the creator with his creatures. The crowning moment of the issuance of being, life, and relationality from his own being, life, and relationality came when God in singular plurality made man in his—that is, in *their*—image.[61] Spirit and matter are, in the action and intention of the creator, not opposites but rather a union born of his will and action; dust and breath (the spirit of life) belong together.[62] Man, as made

---

[59]Genesis 1:1; Revelation 21:5–6.

[60]Cf. Joseph Ratzinger, *Auferstehung und Ewiges Leben*, Gesammelte Schriften, ed. Gerhard Ludwig Müller (Freiburg: Herder, 2012), 10:34: "The bodiliness of Christ, who retains body eternally, means taking history and the material seriously" (trans. JM).

[61]Genesis 1:26.

[62]Genesis 2:7.

in the image of God, cannot be reduced either to dust or to spirit, to body or soul.[63] Man is man in the image of God, in a divine joining of things once not perceived as opposites. For man to be what God intended and made him to be, physical and spiritual, body and soul, matter and the breath of life cannot be permanently and irreversibly separated.

Separation from God, accounted for in the greater story under the language and concept of "sin," means the separation of that which he, as creator, brought together; it means the separation of body and soul,[64] the material and the breath of life. This separation that is sin brings about death. In this divinely unwilled separation, ample complexity crops up, a complexity that is the stuff of human existence in a fallen world. The beginning and end of the story, however, are abundantly simple. In both the Christian Scriptures (Genesis 1–2, Revelation 20–21) and the Christian creeds, origin and end can fall out rather quickly: "maker of heaven and earth" and "the life of the world to come."[65] It is the bits in the story between creation and new creation that mount up, as witnessed by the elongated second article of the creed and the many books of the canonical scriptures, not recounting creation per se but dealing with the complexity of existence in a broken creation while hoping in the faithfulness of a creator whose will was not separation but communion. This will is realized in the person of Christ, who as life eternal takes to himself human life[66] by the working of the Spirit[67] in such a way that when the brokenness of the creation breaks over him, the Father yet

---

[63]Cf. Richard Bauckham, "Eschatology," in *The Oxford Companion to Christian Thought*, ed. Adrian Hastings (Oxford: Oxford University Press, 2000), 206–9, especially 206f. Such splitting, with the soul being weighted as the important aspect of a human being, was characteristic of ancient pagan thought after Plato; see Wright, *The Resurrection of the Son of God*, 47–55.

[64]Cf. Rudolf Bultmann, *The Gospel of John: A Commentary* (Louisville, KY: Westminster John Knox Press, 1971), 154–56.

[65]Nicene Creed. The Apostles' Creed is yet pithier: "the life everlasting."

[66]John 1:1–4, 14.

[67]Luke 1:35; Matthew 1:18, 22.

proves himself faithful in finally holding this human and eternal life together.[68]

No Christian would say that Jesus is not the center of his or her faith, his or her hope. The question has always been, however, "What Jesus?" The offensive but creationally restorative answer comes in a Jesus in whom there is no separation between God and man.[69] As the doctrine of the incarnation aptly notes, God's becoming man did not leave the dust, into which human flesh and bone had long since been falling,[70] behind. As born of the Virgin Mary, Jesus is man; as conceived by the Holy Spirit, he is new man, new humanity, but never in a way that leaves the dust-bound bodies of humanity behind.[71] Though, historically speaking, the resurrection did not directly establish the divinity of Jesus,[72] incarnation and resurrection are certainly of a piece. The Son of God, who took on a human nature (which is not human without flesh and bones) in order to restore humanity to communion with its creator, did not simply leave his flesh and bones in the grave. It is manifest that Jesus of Nazareth lived and died, that at some point the breath/spirit, on a cross, left a body,[73] which was then on its way to being dust. If this Jesus is salvifically significant

---

[68]John 21:14; Acts 2:24, 32; 3:15; 4:10; 5:30; 10:40; 13:30, 34, 37; Romans 4:24f; 6:4, 9; 7:4; 8:11; 8:34; 10:9; 1 Corinthians 6:14; 15:4, 12–20; 2 Corinthians 4:14; 5:15; Galatians 1:1; Ephesians 1:20; Colossians 2:12; 1 Thessalonians 1:10; 1 Peter 1:21. In union with this Christ, often expressed in baptismal language in the New Testament (Romans 6:3–11; cf. 8:11 [with Trinitarian framework]; Galatians 3:27; Colossians 2:12, cf. 3:1); Christians enjoy communion with God, which entails his eternal faithfulness to their lives as well.

[69]Cf. the Chalcedonian Definition: "ἀδιαιρέτως, ἀχωρίστως" ("not divided, not separated") in Henrici Denzinger, *Enchiridion symbolorum, definitionum et declarationum de rebus fidei et morum*, 39th ed. (Freiburg: Herder, 2001), 143 nr. 302.

[70]Cf. Genesis 3:19.

[71]The fate of bodies consigned to the dust was an important component of the unfolding hope of resurrection among the Jews before the birth of Jesus; cf. Wright, *The Resurrection of the Son of God*, 108–19 on Daniel 12:2 and Isaiah 26:19.

[72]Cf. Ibid., 23–26 and 83.

[73]See Luke 23:46.

in the sense of the creator's will coming to fruition, then the dust-bound flesh and bones of the tomb are not insignificant. As Hans Urs von Balthasar insightfully notes, God did not in the resurrection "go back on the Incarnation."[74] Indeed, he therein fully and restoratively embraced fallen humanity. In the overarching story of creation and new creation, the bodiliness of Jesus's resurrection is no indifferent matter; it—along with its counterpart, the incarnation—is one of two hinges on which the whole story swings, if this story story swings at all.

The resurrection of Jesus from the dead is an act of new creation.[75] Wright convincingly shows how 1 Corinthians 15, containing in its creedal material the New Testament's earliest witness to the resurrection, is based on the creation account of Genesis.[76] Jesus as the firstborn *from* the dead is not the firstfruits of those whose bodies are to remain dead[77] but of a new creation. And for what was wrought in him and through him for those whom he joins to himself, the whole creation is groaning.[78]

As an act of new creation, past and future enter the present with the resurrection of Jesus from the dead. In a historical event, history, as a linear progression of causalities and consequences known to and comprehensible by human beings, is interrupted, exploded, without coming to a halt. Beginning and end, creation and new creation reside with the resurrection of Christ in the middle of human history—"middle" not in the sense of quantifications of measurable time before and after Easter but in the sense of an epicenter, that point from which all of separated and broken human history is shaken into the union first wrought and finally rendered by the creator's faithful will to have human beings, the crown of his creation, in communion with himself.[79] The question then is not so

---

[74]Balthasar, *Mysterium Paschale* (as summarized by Nichols), 8.

[75]Cf. Wright, *The Resurrection of the Son of God*, 271–76.

[76]Ibid., 312–61.

[77]Colossians 1:18; 1 Corinthians 15:20–23.

[78]See Romans 8, especially verses 9–11 and 19–23.

[79]The unified event of Christ's incarnation, birth, ministry, death, and resurrection is a matter toward which history pulls, not just in terms of what

much how to understand the resurrection in history (though it is there) as it is to understand history in the resurrection, for history's beginning and end are present here—both present in the resurrection. The day of Jesus's resurrection is both the third day of a broken human history, counting time in view of death, and the first day of a new creation, where death is no more; on the third-first day that is Easter, time is redefined, returned to its former definition and bearings, within time. The resurrection is both historical and metahistorical, for precisely at this moment in the broken history of being human, a new and ancient mode of human-being was opened by this man being raised from the dead.[80]

In pagan thought, at least after Plato, present human existence was infused with a certain connection to the future on the basis of the soul's immortality. The hope of Second Temple Judaism was decidedly more eschatological, in that the object of hope actually set an end or bound—an *eschaton* that demarcated the present. Christian hope for the future also involves an *eschaton*—not one that simply ends the present but has rather invaded it and redefined it; its eschatology is an inaugurated eschatology.[81] On the day of Easter, an end has come, and humanity is here coming to its proper end. Historical investigation into the resurrection of Jesus that concludes his bodily resurrection to the be the best explanation for the faith of the early Christians (as presented in Wright's work) brings with it a metahistorical corollary, just as the physicality of the resurrection entails metaphysical consequence. If Jesus was indeed raised from the dead, then humanity's approach to its history and its story are essentially upside-down or backward because humanity's humanity itself is not full but broken. If Jesus was raised from the dead, then origin and end are not subject to the present; the present has instead been and is being subjected to origin and end. Presumably no

---

preceded them but also in terms of what follows; cf. "the fullness of time(s)" in Galatians 4:4 and Ephesians 1:10.

[80]Regarding historical moment and human-being, cf. Joseph Ratzinger, *Jesus von Nazareth: Beiträge zur Christologie, erster Teilband*, Gesammelte Schriften, ed. Gerhard Ludwig Müller (Freiburg: Herder, 2013) 6/1:42–59, 597–623.

[81]See Bauckham, "Eschatology," 208f.

Christian is interested in a Christian story that is not finally metahistorical, an account that has nothing to say about human origin and end, but it is theologically inconsistent to lay claim to Christianity's account of origin (creation and life) and end (new creation and "the life everlasting") while denying that these metahistoricals have so wondrously disrupted broken human history as to heal something indeed in need of healing. Call it what you will, but the story, the metahistory, the metanarrative of the Christian faith works as little without the historicity of the resurrection as does its metaphysics without the physicality of the resurrection. A "resurrection" that need not entail the tomb's emptiness, such as understood by Allison, is not only an ahistorical category; it fully fails history according to the Christian story.

If indeed something beyond the bounds of our current historical categories—namely, history's origin and end—did break into history in a wondrously disruptive, "shocking but satisfying"[82] way with the resurrection of Jesus from the dead, then indeed something "meta" to the human "historical" has taken place. But that which human beings living in the broken history of a broken world label "historical" would then, in fact, be something else, something that we might (in view of origin, end, and the epicenter of the resurrection) call "subhistorical." Time and history as human beings now experience them would be flawed categories of experience broken by death. The same then could also be said of "physical." Allison resists in a certain sense Wright's use of the term "transphysicality" to describe the resurrected body of Jesus and its characteristics as attested by the New Testament documents.[83] Though Wright certainly is not incorrect in searching for a term that cuts across the grain of normal speech to describe something that cuts across the grain of normal experience, on a theological level, the matter actually goes a step further. Were Christian speech, taking its cues from the resurrection, rigorously consistent, one need not append "trans-" to the physicality of the resurrected Jesus but rather "sub-" to the physicality now belonging

---

[82]Wright, *The Resurrection of the Son of God*, 274.

[83]See Allison, "Resurrecting Jesus," 292f; cf. note 51 above.

to all sons and daughters of the first Adam.[84] In modern theology, the historicity and physicality of Jesus's resurrection came to be discounted along with miracles, the miraculous being aligned with the mythical and thereby the nonhistorical or actual/factual.[85] The "super" of the "supernatural" led to its disregard. But if Jesus was in fact raised from the dead, which is the best historical explanation for the faith of the early Christians, then we need not speak of his body as "transphysical" or its characteristics as something "supernatural"—instead we are led to question why our bodies need something like boats to cross water that would otherwise drown them;[86] why they can be bruised or crushed by the stuff of which doors and walls are made, instead of being able to interact with these materials in such a way as to, say, immediately enjoy a meal thereafter;[87] why food for five of them shouldn't satiate a thousand times more.[88] The physicality of Jesus's resurrection is theologically consistent with the greater Christian story in a way that its nonphysicality is not, but such physicality as his body exhibits calls the physicality of other human bodies into question. Conversation with animals would, for instance, supersede present human capacity, but according to the greater story's account of prelapsarian human condition, a conversation with a snake is natural.[89]

The difficult thing about the historicity of the resurrection of Jesus is not its historicity or his historicity as a resurrected person; these are well attested. The difficulty lies in the historicity of all other human beings, who, quite understandably, approach time and history in categories bounded by the bounds of their own interactions with time—that is, by their mortality. Similarly, the difficult thing about the physicality of Jesus's resurrected body lies not with that body but with the bodies of those who contemplate it, which, as a

---

[84]Cf. 1 Corinthians 15:42–49.

[85]See Williams, "Resurrection," 617; on "miracle" cf. O'Collins, "The Resurrection," 97–104.

[86]See Matthew 14:22–33.

[87]John 20:19 and Luke 24:36–43; cf. Judges 16:25–30.

[88]Mark 6:34–44 and parallels.

[89]Genesis 3:1–5; cf. 2:19–20.

very established rule, do not come back to life after being dead. Our difficulties with the historicity and physicality of the resurrected Jesus point to a difficulty with the humanity of the Son of God: the uninhibited union or communion of God and man is not problematic to that man who fully knows and exhibits this union and communion but to those human beings who do not. So the problem is not that the resurrection is metahistorical but that nonresurrected life is subhistorical—out of touch with time as eternity; the problem is not that the resurrected body of Jesus is or would somehow be "transphysical" or "supernatural" but that bodies bound to graves are actually subphysical and subnatural—matter disconnected from spirit. The problem with the humanity of the Son of God is not with his humanity but with the humanity of all others, which is then, as revealed by his humanity, subhuman. Creation and new creation, resonating in and from the resurrection of Jesus, set bounds to the derogating prepositions. Recognizing our own history and physicality, and indeed even our own humanity, as now impinged is perfectly in accord with the greater Christian story and Christian thinking about God (theology). The Christian account of sin entails both a separation from God (and so from time and matter as he knows, made, and intends them) as well as a privation of what it means to be human. Such privation is evil; it is the loss of what God originally made in his image, for communion with himself, calling that "very good."[90] It is not least in view of the physical resurrection of Jesus Christ that humans, being as they are (or not-being aren't), come to contemplate and fully recognize their own impinged physicality and finally their impinged humanity in view of him who alone is fully and truly human. The teachings and example of a Jesus whose body stayed in a tomb might be worth a following—a religion. But one can see that a resurrected Christ would necessitate proclamation, for the depth of challenge and the hope of possibility that this true human

---

[90]Genesis 1:31. The understanding of sin as a privation of good evidences itself, for example, in the Solid Declaration of the Lutheran Formula of Concord (1577): see SD I:26–29 in *The Book of Concord: The Confessions of the Evangelical Lutheran Church*, ed. Robert Kolb and Timothy Wengert (Minneapolis, MN: Fortress Press, 2000), 536.

being poses to our subhuman nonbeing could finally only come to us from outside of us. Such is the heart of Christianity.

If Jesus was raised from the dead, that resurrection would mean a radical shift of landscape that catches those cruising the track of human existence rather by surprise.

Metanoetic Metamorphosis:
The Resurrection of Jesus as Shifter of the Grid

Along the trajectory of a human life, can a marker surface on the landscape that shifts the whole grid and turns everything without ever stopping the drive? Encounter with the resurrected Jesus, body and all, is such as this. It's a metaturn, a turn of such character that human beings bound for the dust have no direct way of talking about it, a turn in which they are turned. Balthasar notes that the encounters with the risen Christ witnessed in the New Testament bear the marks of sacramental confession: fear, blame, sorrow, joy, and finally paschal joy.[91] Sacramental confession, of course, entails repentance. Μετανοέω, a change of mind, comes on the receiving end of what the risen, tangible Christ gives, when he, in a mandating act of new creation breathes the Holy Spirit unto forgiveness of sins and so to the defeat of death.[92] Such encounter works a metamorphosis of mind[93] and sets hi-story on a true-north trajectory of new creation.

A certain skepticism is a proper mind-set for a traveler navigating from point A to point B by way of landmarks. It entails intent gazing and giving attention to things that might otherwise just slip past. Dale Allison's digestion of modern apparitional research is a worthy endeavor, making the case that experiences of deceased persons need not be characterized as hallucinations and by extension, as evidence for a mode of existence that (to borrow

---

[91]Balthasar, *Mysterium Paschale*, 219–21.

[92]John 20:22f.; cf. Romans 5–6 and Bultmann, "θάνατος," in *Theological Dictionary of the New Testament*, ed. Gerhard Kittel, trans. Geoffrey W. Bromiley (Grand Rapids, MI: Eerdmans, 1965), 3:7–21, especially 14f.

[93]Romans 12:2.

N. T. Wright's terminology) can be labeled life-after-death. What Allison's work does not establish, however, is that the postmortem experiences of Jesus by his followers were appearances, apparitions of a sort that need not have entailed an empty tomb. This can, given conclusions of the truly monumental and yet very basic work of N. T. Wright, simply not be the case. He has convincingly showed that "resurrection" in both Second Temple Judaism and ancient paganism always referred to a renewed bodily existence after a state of life-after-death, with "resurrection" being thereby not a new construal of the state ensuing after death but rather an outright overturning of death by a return to embodied life. Very simply, if the followers of Jesus had only experienced some sort of apparition, they (as Second Temple Jews living in an ancient pagan milieu) had categories under which to appropriate and speak about such phenomena. But they did not speak in such a way;[94] they said that Jesus had risen, that he was raised from the dead, and this, at that time, had no other referent than a reality necessarily entailing an empty tomb. Wright's keen observation is both simple and monumental, pointing to a "true north" of Christian belief around which a grid of creation and new creation aligns. That is to say that the orthodox Christian teaching of the physical, bodily resurrection of Christ fits with Christianity's overarching narrative of creation and new creation in a way that apparitions and an occupied tomb (Allison's best guess) do not. The renewed bodily existence of Jesus, ensuing on the third day after his death, is monumental in its capacity to interpret bounded history in a different way and radically question bounded human existence. Therein it shows metanoetic potential, rightly causing many who take a serious look at it to turn from how they had understood themselves and the landscape of human existence and history around them to a course then dictated by the hope of renewed human (and so bodily) existence in a renewed creation. This shift of the grid, effected by the bodily resurrection of Jesus, is nothing short of a metamorphosis.

---

[94]Joseph Ratzinger, Gesammelte Schriften, 6/1:598 notes the exploding of experiential horizons.

Recommended Reading

Eckstein, Hans Joachim, and Michael Welker, eds. *Die Wirklichkeit der Auferstehung*. Neukirchen-Vluyn: Neukirchener, 2002.

Lapide, Pinchas. *The Resurrection of Jesus: A Jewish Perspective.* Translated by Wilhelm C. Linss. Minneapolis, MN: Augsburg, 1983.

Licona, Michael R. *The Resurrection of Jesus: A New Historiographical Approach*. Downers Grove, IL: InterVarsity Press, 2010.

O'Donovan, Oliver: *Resurrection and Moral Order: An Outline for Evangelical Ethics*. Grand Rapids, MI: Eerdmans, 1986.

Ratzinger, Joseph (Pope Benedict XVI). *Eschatology: Death and Eternal Life*. Translated by Michael Waldstein and Aidan Nichols, O.P. Washington, DC: Catholic University of America Press, 1988.

———. *Jesus of Nazareth: Holy Week: From the Entrance into Jerusalem to the Resurrection*. San Francisco, CA: Ignatius, 2011.

Swinburne, Richard. *The Resurrection of God Incarnate*. Oxford: Clarendon, 2003.

von Balthasar, Hans Urs. *Mysterium Paschale: The Mystery of Easter*. Translated by Aidan Nichols, O.P. Edinburgh: T&T Clark, 1990.

Wright, N. T. *The Resurrection of the Son of God*. Christian Origins and the Question of God, vol. 3. Minneapolis, MN: Fortress Press, 2003.

7

Myth and Resurrection

C. J. Armstrong and Andrew R. DeLoach

> *I believe that legends and myths are largely made of 'truth,' and indeed present aspects of it that can only be received in this mode.*
>
> —J. R. R. Tolkien[1]

> *These are the myths: and he who has no sympathy with myths has no sympathy with men.*
>
> —G. K. Chesterton[2]

Introduction

The religious landscape of the West at the beginning of our twenty-first century appears to be as pluralistic as its counterpart at the time of Christ. A backdrop of divine activity saturated everyday existence in the Roman-dominated Mediterranean, a backdrop populated by the gods that Rome, over its many years of inhabiting and

---

[1]J. R. R. Tolkien, *The Letters of J. R. R. Tolkien*, ed., Humphrey Carpenter with Christopher Tolkien (New York: Houghton Mifflin, 2000), 147.

[2]G. K. Chesterton, *The Everlasting Man* (San Francisco, CA: Ignatius, 2008), 109.

eventually entirely ruling the area, had discovered, invented, inherited, borrowed, adopted, coopted, or otherwise known of. These were divinities that were celebrated formally at family ceremonies and ceremonies of state. They were prayed to and offered gifts of devotion in temples, shrines, and household *lararia*. They were also depicted in sculpture, painting, poetry, drama, and other forms of art. The Greek Olympians in Roman togas, the indigenous gods of Etruria and Latium, divinities of Judea and Egypt and Persia, ancestors, heroes, and the genius of the emperor were accepted as cultural forces by devotees and skeptics alike—even as philosophical religions such as Stoicism and Epicureanism engaged questions of life and death, the existence of the afterlife, and the nature, number, and relative concern of gods. All these had their place in not so much a common pantheon as a common cultural presence in the pluralistic first-century empire.

But despite the number of deities the first-century Mediterranean could boast, none share in common with the story of Christ a resurrection of the body. Religions predating and contemporary with Christianity may indeed correspond in various other ways with the Christ we know from the first-century New Testament documents, but bodily resurrection is unique to Christ. This truth proves an essential difference between the ancient religions and Christianity, one we do well to heed, particularly in light of at least two assumptions that tend to cast doubt on the claims of Christianity. The first is the perceived difficulty in saying anything certain about antiquity in general (and the New Testament in particular); after all, it is argued, these things happened long ago, and therefore conclusions ought to be considered suspect when based on fragmentary evidence, oral tradition, and other artifacts of belief and practice. The second assumption lionizes "science" but patronizes religion as a moral system at best or mythology (by which a critic would mean magic or falsehood) at worst. It is of course the current fashion to consider all such ancient story as religious myth or mythological religion, either of which insufficiently measures up to the modern, rational way of understanding the world. The first assumption leads the uncritical observer to take first-century Christianity, Judaism, mystery religions like the Orphic mysteries or Mithraism, Zoroastrianism, and what came to be known in the later Christian era as traditional pagan religion (the public worship of the major gods of the Greco-Roman pantheon); categorize them under one heading; and declare it "ancient religion"—no wonder then that there are so many "parallels" between, for example, the mythology of Christ and the mythology of Osiris, another divine being who (according to the Egyptians) underwent a death and an underworld journey. The second assumption pits science against religion and science against myth in an epistemological *agon* that neither religion nor myth can hope to win if the goal is to validate a way of seeing the world as it really is from a human point of view, in a way that can be tested, proved empirically, and is consonant furthermore with what have come to be imposed by the purveyors of this modern, rationalist world view as acceptable limitations of humanistic inquiry.

It is not our intention simply to bemoan the fact that our four most recent centuries of human history have moved the agenda for understanding the cosmos and our place in it from one in which religious experience and vocabulary were at the center to one in which they are at the extreme margin. Nor can we hope to satisfy every skeptic or conspiracy theorist in regard to the distinctions among ancient religions and the significance of Christianity's unique claim from its very origins. But we do hope to inform the conversation on both counts by a focus on the uniqueness of the resurrection in Christianity. This claim of resurrection among ancient religions is not only the central event in Christianity but also the heart of a robust *apologia* that is entirely comfortable with the relationship between Christianity and myth and with using the idiom of myth in apologetic discourse. Indeed, numerous Christian thinkers—C. S. Lewis, J. R. R. Tolkien, G. K. Chesterton, and others—have engaged extensively in this task both as lovers of myth (and mythmaking) and as firm believers in the factual nature of Christ's life, death, and resurrection. For each of them was well aware of early criticism of myth as well as the modernist criticisms in their own day, and they engaged with those critics as devout Christians who believed that the Gospel story is the paramount myth that entered history as fact. Tolkien, for example, believed that myth is made up of truth and that aspects of truth could only come through myth.[3] In fact, he argued that

---

[3]Tolkien, *Letters,* 147; see also J. R. R. Tolkien, "On Fairy-Stories," in *The Monsters and the Critics and Other Essays,* ed. Christopher Tolkien (London:

in Jesus's incarnation and resurrection, we encounter myth that has entered history: "Here God tells—indeed, enacts—a tale with all the beauty and wonder and symbolic power of myth, and yet a tale that is actually true."[4] Lewis agreed, calling myth a *"preparatio evangelica,* a divine hinting in poetic and ritual form at the same central truth which was later focused and (so to speak) historicized in the Incarnation."[5] That it is true is a happy ending that brings overwhelming joy; Tolkien called this *eucatastrophe,* concluding that the resurrection was the greatest eucatastrophe possible.[6]

Not surprisingly, Christianity is today no less a target of criticism based on its alleged parallels with ancient religion and myth. But following Lewis and Tolkien against their critics and with equal confidence, our response to the current crop of critics rests on proclaiming that in Christ's resurrection, *myth entered into history as fact.* That fact dispels the kind of slipshod assumptions and uncritical falsehoods promulgated by pop history and propaganda pieces such as the 2007 film *Zeitgeist: The Movie,* which asserts that Jesus Christ and countless other figures of ancient religion are explicable primarily as astrologically parallel phenomena. Similarly, exponents of conspiracy culture are themselves guilty of the same revisionist history they purport to expose, as in the series of books that includes Dan Brown's 2003 *The Da Vinci Code.* Pop history, alternative knowledge, or plain conspiracy theory are (at least overtly) not given a great deal of credibility by self-identifying skeptics such as Michael Shermer, author and founding publisher of *Skeptic Magazine.* Science, it is claimed, debunks these falsehoods. But while the published tenets of the skeptical stance include rational and critical thought over and against belief in pseudoscience, for the (what seems to us) laudable purpose of "making the world a safer and saner place," nevertheless

---

George Allen and Unwin, 1983), where he explains: "History often resembles 'Myth,' because they are both ultimately of the same stuff" (127).

[4]Philip Zaleski and Carol Zaleski, *The Fellowship: The Literary Lives of the Inklings* (New York: Farrar, Straus and Giroux, 2015), 188–89.

[5]C. S. Lewis, "Religion without Dogma?," in *God in the Dock,* ed. Walter Hooper (Grand Rapids, MI: Wm. B. Eerdmans Publishing Co., 1970), 132.

[6]Tolkien, "On Fairy-Stories," 156.

all that passes for "religion" likewise is eliminated from discussion as myth (i.e., magic or falsehood) instead of science. A (perhaps justifiable) fear of oppression by social systems like organized religion, particularly conservative American Evangelical Christianity, drives these pop history and conspiracy theorists; witness the titles on the suggested reading list for skeptics (catalogued on Shermer's blog): Robin Morgan's 2006 *Fighting Words: A Toolkit for Combating the Religious Right* and Sean Fairclough's 2012 *Attack of the Theocrats! How the Religious Right Harms Us All—And What We Can Do about It*. The list continues with material for the college syllabus and for younger budding "junior skeptics" as well. This kind of "mythbusting" in our own pluralistic context may be the major distinction between first- and twenty-first century pluralism—we have a different sort of atheist than any that Hellenistic imperial Rome could produce, different too than we produced in the last century, and we have them in droves.

From the beginning, the term "myth" is a major point of contention. We have noted what critics mean when they say "myth"—generally magic or falsehood. But the stuff of ancient religion, the narratives that form the content of belief and practice, is also denoted by the word myth in what is more than a subtle distinction from its pejorative usage. Much of what we call myth in ancient narrative has nothing to do with magic; furthermore, to call a story patently false because of its age or its content is as academically naïve as accepting one as true because of perceived cultural authority or identification with a political party or religious dogma. On the other hand, myth and mythology also denote a branch of rational humanistic inquiry in the modern academy, a focus of serious study for anthropologists, sociologists, classicists, and scholars of religion, culture, and literature.

We seek to define "myth" more specifically to aid further conversation with skeptics of many stripes and thereby reclaim for myth a definition that both honors its ancient usage and that also might become more useful in our modern parlance than just a dirty word under which to subsume falsehood, pseudoscience, and uncritical assumption. Our examination, which cannot be exhaustive, therefore considers a few myths that have been "paralleled" with Christ. We attempt to summarize a few of these ancient stories themselves and the religions contemporary with early Christianity that held them as a matter of belief. We conclude that myth remains the inevitable idiom for engaging the unique historical event of Christ's resurrection, not only (as may be assumed) in its ancient milieu but also as a natural human practice of handing down the story even to our own time.

What We Mean by "Myth"

We have inherited ways of talking about myth from the nineteenth and twentieth centuries that assumed that myth was generally a way that the ancients explained natural phenomena in the world. The term *aetiology*—myth as an explanation of causes—may be a helpful designation for that presumed method. This notion was taken to be the "primitive" antecedent to science, the modern "rational" way to explain the world. The result of the assumed primitivism of mythology as literal explanation was to place science wholly above, and consider it wholly other than, myth. This assumption still emerges today in certain forms. One result is the prevailing synonymous usage of the vocabulary "myth" with "falsehood." Indeed, if science is shown to explain the workings of the world in contradistinction to a myth's attempt literally to assign a cause to something incompatible with that science, it is easy to understand why a skeptic would throw his lot in with science and consider a myth insufficient or false. This assumption has given birth to an accepted way of talking about myth as if it means a false conviction.

More recent critical approaches to myth question the assumption that compares myth and science as incompatible and myth as a "primitive" antecedent to science. Even the ancients themselves were critical of their own received myths; the Socratic school declaimed stories about gods involved in salacious crimes like rape, and later philosophers allegorized these stories both to mitigate the dilemma and to use them for their own didactic purposes. Allegorizing is one means of reconciling myth and science today as well. Our recent history has produced proponents of scientific "readings" of flood narratives, for example (including the Noahic flood). Intelligent design talk by self-identified creationists purports at least on some level to legitimize scientifically what cultures have described with mythic language, including the origin of the universe. This is an attempt to equal a playing field between biblical accounts and scientific dogma (which is accused by fundamentalists of following its own "myths").

We contend to the contrary that we do myth a disservice when we reduce it either to a false conviction, however sincerely held, or on the other hand to an allegorizing reconciliation with what humans can know and how we explain the world from science—whether modern or ancient science and natural philosophy. Myth is neither imaginary fabrication nor bare allegory. As Chesterton quipped, Father Christmas is not an allegory of snow, but something that infuses deeper meaning into the world of snow "so that snow itself seems to warm."[7] We have been so bent on using the word "myth" as a means of explaining the world that when a reasonable challenge to that world view comes along, it's either baby out with the bath-water or figure out how best to reconcile them. The problem lies in limiting "myth" to this aetiological definition. Myth is indeed about story, but it is more than its possible origin and function as explanation of cause. Myth is the story that is so significant to a people that it brings about narrative, art, and other means of telling the story (mythopoesis) of the event(s) at the center of the myth. We are therefore on surer ground when talking about myth when we accept the idea that myth points to a conviction of a people, but that conviction need not be false. Myths indeed are usually retold without recourse to authority (empirical evidence, historical fact) besides tradition, though historical facts may have engendered the tradition (cf. the Solon and Croesus story of Herodotus 1). This is one of the ways that myth differs from history, in that myth often depends on tradition or oral transmission, not on written record; written (or artistic) record is more a result, rather than the cause, of a people's conviction of the significance of myth.

And the means of transmission—which of course makes the myths no less true—is bound up in the momentous subject of the story. In myth, we are confronted with the transcendent; we approach—or are approached by—the frontier of the eternal. Myth explains and adorns seemingly ordinary stories with a numinous

---

[7]Chesterton, *The Everlasting Man*, 104–5.

quality, and it is therefore a defiance of the concrete time of the everyday. Yet it is a means by which eternity—and our nostalgia for it—is embodied (incarnated!) in ordinary time. Thus Eliade describes myths as hierophanies, "breakthroughs of the sacred into the World," traces of the divine in real time.[8] Likewise does Tolkien praise mythic poetry that "glimpses the cosmic." For Christian thinkers like Tolkien, Lewis, Charles Williams, and others, myth points to a higher and purer world, and mythopoesis is "a pathway to this higher world and a way of describing . . . its felt presence."[9]

And yet myth is necessarily abstract. As Owen Barfield described it, myth is "the ghost of concrete meaning."[10] The myths were not merely the frivolous creations of ancient storytellers but were the expression of their spiritual perceptions and a communication of reality as they conceived it. What we now receive in the myths is true metaphor, but metaphor nonetheless. Faërie, "the Perilous Realm" of the eternal, cannot be "caught in a net of words."[11] Attempts to explain are always inadequate; the more one endeavors to define myth, the further one draws from a satisfying reality.[12] Thus myth is impervious to rational (and rationalist) analysis, particularly of the kind of quasi-scholarly literary criticism practiced by contemporary critics of Christianity that attempts to debunk myth as either confused history at best or euhemeristic religious lies at worst. For myth is extraliterary; it is "a particular kind of story which has value in itself—a value independent of its embodiment in any literary work."[13] Divine truth, ultimate reality, the fulfillment of humankind's deepest yearnings—these are not the legitimate objects of scientific examination, and they cannot (as Tolkien

---

[8]Mircea Eliade, *Myth and Reality* (New York: Harper & Row, 1963), 6.

[9]Zaleski and Zaleski, *The Fellowship*, 11.

[10]Owen Barfield, *Poetic Diction: A Study in Meaning* (Oxford: Barfield Press, 2010), 84.

[11]J. R. R. Tolkien, "On Fairy-Stories," 114.

[12]Clyde S. Kilby, foreword to *Christian Mythmakers*, by Rolland Hein (Eugene, OR: Wipf & Stock, 1998), x.

[13]C. S. Lewis, *An Experiment in Criticism* (Cambridge: Cambridge University Press, 2012), 41.

hinted) be precisely defined or described, though we can readily perceive them. In his typical wit, Chesterton explained it thus: "I knew the magic bean stalk before I had tasted beans."[14] But myth conveys more than arbitrary morals or entertainment. What Chesterton was describing—and what countless many have experienced—is an encounter with Elfland, Faërie, the transcendent. In myth, "we come nearest to experiencing as a concrete what can otherwise be understood only as an abstraction."[15] Myth is important, necessary, to this extraliterary and extrarational encounter, because "reality is so much larger than rationality."[16]

Here the critic balks. The myth-hater ("Misomythos," as Tolkien called a then-agnostic Lewis and those like him) claims that because myth is not rational, it must be imaginary, and it is therefore unscientific and necessarily false. But this is precisely the problem, as Lewis well understood: if one begins by knowing on some other ground that Christianity is false, then the parallels to pagan myths will only confirm this falsity; but when the veracity of the Christian claim is the very issue under investigation, then the argument from correlation clearly begs the question.[17] When the critic insists on looking at the myths as specimens in a lab, all hope is lost of understanding meaning—much less apprehending truth—in them. But this is the favored objection: that the Christian story cannot be true because it so obviously borrowed from the ancient myths (themselves obviously fabricated for one purpose or another), with which it shares several key features. Frazer's *The Golden Bough*, for example, points to the numerous parallels of the "dying god" in the history of ancient

---

[14]G. K. Chesterton, *Orthodoxy* (New York: Doubleday, 2001), 46. Elsewhere, Chesterton expands on this idea: "Therefore do we all in fact feel that pagan or primitive myths are infinitely suggestive, so long as we are wise enough not to inquire what they suggest. Therefore we all feel what is meant by Prometheus stealing fire from heaven, until some prig of a pessimist or progressive person explains what it means. Therefore we all know the meaning of Jack and the Beanstalk, until we are told." Chesterton, *The Everlasting Man*, 111.

[15]C. S. Lewis, "Myth Became Fact," in *God in the Dock*, 66.

[16]Kilby, *Christian Mythmakers*, x.

[17]Lewis, "Religion without Dogma?," 132. It also commits the "false cause fallacy," confusing correlation for causation.

religions. The myths of Adonis and Osiris, for instance, are meant to signify natural growth.[18] These intentionally imagined gods, who died and "returned" to renew the world, are symbols of the grain that dies and falls into the earth and rises with each new harvest. The myths, then, apply this natural process to the life of humanity: each of us must die to live again.

As an atheist, Lewis believed the Gospel narratives were myths of this kind, telling of the natural cycle of birth, death, and renewal. After all, Jesus says that the wheat must die to bear fruit, and after he breaks the bread he calls his body, he dies and rises to new life. Isn't he just one more dying harvest god offering his life for the world? But Lewis came eventually to doubt this idea:

> [W]hy was it that the only case of the "dying God" which might conceivably have been historical occurred among a people . . . who had not got any trace of this nature religion, and indeed seemed to know nothing about it? Why is it among *them* the thing suddenly appears to happen? . . . The principal actor, humanly speaking, hardly seems to know of the repercussions His words (and sufferings) would have in any pagan mind. Well that is almost inexplicable, except on one hypothesis. How if the corn king is not mentioned in that Book, because He is here of whom the corn king was an image? How if the representation is absent because here, at least, the thing represented is present? If the shadows are absent because the thing of which they were shadows is here?[19]

What troubled Lewis, and ought rightly to trouble the anthropological critics of Christianity, is the fact that it *happened*—God in Christ actually "dived down" into nature, was present here with humanity, and among them died and rose to life again. The anthropological criticism based on parallels flagrantly ignores the facticity of this narrative and avers that for Christianity to be true, every

---

[18]To the naturalist critic, this is *all* they are meant to signify. To Philomythos (myth-lover), this is plainly reductionistic: "The naturalist is right when he connects the myth with the phenomena of nature, but wrong if he deduces it solely from these." Barfield, *Poetic Diction*, 84.

[19]C. S. Lewis, "The Grand Miracle," in *God in the Dock*, 83–84.

other religion in the world must be 100 percent false. This is the only way that Christianity could avoid all coincidence with other religions and myths.[20] The universal human desire to tell stories undeniably makes many of them sound similar, but despite this, they may to some degree be both original and true. But to seize on similarities between ancient religion and Christianity and claim that fabrication is the *sine qua non* precludes all mythmaking—indeed all narrative. But this is neither rational nor realistic, for the parallels—regardless of how closely they do coincide—argue neither for nor against the truth of Christianity. And if the parallels say nothing for or against its truth, we ought to reverse the conclusion of modern science: rather than the parallels necessitating that the stories must all be false, we are justified in viewing the parallels as indicating that the myths all touch on some truth (inexplicable though it may seem) and that Christianity lands squarely on and completes it. For Lewis, "who first approached Christianity from a delighted interest in, and reverence for, the best pagan imagination, who loved Balder before Christ and Plato before St. Augustine," acknowledging the historical truth of the Christian narrative did not require that he (and we) confess that of a thousand religions in the world, 999 are "pure nonsense and the thousandth (fortunately) true"; rather, it "depended on recognizing Christianity as the completion, the actualization, the entelechy, of something that had never been wholly absent from the mind of man."[21]

Moreover, the critic misunderstands the myths as myth, as literature. Some are cultic while others have no relation to religion at all. Some are concerned with heroes and others harvest. Notwithstanding this, many of the myths seem to be meant largely for entertainment rather than explanation, and just as many have no connection to nature whatever. But the critic misses this entirely by reducing all myth to narrative falsehood. What must be remembered is that myth

---

[20]C. S. Lewis, "Is Theology Poetry?," in *The Weight of Glory* (New York: Harper Collins, 2001), 127.

[21]Lewis, "Religion without Dogma?," 132. Likewise, Chesterton's awareness of the myths preceded his belief in their truth; see Chesterton, *Orthodoxy*: "I am concerned with a certain way of looking at life, which was created in me by the fairy tales, but has since been meekly ratified by the mere facts" (47).

is not a work of empirical observation and systematized results. It is a work of the creative intellect and imagination, and while it in no way follows that myth must necessarily be false (for imagination does not mean imaginary, as Chesterton insisted), myth is nonetheless a work of the *poetical* aspect of human action and thus requires the critic check his presuppositions and understand it as such.[22]

We may point out the terrible irony in the criticism of Christianity as an unoriginal copy by contemporary critics, who are themselves parroting Gerald Massey, James Frazer, and Joseph Campbell. It would be just as easy to apply the argument about parallels to their critical scholarship of the history of religions and turn it into what Chesterton called "a vulgar monomania of plagiarism."[23] But we need not go this far, for while we may acknowledge their learning, they make clear for us that their judgment of myth, literature, and the Christian narrative is not equally deserving of respect. Lewis speaks here for us: "[W]hatever these men may be as [scholars], I distrust them as critics. They seem to me to lack literary judgment, to be imperceptive about the very quality of the texts they are reading. . . . If he tells me that something in a Gospel is legend or romance, I want to know how many legends and romances he has read. . . . I have been reading poems, romances, vision-literature, legends, myths all my life. I know what they are like. I know that not one of them is like this."[24] And while it is no indication of the merit of their criticisms, we find further irony in certain contemporary attempts at explicitly secular myth and fantasy that borrow on divine capital—like Phillip Pullman's *His Dark Materials* trilogy (from which came the 2007 film *The Golden Compass*), which relies not on classical pagan myth but on Christianity, and particularly

---

[22]In this regard, Chesterton explains that myth "needs a poet to make it. It needs a poet to criticize it. . . . But for some reason I have never heard explained, it is only the minority of unpoetical people who are allowed to write critical studies of these popular poems. We do not submit a sonnet to a mathematician or a song to a calculating boy; but we do indulge the equally fantastic idea that folk-lore can be treated as a science." Chesterton, *The Everlasting Man*, 101.

[23]Ibid., 103.

[24]C. S. Lewis, "Modern Theology and Biblical Criticism," in *Christian Reflections* (Grand Rapids, MI: Eerdmans, 1994), 154–55.

Milton's *Paradise Lost*—to create an intentionally anti-Christian allegory. The result of the superficial and cynical de-mythologizing process is to strip the myths of their wonder and value. In Tolkien's poem "Mythopoeia," he warns of the danger of taking everything in life for face value (as the "rationalist" does):

> You look at trees and label them just so,
> (for trees are "trees," and growing is "to grow");
> you walk the earth and tread with solemn pace
> one of the many minor globes of Space:
> a star's a star, some matter in a ball
> compelled to courses mathematical
> amid the regimented, cold, inane,
> where destined atoms are each moment slain.[25]

This is the indifferent and insipid world offered by the materialist critics of Christianity. But true, ultimate reality is that which pulls at the deepest yearnings of the human heart, which presses us beyond mere living into *being*. This reality is the antithesis of the trivial and soulless world of the materialist skeptic who wishes to be good and happy without the sacred and eternal.

A graduate professor of classics who self-identified as a "very lapsed Catholic" once told me (C. J.) that she was no longer a Christian because she could no longer "believe in the myth." As a scholar very well entrenched in the academic study of mythology, she was no doubt aware of the possible slippage of the term "myth" when she made this statement, but I have to believe she meant more than simply "magic" or "falsehood," not least because she did not say "I don't believe in myths." This was a different response than the facile, skeptical stance that defuses dialogue regarding ancient events and their narrative tradition by suspiciously considering them either as the product of an irremediably backward world view just waiting for science to show us the light, or even worse, as impossible to get at with any degree of objective accuracy and so not worth the effort.

---

[25] J. R. R. Tolkien, *Tree and Leaf: Including the Poem Mythopoeia* (London: George Allen and Unwin Hyman, 1964), 97.

In other words, skeptical dismissal of ancient event and story is arrogant at best and willingly, blissfully ignorant at worst. It is one thing "not to believe in the myth." It is another thing to ignore myths completely, or even treat them uncritically as indistinguishable.

So also with reducing the proclamation of Christ's resurrection to simply one of many equally false ancient dying-and-rising-god myths. Not only is the resurrection event recorded in the New Testament an event distinct from other historical events in the ancient world, but the way the story of it is told (and rites associated with its import) is quite distinct from the ways in which the ancient Greco-Roman myths were told. The criticism assumes *a priori* that the people among whom the Christian proclamation arose were either entirely ignorant, or immediately misunderstanding, of the events surrounding Christ's death and resurrection. Apparently the followers of Jesus could not possibly have recognized his actions, teachings, or purpose—much less the correspondence of certain of his actions to the ancient myths, for it *is* there—and yet our modern critics have managed to divine and debunk all of it. Here again we concur with Lewis: "The idea that any man or writer should be opaque to those who lived in the same culture, spoke the same language, shared the same habitual imagery and unconscious assumptions, and yet be transparent to those who have none of those advantages, is in my opinion preposterous."[26]

The vocabulary of mythopoeia refers to the way we rehearse, repeat, represent, and deliver the story of an event of great import for a people. Christianity claims that the people in question is universal; indeed Luke reports that the resurrection of Christ both has meaning beyond an empty grave and demands a response:

> Now when they heard this they were cut to the heart, and said to Peter and the rest of the apostles, "Brothers, what shall we do?" And Peter said to them, "Repent and be baptized every one of you in the name of Jesus Christ for the forgiveness of your sins, and you will receive the gift of the Holy Spirit. For the promise is for you and for your children and for all who are far off, everyone whom the Lord our God calls to himself." And with many other words he bore witness and continued to exhort them,

---

[26]C. S. Lewis, "Modern Theology and Biblical Criticism," 158.

saying, "Save yourselves from this crooked generation." So those who received his word were baptized. (Acts 2:37–41)

Luke's "those who received his word" implies furthermore that there were people in the crowd who did not receive his word. This does not mean there were people in the crowd at Pentecost who just didn't believe in myths, meaning souls too rational to be tricked by miracle stories, magic, or slick rhetoric. We do not see argument against the resurrection event here. Rather, we see only some who receive it—that is, believe it to their salvation (accepting not only the fact of Peter's current events review but also the consequences he lays out in the proclamation of Joel's prophecy fulfilled)—and others who do not. Rejection of the story may involve simply demurral regarding its meaning or its intended beneficiaries. But this bit of documentary evidence does not leave us with a sense that there is disbelief in the fact of the event itself. For Lewis, and for us today, the word is received thus: "Here is the very thing you like in poetry and the romances, only this time it's true."[27]

Christianity and the Romans

One further distinction to consider between the pluralism of the first century AD and our own is the notion of religions in competition. Roman religious practice was not so much a matter of choice among alternatives as it was a religious life of many dimensions. There was little for the religious participant to be anxious about in moving from celebration of state cult to family worship to mystery-club devotion to philosophical rumination, as the tolerant cultural context of polytheism was the general rule for the religions in question rather than claims of exclusivity or prohibitions against idolatry. It is helpful therefore to consider the particularly Roman lens through which Christianity was perceived with a brief survey of the religious backdrop of the Roman world.

---

[27]Walter Hooper, ed., *The Collected Letters of C. S. Lewis, Volume II* (San Francisco, CA: HarperSanFrancisco, 2004), 5.

The broad strokes of belief in the existence of the divine and the need to pray to and propitiate gods through offering and ritual sacrifice were as common to religion in Rome as they were throughout the Hellenistic world and the ancient Near East, a point basically held in common with Judaism and Christianity. Roman civic religion boasted several colleges of priests devoted to their many gods, and the office of these priests was to ensure the public good. Hence the priesthoods, managed at the top of the Roman state's hierarchy by one chief priest (*pontifex maximus*), were public in nature (priestly offices were in fact public magistracies). Peoples' prayers to gods were supplemented with a tangible offering (a *votum*) dedicated to a deity's temple. More substantial offerings included animal sacrifice—the larger and more public the need, the larger, more public, and more official the offering—to the gods whose cultivation reinforced their patronage of the state. A Roman's participation in ceremonies of the state's major patron gods also reinforced the community's allegiance to the state, as much as the later sacrifice of a bit of incense and prayer to the genius of the emperor would confirm an individual's identity as a citizen loyal to the empire.

Roman civic religion took as given that people, and indeed the entire state, were under obligation to the gods. This relationship of obligation, reflected in the worship practice of sacrifice, reveals a *do ut des* way of cultivating their religion: I give (to you gods) in order that you (gods) may give to me (i.e., as individual or community). The important role of the human agent or agents doing the giving on the front end of that contract is reflected in the need to perform sacrifices perfectly, according to procedure known by the various priesthoods to honor their particular gods at their particular shrines and temples. Imperfect sacrifices needed to be repeated with new victims until ceremonies were completed without flaw; to do otherwise was to risk the disastrous outcomes of such ill-omened, deficient ceremony.

Jewish cult of course also included priesthood and sacrifice of victims, localized at the Jerusalem temple until its destruction by the Romans in 70 AD. But the Roman perception of Christianity vis-à-vis Judaism is not colored so much by Jewish sacrificial practice as by the other Jewish distinctives Rome found hard to swallow. As a Jewish sect, Christianity shared in common its insistence on monotheism. Limiting worshipers to cultivation of one deity exclusively amid so many options—and under threat of punishment for idolatry—not to mention Sabbath worship centered locally in the synagogue, ritual purity including dietary regulation, and devotion to the Torah were, frankly, odd to the Romans. Odd as these elements were to rank polytheists, the very nature of polytheism demands broad toleration, and Romans were in fact generally quite tolerant of exclusive religious groups such as Judaism and Christianity. Up to a point, that is. Conformity to municipal peace was the *sine qua non* of the *pax Romana*, conformity established and enforced by its peacemakers, the Roman military presence in every municipality, ready to put down riots violently, up to and including systematic persecution of troublemakers. Perceived oddity probably did not help mitigate the stigma attached to these groups, attracting the focus of a Nero who scapegoated the Jews and Christians in 64 AD as the arsonists in Rome's conflagration.[28] But the Jewish state was later obliterated by Roman armies not because of its insistence on monotheism but because of the Jewish revolts of the first and second centuries AD. So also, Christians were not systematically persecuted under Nero, Decius, or Diocletian because of their proclamation of and insistence on Christ's bodily resurrection from the dead but because of their perceived nonallegiance to the well-ordered state[29] and as a response to riots.[30]

Early martyrs of Christianity were, not surprisingly, remembered by fellow Christians as local heroes, having died a death worthy of emulation. Indeed, becoming (or remembering) a Christian martyr was at the same time a remembrance of Christ's sacrificial death. Early Christian writing casts death in a light quite different than that promoted by their pagan contemporaries, however, who saw death as an evil to be avoided or mitigated by a hopeful afterlife.[31] "What

---

[28]Tacitus, *Annales* 15.44.

[29]Pliny, *Epistulae* 10.96–97.

[30]Suetonius, *Claudius* 25; cf. Acts 18:1–18.

[31]The general attitude toward death and pessimism regarding the afterlife, which Rome inherited from archaic and classical Greece, is summarized and

was different" in ordinary Christian funeral practice from that of their non-Christian neighbors,

> was the centrality of the resurrection of Christ as the witness, the exemplar, of personal and physical resurrection for each Christian. Resurrection was . . . *part* of the Jewish inheritance, but it was enunciated now as *the* central indisputable proposition of the new faith. It was enunciated so strongly that (much to the amazement of the Roman authorities) large numbers of Christians came forward to claim their resurrectional rights, as it were, by offering to die, and to do so in the most public and painful of ways.[32]

Correspondence to pagan remembrance of a hero's death ends here, then, at remembrance. Certainly in Greece and during the Roman period, minor deities as well as patron demigod heroes were cultivated in worship that focused on the memory of eponymous founders of cities and family lines, or those who had shown great service to a locale through good work, service in war, or martyrdom. These localized cults are traceable as antecedents of the later cult to the dead and deified emperors of Rome. The Greeks could point to big names (Heracles, for example) as enjoying some kind of blessed afterlife on Olympus or the Isles of the Blessed, and the Romans considered emperors whose honors surpassed other living mortals to have been catasterized (turned into stars or constellations and therefore having an afterlife existence in the heavens). On a smaller scale, local heroes received ritual attention at their graves, more in the Greek world than in the later Roman one. The later popularity of mystery cult in Rome may be related to this more ancient Greek phenomenon.

In our normal usage, we employ the word "mystery" generally to refer to riddles or secrets that are obscure, difficult to understand, or hidden from view, hence the genre of modern "mystery" fiction

---

convincingly established by N. T. Wright, *The Resurrection of the Son of God* (Minneapolis, MN: Fortress Press, 2003), 32–45.

[32]Jon Davies, *Death, Burial, and Rebirth in the Religions of Antiquity* (London: Routledge, 1999), 199–200.

that includes detective stories like Doyle's Sherlock Holmes books or thrillers by Agatha Christie. And indeed when we talk about the so-called "mystery religions" of the ancient world, we are on ground that, well trod as it is, nevertheless is yet riddled with much that is unknown—we can only hope that further generations of scholars will shed more light on a field that at present is rather more dark than other aspects of ancient society. When we use the term "mystery" to categorize these religions, however, scholars are not referring to their own ignorance or the obscurity of the subject, but rather to what the ancients considered a club, the inner workings of which were exclusively the experience of the initiated (the Greek verb *myein* means to shut or close; a *mystēs* was an initiate, plural *mystai*; hence the activities of the club come to be known as *mysteria*).

Mystery religions were popular among many (though not all) ancients, as they offered worshiper-club-members a more intimate association with a society of fellow thinkers than what was provided in the ritual ceremonies of state. Not all were of Eastern origin, like the devotion to Mithras (probably Persian in origin) or Isis (Egyptian); the Greek cult of Demeter at Eleusis originating in at least the seventh century BC, though possibly older, still existed through the duration of the Roman Empire as well. The diversity of origin and variety of practice among these religions to a great extent defies identifying them together beyond the common attributes of initiation for membership (and therefore secrecy regarding their inner workings) and their position as voluntary practices vis-à-vis other facets of religious life in ancient Rome. Nevertheless, studies of the nineteenth and twentieth centuries conjectured that Christianity was viewed by the Romans (sometimes with suspicion) as a mystery cult because of elements it shared in common with other known cults, including the rite of initiation (holy baptism) and what came to be known in Christian parlance as the *mysteria* (sacraments, particularly the Lord's Supper).[33] While we are on surer ground in chalking up Roman suspicion of Christianity to Christian demurral of allegiance to the

---

[33]Selected bibliography is included in Walter Burkert, *Ancient Mystery Cults* (Cambridge, MA: Harvard University Press, 1987), 134–35 (nn. 13–14); he is right to caution that "the constant use of Christianity as a reference system when dealing with the so-called mystery religions leads to distortions as

emperor due to the prohibition against idolatry, linking Christianity with mystery religions still entices scholars and skeptics alike with the possibility of discovering correspondence with them beyond initiation and secrecy. The death and underworld journey of the god Osiris can be thought, for example, to compare with the death of Christ. The focus on the agricultural cycle of Persephone / Kore in the Eleusinian cult could similarly compare with resonances of death and life in the myths of other mysteries, as well as the death and life motif in the Christian story.

In addition to the possible mythic correspondence between Christianity and the mystery religions (i.e., comparing the stories upon which the cults derive their reason to be), one major social factor also invites comparison—namely, the ordinariness of the worshipers involved. Initiates of these religions cultivated worship in expectation of personal blessings from their patron deity, including individual deliverance from anticipated dangers and sorrows of the afterlife, a reflection of (in the case of devotion to Isis and Osiris, for example) earlier practice that was more limited to the ruling class. In ancient Egypt, for example, only pharaohs and their ilk could expect pyramids and grave goods replete with spell-scrolls to help them map out their underworld experience and succeed in their death journey. But the development of mystery cults promised delivery of these blessings to the average citizen, soldier, or even slave. Christianity also arguably succeeded on the score of its egalitarian and universal proclamation, reflected in such texts as Paul's conclusion regarding the good of initiation into the body of Christ:

> But now that faith has come, we are no longer under a guardian, for in Christ Jesus you are all sons of God, through faith. For as many of you as were baptized into Christ have put on Christ. There is neither Jew nor Greek, there is neither slave nor free, there is no male and female, for you are all one in Christ Jesus. And if you are Christ's, then you are Abraham's offspring, heirs according to promise. (Galatians 3:25–29)

---

well as partial clarification, obscuring the often radical differences between the two" (3).

The social parallel might suggest further correspondence, and indeed we make no claim that the average practitioners of these religions met the distinctions between cults with anything like critical observation of their competing philosophical or theological claims. These distinctions nevertheless existed, forming the basis of early Christian apologetic (cf. Acts 17:18ff; 1 Peter 3:13–17; 2 Peter 1:16–21). The need to be aware of these distinctions is no less demanding today, as many frankly find it easier to fudge the details of ancient belief into one amalgam and assume Christianity's debt to the substance of early cultic belief. So what did they believe? We limit ourselves to a brief survey of the cults we hear brought up from time to time as "parallels to" or "corresponding with" Christianity, through what little evidence they offer us, in order to get some sense of their content and present some distinguishing characteristics. Our survey does not pretend to be exhaustive; suggestions for further reading follow at the end of our study.

Isis and Osiris

Writing in the early second century AD, Plutarch's *Moralia* includes a philosophical essay known as *Isis and Osiris*. The latter part of that century attests to the popularity of the Hellenized Egyptian cult within Rome in the entertaining novel *Metamorphoses* (also known as the *Golden Ass*) by Apuleius. Together, these ancient *testimonia* present a picture of cultic practice and an edited history of the story at the center of the religion.

Central to the story of Isis is the dismemberment of the god Osiris by his brother Set (whom Plutarch calls Typhon), his scattered burial, and the reintegration of his dismembered parts into one body by Isis.[34] Plutarch's allegorical observations relate the dismembering and reintegration of Osiris and the eventual revenge of his son Horus over the evil Typhon to metaphysical processes of reason creating order out of disorder.[35] We are most interested in the substance of the myth that deals with death and afterlife, for which the

---

[34]Plutarch, "*Isis and Osiris*," in *Moralia*, Loeb Classical Library vol. 5 (Cambridge, MA: Harvard University Press, 1936), 18, 54.

[35]Ibid. *passim*, cf. 54–55.

story of Isis and Osiris offers a unique picture in the ancient world.[36] Osiris, reintegrated and revived by Isis, becomes (according to the Egyptians, the lord of the underworld) the deity with whom the dead hoped to identify in order to experience some kind of living experience while dead (instead of oblivion—that is, a second death), a translation from one form of living (mortal, with others on this side of death) to another (the "new day," as reflected in the spell scrolls known as the Egyptian "books of the dead"). The uniquely Egyptian practice of mummification reflects belief in the Egyptian afterlife experience (which is also unique to the ancient world), but it was not one in which Egyptians expected their dead to come back to a bodily life in this mortal world. The upshot of the myth's pertinence to the anxiety of life and death is not that it offers a believer a way to beat death or come back to life; rather it presents a model for how to live once one has died. Employing the term "resurrection" to this myth in the context of the Hellenistic Roman world is seriously problematic, therefore, as it confuses a uniquely Egyptian concept of the afterlife with bodily resurrection, about which Paul and the New Testament authors wrote many decades *before* Plutarch's writings.

Mithras

As often as we hear that Christian talk about resurrection has its source in the dying and rising gods of Egypt, we hear the claim that Mithraism was a major contender for the dominant Western religion of late antiquity.[37] Apologetic engagement with this claim is relatively simple, as the burden of proof falls on the one making the claim, which at best is based on interpreting the limited (mostly iconographic) extant evidence. A myth must have existed consistent with what is represented carved in stone in *mithraea*, the caves or other spaces adapted for communal eating and celebration of Mithras's mysteries. More than four hundred ancient sites witness

---

[36]Here we simply suggest that the myth is central to the mysteries, whether or not a worshiper is consciously aware of the death-life motif.

[37]Burkert dismisses the claim: "Most scholars today agree there never was a chance for that, since Mithraism was not even a religion in the full sense of the word" (*Ancient Mystery Cults,* 3).

Mithras devotion. The central image of Mithras iconography represents the hero slaying a bull; others depict him wearing a Phrygian cap, birthed from a rock, seeking and subduing the bull, and feasting on the bull.

But the picture of Mithraism at present is a puzzle missing too many pieces to call it clear. The process of making connections between uncertain Mithraisian origins and assumed practices and what can be surmised from Mithras iconography results at best in tenuous, provisional conclusions regarding the myth.[38]

In the absence of anything like a literary narrative or synopsis of Mithraic theology, it is nearly impossible to say anything with certainty about the mythical origins or purpose of the cult. Furthermore, we may point out that if the narrative were to include robust references to dying and rising or even a central point about the agricultural cycle, even then we would be hard-pressed to observe clear correspondence to the iconography to which we are limited at present, so connections with Christianity are at best abject conjecture and at worst completely misplaced.

The Suffering Gods: Persephone, Orpheus, Dionysus

Students of Greco-Roman mythology generally stand more confidently on the well-known stories of the gods known from the classical West than on those from Egypt or Persia. Persephone, Orpheus, and Dionysus all make their appearances in plays, hymns, epics, and other songs extant from the Greek and Roman world. We are therefore in a position to say more about the myths from which their cults derived, even where little is known about the actual mystery religions themselves.

The most thorough treatment of the Persephone myth is the archaic Greek *Homeric Hymn to Demeter*; a Latin-speaking Roman audience could also enjoy Ovid's treatment of the myth in Book Five of his *Metamorphoses*. The hymn recounts how Persephone, daughter of Zeus and Demeter, was abducted by Hades and taken to the

---

[38]Marvin W. Meyer, ed. *The Ancient Mysteries: A Sourcebook of Sacred Texts.* (Philadelphia: University of Pennsylvania Press, 1999. [By arrangement; originally NY: HarperCollins, 1987]), 201.

underworld. Demeter, goddess of agriculture and fertility, frantically searches for her daughter, during which time the world suffers famine. When Persephone's whereabouts are finally discovered, Zeus brokers a deal: Persephone will spend a portion of the year above with her mother and the other portion below as the consort of Hades. Among other interpretations, the myth is read as an obvious *aetion* for the cycle of the seasons and agriculture, seedtime, and harvest.

Orpheus, a demigod hero associated especially with song, is especially famous as the bereft lover of Eurydice, the nymph who died on their wedding day, as Ovid recounts in Book Ten of his *Metamorphoses*. Orpheus descends to the underworld, where his magical song convinces the lords of the dead to allow Eurydice to return to the land of the living on the condition that Orpheus not look at Eurydice until they have reached the farther shore separating the world of the dead from his own. This condition Orpheus fails to observe, and he is twice bereft. His lamentation leads him to eschew all association with women, driving mad the Thracian maenads who tear him limb from limb (Dionysiac *sparagmos*), though his head still sings. Besides this primary story of Orpheus's mythology, ancient Orphic sources also include theogonic and philosophical hymns attributed to him, which form the basis of the mystery rites of the Orphic cult of Dionysus.

Dionysus was celebrated in the Greek world as the god of seeing things that were not actually there and was therefore associated with ecstatic experience, drama, and wine. Greek drama is replete with narrative about Dionysus's birth and powers. Conceived of the union between Zeus and the Theban Semele, who was killed after demanding Zeus's theophany, Dionysus's embryo was saved by Zeus, who gave birth to the new god from his own thigh and entrusted his upbringing to nymphs. Dionysus is consistently portrayed as young and accompanied by a retinue of ecstatic worshipers who enjoy his wine and the wilder aspects of nature (as opposed to civilization). The Orphic hymns honor the circumstances of Dionysus's birth and rebirth, the central event relevant to the mysteries of Dionysus.

The myths at the center of these dying gods' stories no doubt influenced both the beliefs and the religious practices of their cult members. But the myths of a god's demise and afterlife do not directly correspond to a worshiper's individual hopes for a blessed afterlife, much less offer hope in a resurrection comparable to that proclaimed by Christians at their funeral rites or in the New Testament documents. Egyptian afterlife was the life lived while dead; the most explicit texts in this regard from the Greco-Roman cults are the Orphic hymns, which point rather to the ecstatic experience sought by worshipers in the here and now of Dionysiac cultic rite rather than a hope of experiencing a second birth like Dionysus had. The bleak afterlife of Hades established by ancient authority still resounds in the Orphic hymns as worshipers sing to Hermes *psychopompus*, who will lead their shades to the realm of the dead, as well as bring their ecstatic rites in honor of Dionysus to a proper close. The Roman philosophical conceit of passing through death to something not to be feared, or to nothing at all, or to a more rarefied form of soul existence that leaves the burdensome body behind, owes more to Plato's demurral of mythology and teaching of metempsychosis than any idea about a bodily resurrection. Indeed it would be surprising to find someone in the world of the Roman Empire who interpreted any myth literally, much less expected something like a bodily resurrection as a result of that reading.

The myths nevertheless did exist and influence the religious life of the Roman world during the nascent stage of Christianity. What might we conclude from this brief review of the basic myths? We anticipate the inquirer or the critic thus:

Question: Isn't it true that Christianity was seen by the Romans as just another quirky mystery cult?

Answer: No. A discerning Roman might well consider the Christian cult as similar to other cults to the extent that its requisite initiation and sacramental exclusivity resembled certain aspects of other religions, but the variety of cults that make up the religious backdrop of Roman cultural experience is not limited to just the "mystery" subset. Moreover, its connection to Judaism textually and culturally meant *Christianity was seen as quite distinct from mystery religions* in that it was exclusively monotheistic and not tolerant of idolatry.

Question: Isn't it true that all mystery cults baited believers with a better afterlife?

Answer: No. While in general the prevailing belief about death in the ancient world was not one that was optimistic, and while various

philosophical schools and cults of the Roman Empire promoted doctrines that mitigated the fear associated with mortality, not every mystery was focused primarily on death and the afterlife, in spite of what
connections we may want to make based on our interpretation of the
myths from which they developed.[39] More to the point, the mysteries
were opportunities for ecstatic religious experience in the here and
now, for the worshiper living on this side of mortality. Identification
with any particular cult did not necessarily go beyond the one initiat-
ing encounter (e.g., the Eleusinian rite) to affect a sense of identity in
everyday life or grant extra confidence in a life after death.

Question: Isn't it true that all mystery cults simply rehashed old
ground with myths centered on agriculture?

Answer: No. It was once the fashion to attempt to discover as many
parallels as possible to archetypal myths, and Frazer's *Golden Bough*,
published in subsequent editions through the turn of the nineteenth
to twentieth century, brought the agricultural death-life cycle to the
foreground as the *ur*-myth of all ancient religion. This kind of paral-
lelomania spins an attractive story, as it suggests not only a common
source for many ancient religions (fertility cult) but also a natural
progression or evolution from religion to the scientific thinking of
Frazer's own day. But the devil in the details is that agricultural concerns do not appear at the center of all myths. Mithras devotion,
for example, may have in fact nothing to do with agriculture at all
(not to mention the afterlife), or at most tangentially (we are limited to considering iconographical representation of wheat sprouting
from the bull's tail), and any alimentary focus in Dionysus worship
seems to have been more about eating meat (raw, *homophagia*) than
about the harvest cycle.

Question: Isn't it true that all mystery cults believed in resurrection,
one more point in favor of thinking that Christianity owes a debt to
these religions?

---

[39]The assumption that all mystery cults primarily engaged an anxiety about
death and the afterlife has been challenged successfully by Burkert (*Ancient
Mystery Cults*, ch. 1), and more recently Hugh Bowden, *Mystery Cults of the
Ancient World* (Princeton, NJ: Princeton University Press, 2010), 22–23.

Answer: No, and no. For those religions that did teach something like a blessed afterlife, resurrection may be approximated as reincarnation / metempsychosis (a la the teaching of Pythagoras or Plato's myth of Er, *Republic* 10), a spiritual "resurrection" meaning a better existence after death (though not a bodily one) or a dead kind of life (the teaching about death and its journey particular to the tradition coming from Egypt). In all these cases, there is not taught a bodily resurrection in which people are reanimated, revived, to live in the here and now as Jesus is said to have done and as the dead in Christ are promised to be. What little evidence there is that associates mysteries with Christianity does not point to influence or debt in the direction of Christian borrowings from the myths or practice of these cults.

Conclusion: Myth and Christianity

On the cusp of his conversion, Lewis wrote to his childhood friend, Arthur Greeves, admitting (which Tolkien and Hugo Dyson had recently helped him see) that he had always liked the idea of the dying-and-rising god provided he didn't meet it in the Gospels. He then confessed: "Now the story of Christ is simply a true myth: a myth working on us in the same way as the others. But with this tremendous difference that *it really happened*."[40] For Christians of every age, the fact that God in Christ entered into humanity, into our history, is at once our central claim and apologetic. And yet it is myth—*true* myth. We have in this brief examination considered several ancient myths that popular opinion assumes correspond to Christianity in more significant ways than they actually do; our analysis has attempted to point out certain elements that distinguish them from the story of Christ. In the end, the parallels neither confirm nor deny the fact that it is true myth and therefore ought not to trouble us. "The old myth of the Dying God, *without ceasing to be myth*, comes down from the heaven of legend and imagination

---

[40]Hooper, *Letters,* 1:976–77. Later, in "Myth Became Fact," Lewis exhorted: "To be truly Christian we must both assent to the historical fact and also receive the myth (fact though it has become) with the same imaginative embrace which we accord to all myths" (67).

to the earth of history. It *happens*—at a particular date, in a particular place, followed by definable historical consequences. We pass from a Balder or an Osiris, dying nobody knows when or where, to a historical Person crucified (it is all in order) *under Pontius Pilate*. By becoming fact it does not cease to be myth."[41] As Lewis (with our creeds) recognizes, Christianity rests on solid historical bedrock. Therefore we need not be put off by claims of parallels with pagan myths: "[T]hey *ought* to be there—it would be a stumbling block if they weren't."[42]

But Christianity does not rest only on cold, hard facts like the objectively verifiable claim of Christ suffering under Pontius Pilate. Its life is the union of the transcendent and the mundane, which is indeed parallel to the mythological backdrop of the ancient Greco-Roman world and common also to human experience of every time and place. Christians need not shy away from "myth" language; indeed such stories cannot be told without the language of mythology. Of course, the doctrines we derive from this true myth are not the myth itself, but "translations into our concepts and ideas of that which God has already expressed in a language more adequate, namely the actual incarnation, crucifixion, and resurrection."[43] This point, with the aid of Lewis and other Christian lovers of myth, is what we have here attempted to demonstrate: what we may call the "inevitability of myth," the fact that myth is the necessary idiom for dealing with the central claim of Christianity. There is no sense that those who rejected Peter's Pentecost plea were disinterested in stories, narratives, or myths. Nor ought we to be. The story of Christ cannot make sense apart from the context of the stories of the Greeks and the Romans and all others who have left us their myths. For myth is the grammar of incarnation, crucifixion, and resurrection. And every Christian ought gladly to take the name of philomythos—lover of myth—without fear of losing the

---

[41]Lewis, "Myth Became Fact," 66–67. Lewis reminds us also that "what became Fact was a Myth, that it carries with it into the world of Fact all the properties of a myth. God is more than a god, not less; Christ is more than Balder, not less."

[42]Ibid.

[43]Hooper, *Letters*, 1:977.

historic fact of the Gospel. The resurrection is the eucatastrophe, the overwhelmingly joyous happy ending of the Christian myth-become-fact, in which everything sad has come untrue.

Recommended Reading

Alvar, Jaime. *Romanising Oriental Gods: Myth, Salvation, and Ethics in the Cults of Cybele, Isis and Mithras.* Religions in the Graeco-Roman World. Translated and edited by Richard Gordon. Leiden, Netherlands: Brill, 2007.

Bernthal, Craig. *Tolkien's Sacramental Vision: Discerning the Holy in Middle Earth.* Kettering, OH: Second Spring, 2014.

Bowden, Hugh. *Mystery Cults of the Ancient World.* Princeton, NJ: Princeton University Press, 2010.

Burkert, Walter. *Ancient Mystery Cults.* Cambridge, MA: Harvard University Press, 1987.

Chesterton, G. K. *The Everlasting Man.* San Francisco, CA: Ignatius, 2008.

———. *Orthodoxy.* New York: Doubleday, 2001.

Davies, Jon. *Death, Burial, and Rebirth in the Religions of Antiquity.* London: Routledge, 1999.

Graf, Fritz and Sarah I. Johnson. *Ritual Texts for the Afterlife: Orpheus and the Bacchic Gold Tablets.* London: Routledge, 2007.

Hein, Rolland. *Christian Mythmakers.* Eugene, OR: Wipf and Stock Publishers, 2014.

Lewis, C. S. "The Grand Miracle." In *God in the Dock: Essays on Theology and Ethics.* Grand Rapids, MI: Eerdmans, 1970, 80–88.

———. "Is Theology Poetry?" In *The Weight of Glory.* New York: Harper Collins, 2001, 116–40.

———. "Modern Theology and Biblical Criticism." In *Christian Reflections.* Grand Rapids, MI: Wm. B. Eerdmans, 1994, 152–66.

———. "Myth Became Fact." In *God in the Dock: Essays on Theology and Ethics.* Grand Rapids, MI: Eerdmans, 1970, 63–67.

———. "Religion without Dogma?" In *God in the Dock: Essays on Theology and Ethics.* Grand Rapids, MI: Eerdmans, 1970, 129–46.

Meyer, Marvin W., ed. *The Ancient Mysteries: A Sourcebook of Sacred Texts.* Philadelphia: University of Pennsylvania Press, 1999. [By arrangement; originally NY: HarperCollins, 1987.]

Tolkien, J. R. R. "On Fairy-Stories." In *The Monsters and the Critics and Other Essays*. Edited by Christopher Tolkien. London: George Allen and Unwin, 1983.

Wright, N. T. *The Resurrection of the Son of God*. Minneapolis, MN: Fortress Press, 2003.

Zaleski, Philip and Carol Zaleski. *The Fellowship: The Literary Lives of the Inklings*. New York: Farrar, Straus and Giroux, 2015.

Suggestions for reading in the kind of "new" mythopoeia discussed in this chapter (leaving out Tolkien's *The Hobbit* and *Lord of the Rings* and Lewis's *The Chronicles of Narnia* and the Space Trilogy):

Lewis, C. S. *The Pilgrim's Regress*. Grand Rapids, MI: Wm. B. Eerdmans, 2014.

———. *Till We Have Faces: A Myth Retold*. Orlando, FL: Harcourt, 1980.

MacDonald, George. *Lilith*. Grand Rapids, MI: Wm. B. Eerdmans, 2000.

———. *Phantastes*. Grand Rapids, MI: Wm. B. Eerdmans, 2000.

———. *The Wise Woman and Other Stories*. Grand Rapids, MI: Wm. B. Eerdmans, 1980.

Stoddard, James. *The False House*. Hampshire, UK: Ransom Books, 2015.

———. *Evenmere*. Hampshire, UK: Ransom Books, 2015.

———. *The High House*. Hampshire, UK: Ransom Books, 2015.

Tolkien, J. R. R. *The Children of Hurin*. Edited by Christopher Tolkien. New York: Houghton Mifflin, 2007.

———. *The Legend of Sigurd and Gudrún*. Edited by Christopher Tolkien. New York: Houghton Mifflin, 2009.

———. *The Silmarillion*. Edited by Christopher Tolkien. New York: Houghton Mifflin, 2014.

Williams, Charles. *Descent into Hell*. Grand Rapids, MI: Wm. B. Eerdmans, 1980.

———. *Many Dimensions*. Grand Rapids, MI: Wm. B. Eerdmans, 1993.

———. *War in Heaven*. Grand Rapids, MI: Wm. B. Eerdmans, 2004.

8

Tactile and True:
The Physicality of the Resurrection

Carolyn Hansen

Introduction

In his first epistle to the Corinthians, the apostle Paul readily conceded, "If Christ has not been raised, our preaching is useless and so is your faith" (1 Corinthians 15:14). He could not have been more explicit. Christ's bodily resurrection is absolutely essential to the Christian faith; it's the *sine qua non* of Christianity. No resurrection, no biblical Christianity. Period. If the once-crucified Jesus of Nazareth did not rise from the grave with a resurrected body after a certifiable death, then this same Jesus did not defeat death, he was not the Messiah of God, and our faith is not binding as universally true with cosmic consequences. Paul himself summarized the not only disastrous but also blasphemous consequences of a resurrectionless Christianity with these words:

> We [Christians] are even found to be misrepresenting God, because we testified about God that he raised Christ, whom he did not raise if it is true that the dead are not raised. For if the dead are not raised, not even Christ has been raised. And if Christ has not been raised, your faith is futile and you are still in your sins. Then those also who have fallen asleep in Christ have perished. If in Christ we have hope in this life only, we are of all people most to be pitied. (1 Corinthians 15:15–19)

Simply put, without a bodily resurrection, death reigns, sin condemns, and Christians are peddling dangerous deceits. There's no relief from judgment or guilt or bondage because the Christian message is a lie and the worst sort of lie—one propagated in the name of Almighty God. But that's exactly the bold proclamation of Christianity: Christ is risen from the dead by the will and power of God Almighty as *the* hallmark of divine authenticity. And it is precisely *that* sweeping claim, Paul asserted, which brings comfort, confidence, and assurance that Jesus Christ is the world's rightful king, only redeemer, and Lord of life (1 Peter 1:3–5; Romans 6:9; John 11:25).

The bodily resurrection of Jesus of Nazareth, then, is a truth claim like no other, because if true, it changes everything. If true, mankind is in fact saved by his death and justified through his resurrection (Romans 4:25), and the cosmos will never be the same (8:22) because God has visited us for the expressed purpose of reconciling humanity (2 Corinthians 5:19) to himself and remaking his creation in the image of the Resurrected One (1 Corinthians 15:22; 1 John 3:2). Thus our faith depends on and emerges from what Paul and the rest of the apostles and disciples who encountered the risen Christ meant when they proclaimed that Jesus had been "raised."

But isn't this risky business pinning the verity of a totalizing claim with cosmic implications upon something that is entirely unknown to modern science? Paul seemed to have put all his eggs into quite a vulnerable basket. After all, you don't need to be a scientist of the twenty-first century to know that people don't rise from the dead. Neither is the permanence of human death a new discovery. Mankind has always known that the dead bodies of individuals do not undergo any kind of meaningful bodily transformation that would indicate they've conquered physical death.[1] Quite the opposite: they rot, decay, and disintegrate. Paul knew this, and so did his contemporaries, and yet he and the other New Testament authors

---

[1] N. T. Wright makes much of this apologetical point against detractors in Craig A. Evans and N. T. Wright, *Jesus, the Final Days: What Really Happened*, ed. Troy A. Miller (Louisville, KY: Westminster/John Knox Press, 2009), 76–77, esp. 84.

assert the resurrection as a basic fact. For Christians past and present, that's because it happened in real time and space.

Not so fast, argues Gerd Lüdemann, professor of the New Testament and early Christianity at the University of Göttingen. Lüdemann doesn't think it is worth the trouble trying to defend or even to believe in the facticity of the bodily resurrection precisely because it *is* entirely out of step with modern learning and science concerning what may factually happen. For him, modern scientific knowledge about life and death are incompatible with a literalist understanding of the resurrection of Jesus Christ. "If you say that Jesus rose from the dead biologically, you would have to presuppose that a decaying corpse—which is already cold and without blood in its brain—could be made alive again." And he concludes, "I think that is nonsense."[2] He doesn't even believe that Paul or the other eyewitnesses of the risen Christ actually meant a bodily resurrection anyway. This supernaturalist interpretation, he contends, came later and was superimposed upon the New Testament accounts.

Curiously, for a time, Lüdemann denied the physical resurrection but still considered himself a faithful Christian. This led to a public debate in 1997 with William Lane Craig[3] over whether one can rightly be a Christian according to the New Testament while denying Jesus's bodily resurrection. Lüdemann argued that the immediate postapostolic church misinterpreted the New Testament authors, especially Paul, to understand the resurrection as something truly bodily. In reality, he maintained, their alleged encounters with Jesus were *visions* induced by posttraumatic conditions and their profound desire to perpetuate Jesus's kingdom agenda.[4] This, he claims, is *authentic* Christianity; a bodiless resurrection was the belief of the first Christians, and so this would be the faithful confession of authentic Christians.

---

[2]Lüdemann quoted in William Lane Craig and Gerd Lüdemann, *Jesus' Resurrection: Fact or Figment?: A Debate between William Lane Craig & Gerd Lüdemann*, ed. Paul Copan and Ronald K. Tacelli. (Downers Grove, IL: InterVarsity Press, 2000), 45.

[3]*Op. cit.* note 1.

[4]Evans and Wright, *Jesus, the Final Days*, 80.

Professor Lüdemann's primary goal has been to modernize Christianity, to make it more palatable to a modern audience. In doing so, though, what he does is destroy Christianity. One need only read 1 Corinthians 15 to get that. And Lüdemann understands this clearly enough. So to avoid making a claim that rejects Christianity entirely, he retells the biblical narrative about Jesus of Nazareth in such a way as to appeal to modern sensibilities. He takes up the Pauline challenge of 1 Corinthians 15 and posits an alternative theory of a spiritual or metaphorical "resurrection" using much of the very same biblical language of "seeing the Lord" that orthodox Christianity invokes.[5] He fits his vision hypothesis into the traditional Christian narrative. Such an approach is necessary, he contends, for the "idea of the Son of God's being raised from the dead, getting out of the tomb, staying with the disciples for forty days and then ascending into heaven is a precarious concept."[6] It collapses under its own supernaturalistic weight. "The risen Christ is the skeleton in the closet of the church. In other words, everybody seems to know that Christ didn't rise," Lüdemann writes. "I think this is a first-century myth that makes sense in its historical context but that doesn't make any sense today."[7] And so, with an antisupernaturalistic philosophy underpinning his intellectual commitments, he explains what *originally* happened to the historical Jesus: After Jesus was crucified and buried, his corpse rotted away like every other person who has died. His disciples, struck by the trauma of having suddenly lost their inspirational leader and so desiring the successful establishment of his "kingdom," experienced profoundly moving visions of Jesus alive and well and reigning. These were encounters entirely of a psychological nature, of course, and not at all physical manifestations. This is how the "Jesus is Lord" movement began, he explains—namely, with traumatized disciples envisioning Jesus "living" after his crucifixion and living on through their passion to see the kingdom of God come on earth as it is in heaven.

---

[5]Craig and Lüdemann, *Jesus' Resurrection*, 150.

[6]Lüdemann quoted in ibid., 62.

[7]Ibid., 67.

"I think vision is the primary religious experience that led to the whole Christian movement,"[8] confesses Lüdemann. In this way, Jesus's "resurrection" becomes a metaphor for hope in this life that provided a catalyst for conversion, evangelization, and devotion to Christ among his earliest followers. "A vision can be a force within a person that in many cases leads to a complete reversal and change of one's life."[9] Thus he can continue using visions to explain the rapid growth of Christianity, centered around a story of a "risen Christ" that would still be meaningful to subsequent generations of Christians despite Paul's all-or-nothing injunction in 1 Corinthians 15. But as we shall see, Lüdemann inadvertently proves Paul's point concerning Christianity's *sine qua non* relationship with the bodily resurrection of Jesus. Lüdemann has taken the biblical plot, imposed a faulty methodology, and winds up telling a story that forces conclusions to comply with his presuppositions concerning miracles. While his aim is to make Christianity more palatable to modern minds, he ultimately fails, for it is anachronistic to the core. The New Testament witnesses and authors did not subscribe to an antisupernaturalistic philosophy with anguish-motivated proclivities toward inspirational "visions." Rather, the New Testament witnesses operated in a Semitic philosophical tradition that was *intensely tactile* and defined by a biblical narrative in which God was providential and miraculously active in time and space.

It was the apostles' deep commitment to a Jewish world view that provided them with resources to recognize the difference between trauma-induced visions and a bodily resurrection. Indeed, biblical Judaism had a profound understanding of material reality and, relatedly, its antithesis in terms of nonphysical entities.[10] Gerd Lüdemann's modernist reinterpretation of the resurrection narratives entirely misses this decisive point. Understanding the deeply physical Jewish world view of the New Testament witnesses and authors

---

[8]Ibid., 55.

[9]Ibid.

[10]Thomas Howard, "Recognizing the Church," in James M. Kushiner, ed., *Creed & Culture: A Touchstone Reader* (Wilmington, DE: ISI Books, 2003), 127–28.

gives readers of the New Testament certainty that the disciples of Jesus were not conflating physical and spiritual realities. Far from it. The Jewish disciples of Jesus were steeped in a religious culture given entirely to what was tactile and true, not ephemeral and ambiguous. It really is best to interpret the text the way it presents itself with the philosophical beliefs and world views of the first Jewish Christians, best preserved for us in the writings and legacy of Paul himself, "a Pharisee, descended from Pharisees" (Acts 23:6), who imbibed an advanced Jewish understanding from Rabbi Gamaliel (Acts 22:3).

Put differently, Christian witnesses to the resurrection of Jesus were from the majority house of the Pharisees (who affirmed a bodily resurrection), not the minority house of the Sadducees (who denied any future life whatever).[11] What the Bible presents, in both Testaments, is a thoroughly integrated physical-spiritual reality—heaven commingled with earth, time infused with eternity, spirit suffused with matter. There was a sacramental tapestry to the world of Jews that was taken to a deeper and more profound level with Christianity. For God had become flesh, and flesh—through the resurrection— had become glorified. Paul knew precisely what was presented to him in postcrucifixion bodily form and that his transformed but nonetheless physical presence was the result of resurrection—and that *this* Jesus was no apparition, phantasm, or stress-induced vision. First Corinthians 15 details his entire argument (posited also in 1 Thessalonians 4) over against gainsayers, the confused, the doubting, the skeptical, and, indeed, the school of the Sadducees.

So while Lüdemann refers to the well-known disagreement between first-century Pharisees and Sadducees concerning the resurrection of the dead, he completely ignores its epistemic consequences upon the likes of the apostles, let alone their commitment to the entirety of the Hebrew Scriptures. He cautions that we can't assume that a Jew at the time would immediately think of *bodily* resurrection because "there were various notions of resurrection around, one of which was bodily."[12] N. T. Wright, for example, has

---

[11]N. T. Wright, *The Resurrection of the Son of God* (Minneapolis, MN: Fortress Press, 2003), 131–40, 162–75.

[12]Lüdemann quoted in *Jesus' Resurrection*, 44.

conclusively established that both antiquity's meaning and usage of resurrection "always meant bodies."[13] In fact, Lüdemann's unsubstantiated assertion is precisely the opposite of the historical assessment provided by Wright's benchmark research:

> The ancient world, like the modern world, produced widely differing speculations about what happens after we die. The word *resurrection* designates one and only one of those options: a new bodily existence. A new physical human being, after a time during which that human being had been dead and gone.[14]

And so Paul, whom we know was a resurrection-affirming Pharisee (Acts 23:6),[15] held a set of beliefs about resurrection already set in a historical context over and against those who denied *bodily* resurrection (i.e., the Sadducees).

Lüdemann's thesis is rendered all the more implausible by the fact that the Jewish authors of the New Testament—indeed, it seems *all* Second Temple Jews whatever (including the Sadducees)[16]— were supernaturalists.[17] The miraculous was not precluded from their world view; it was an integral part of it. Lüdemann could hardly be more out of step with scholarly knowledge of the apostles' philosophical and scriptural commitments. His proposal concerning the resurrection disregards these important historical and philosophical details. Ignoring Paul's (to say nothing of Peter, James,

---

[13]N. T. Wright, *Simply Good News: Why the Gospel Is News and What Makes It Good* (San Francisco: HarperOne, 2015), 47.

[14]Ibid.

[15]Acts 26:3: "Now when Paul perceived that one part were Sadducees and the other Pharisees, he cried out in the council, 'Brothers, I am a Pharisee, a son of Pharisees. It is with respect to the hope and the resurrection of the dead that I am on trial'" (ESV).

[16]In Acts 4:16–17, the Sadducees admit that the apostles of Jesus engaged in the miraculous, saying: "We cannot deny that they have performed a miraculous sign, and everybody in Jerusalem knows about it."

[17]Although the Sadducees denied ordinary divine providence, according to Josephus. See Flavius Josephus, *The Works of Flavius Josephus*. ET William Whiston (Auburn and Buffalo, NY: John E. Beardsley. 1895), I: 8, 14.

John, and Luke's) philosophical context is a sin of omission. And once loosed from an obligation to defer to the world view commitments of Jesus's Jewish contemporaries about the material world and its relationship with the spiritual, what then follows from Lüdemann is predictable: a modernist account of the biblical narrative within strictly antisupernaturalistic parameters yet devoid of both philologic support and recognizable intellectual commitments. In short, what Lüdemann offers is antisupernaturalism, not Christianity.

Lüdemann's Body-less Resurrection as Alternative Biblical Narrative

In *Jesus' Resurrection: Fact or Figment*, Gerd Lüdemann introduces his proposal by questioning whether Paul, the oldest written source referencing the burial of Jesus, even knew the story of the empty tomb.[18] Paul writes to the Corinthians to remind them of the tradition he taught them, specifically that "Christ died for our sins, according to the Scriptures, and was buried. He was raised on the third day, according to the Scriptures, and appeared to Cephas and then to the Twelve."[19] This is often cited as the earliest written reference to the resurrection of Jesus, but Lüdemann argues that, notwithstanding, it is unclear what Paul meant by "raised" and "appeared" in this passage, and there is nothing at all said about an empty tomb.[20] He thus concludes that given the impossibility that someone would rise from the dead, it is presumptuous to conclude that these words are sound evidence for a physical/bodily resurrection or the first Christians belief in it.

Lüdemann's arguments about Paul's epistles are not to be taken lightly. He is right to note that Paul does not mention the empty tomb per se in 1 Corinthians 15:3–6, and he argues that if Paul believed in an empty tomb, surely he would have mentioned it to the

---

[18]Craig and Lüdemann, *Jesus' Resurrection*, 43.

[19]1 Corinthians 15:3b–5.

[20]Craig and Lüdemann, *Jesus' Resurrection*, 44. Paul mentions Jesus dying and being raised but not the empty tomb, which Lüdemann cites as evidence that Paul did not believe in a physical resurrection.

Corinthians who struggled with the idea of bodily resurrection: "If he [Paul] had known about the empty tomb, he would certainly have referred to it in order to have an additional argument for the resurrection."[21] Lüdemann also examines Paul's use of the word "appear" in other epistles and finds further reason for doubting a reference to a corporeal resurrection. Paul claimed repeatedly to have seen the risen Lord, even saying so in 1 Corinthians 15:8: "Last of all, as to one untimely born, he appeared also to me."[22] But no one else can corroborate Paul's accounts of encountering the "risen" Christ, and there is no evidence that the two ever met in person. In fact, if there is anything that Paul offers by way of transparency, it is that he never met Jesus during the Nazarene's own lifetime. So Lüdemann leads his readers to ask, how can Paul claim to have seen Jesus and heard from him on multiple occasions unless such encounters were other than physical?[23]

Lüdemann thus asserts that these "encounters" on the road to Damascus (Acts 9) and elsewhere (e.g., Galatians 1:12) support his claim that Paul did not make a clear distinction between physical bodily presence and hyperrealistic, emotionally charged visions. Rather, because of what we now know through the findings of science, we are compelled to understand that Paul was referring to encounters that were *real* visions of Jesus but not of a really transformed-by-the-resurrection Jesus. This is how Lüdemann offers a palatable alternative narrative that allows him to circumvent the persistent problem of defending (what is in his mind) an indefensible bodily resurrection to modern readers. He writes: "[Paul] asserted repeatedly 'I have seen the Lord.' So Paul is the main source of the thesis that a vision is the origin of the belief in the resurrection."[24] Paul experienced (apparently with many hundreds of others over the space of months and in various locations and contexts) hyperrealistic visions

---

[21]Lüdemann quoted in *Jesus' Resurrection*, 44.

[22]Galatians 1:11,12. Luke also reports Paul's Damascus road encounter with the resurrected Jesus in Acts 9:4 and Paul's testimony to the same in 22:7–11 and 26.13–18.

[23]Craig and Lüdemann, *Jesus' Resurrection*, 61.

[24]Lüdemann quoted in ibid., 45.

of "seeing the Lord," and these came to be referred to as encounters of the "risen Christ" and eventually were misunderstood, by the early church, to imply a resurrected body.

Lüdemann's hypothesis is based, at first, on Paul's writings, but he goes further to incorporate all the Gospel accounts into his alternative narrative. He claims that all the surviving apostles were so overcome with grief at the death of their spiritual leader that they had intense visions of Jesus, which were "later replaced by the stories you read, for example in Luke . . . My explanation is that Luke is writing when there are conflicting theories and opinions of Christians who claim that Jesus did not eat, that the resurrection was not a bodily resurrection but a spiritual resurrection."[25]

What is interesting is that he does not think he is making a case *against* true Christianity; indeed, his sincere hope is to preserve the plausibility of authentic, demythologized Christianity that remains "highly meaningful" but "avoids the necessity of basing . . . faith on an historical person and on the Christian myth [of bodily resurrection]."[26] By Lüdemann's reckoning, given that the language about Jesus's postmortem appearances is vague in the New Testament and the bar of evidence required to prove a bodily resurrection unobtainable by the biblical record, the Gospel accounts and Paul himself provide insufficient support for such a belief: hence the need to desupernaturalize the resurrection narratives for the scientific age.[27]

Responding to Lüdemann

The first point Gerd Lüdemann uses to build his case is, he claims, that Paul never mentions the empty tomb. While this may be technically

---

[25]Ibid., 54.

[26]Ibid., 161.

[27]Traditional Christianity continues to grow globally and is finding something of a revival in patches of Europe: England, the Baltic States, and in many second-world countries, too. Consumerism and secularization in Western Europe and the United States continue to eviscerate the Christian presence and heritage in these regions. Communism and atheism have been contributing factors in Russia and many former Eastern Bloc countries.

true, it is really an argument from silence. His requirement that Paul specify that the tomb was empty is too restrictive and requires more than what Paul himself would have considered sufficient detail. What few references we do have from Second Temple Judaism concerning resurrection never reference an "empty tomb" either. It did not need to, for it was a broad cultural assumption that at the resurrection, (1) graves/tombs/ossuaries would be emptied, and (2) resurrection always referred to physical bodies. In saying that Jesus was "raised" in 1 Corinthians 15, Paul needed no further clarification or expansion since the empty tomb and a physical resurrection would have been assumed by his audience. How much more so his intended audience of Corinthian Christians who already heard the Gospel from Paul and were baptized (in some cases by him [vv. 14, 16]) into the death and resurrection of Christ (cf. Romans 6:3–6)!

The supposed necessity of Paul having to mention the empty tomb serves as a diversion from the issue at hand. Paul doesn't use the empty tomb as an argument or even part of his argument for resurrection in 1 Corinthians 15 because his purpose was not proving or substantiating an empty tomb but rather what happens after death—namely, the transformation of our bodies by the process of resurrection. Jesus being "raised" entails a vacant burial plot *because* he was bodily resurrected.

The most recent scholarship on 1 Corinthians 15 has shown that Paul did not rehearse *his* account of things, but rather through the technical terms of "παρελάβετε . . . παρέδωκα . . . παρέλαβον" (vv. 2, 3), he rehearsed a formulaic expression of transmission and reception of the Gospel tradition. It was not his account; it was the apostolic account—it was their "creed."[28] And that creed, leading scholars safely conclude, dates to within a year or so of the resurrection itself.[29] The bodily resurrection of Jesus, it turns out, is the earliest creedal proclamation of the church, and that proclamation,

---

[28]See Paul Barnett, *Finding the Historical Christ* (Grand Rapids, MI: Eerdmans, 2009), 176–209.

[29]Graham Stanton, *The Gospels and Jesus* (Oxford: Oxford University Press, 2002), 289.

originating in Jerusalem itself, knew of a vacant tomb that Christ once occupied.

Lüdemann's second argument is that Paul's use of the word "appear" does not necessitate a corporeal resurrection. Aside from the decisive work of N. T. Wright concerning the *meaning* of resurrection (mentioned above), Gerd Lüdemann fails to recognize that the New Testament consistently differentiates between a vision of Christ and a resurrection appearance of Christ. Here, William Lane Craig is helpful:

> Paul was familiar with "visions and revelations of the Lord" (I Cor. 12.1). Yet Paul, like the rest of the New Testament, did not equate such visions of Christ with resurrection appearances. The appearances were to a limited circle of witnesses at the birth of the Christian movement and soon ceased, Paul's untimely experience being "last of all" (I Cor. 15.8). Yet visions of the exalted Lord continued to be experienced throughout the Church. The question then presses: what essential difference exists between a vision of Christ and a resurrection appearance of Christ? The answer of the New Testament seems clear: a resurrection appearance was an extramental event, whereas a vision was merely in the mind of the percipient. To say that some phenomenon was visionary is not to say that it was illusory. Biblical scholars have found it necessary to distinguish between what are sometimes called "objective visions" and "subjective visions." An objective, or, less misleadingly, veridical vision is a vision caused by God. A subjective or nonveridical vision is a product of the percipient's imagination. A veridical version involves the seeing of an objective reality without the normal processes of sense perception. A nonveridical vision has no extramental correlate and is therefore hallucinatory. Now visions of the exalted Christ such as Stephen's (Acts 7.55–56), Paul's (Acts 22. 17–21), or John's (Rev. 1.10–18) were not regarded as hallucinatory; but neither did they count as resurrection appearances of Christ. Why not? Because appearances of Jesus, in contrast to veridical visions of Jesus, involved an extramental reality which anyone present could experience. Even Paul's experience on the Damascus Road, which was semivisionary in nature, could count as a real appearance because the light and the voice were experienced by Paul's traveling companions (though they were not experienced by them as a revelation of Christ). As I say, this seems to be the consistent answer throughout the New Testament to the question of what the

difference was between a vision and an appearance of Jesus. And this answer is thoroughly Jewish in character: the rabbis similarly distinguished between an angelic vision and an angelic appearance based on whether, for example, food seen to be consumed by the angel was actually gone after the appearance had ceased.[30]

Craig is correct that if this distinction is true, it is devastating to the claim that the postmortem appearances of Christ were visionary appearances. And in a damning concession, Lüdemann concedes that most exegetes recognize this distinction. But rather than reconsider his position, "since he finds himself at a loss to explain it, [Lüdemann] simply . . . den[ies] it."[31]

The third facet to Lüdemann's thesis states that Paul never actually met Jesus before his crucifixion. So how could Paul have known it was a resurrected *Jesus* he encountered on the road to Damascus?[32] It seems this same question may have been on the mind of Saul when he had that transformative experience when he asked, "Who are you, Lord?" To which the response came, "I am Jesus" (Acts 9:5). Jesus announced himself to Paul, performed a miracle on him, and (it appears) conveyed the Gospel to him as well (Gal. 1:12). In other words, while Paul presumably did not meet Jesus before this event,[33] there are multiple occasions when the apostle communicated his personal familiarity with Jesus, and his accounts were never contradicted or corrected by the Twelve. Indeed, as Paul Barnett shows, Paul's close acquaintance with Jesus parallels Peter's intimate association with the Christ on many points of character, doctrine, and ethics.[34]

---

[30]William Lane Craig, "Visions of Jesus: A Critical Assessment of Gerd Lüdemann's Hallucination Hypothesis," *Reasonable Faith,* accessed 4 February 2016, http://www.reasonablefaith.org/visions-of-jesus-a-critical-assessment-of-gerd-ludemanns.

[31]*Op. cit.*

[32]Lüdemann quoted in *Jesus' Resurrection*, 55.

[33]Though some have inferred from 2 Corinthians 5:16 this possibility.

[34]Paul Barnett, *Finding the Historical Christ* (Grand Rapids, MI: Eerdmans, 2009), 184–209.

Gerd Lüdemann uses as his fourth point the well-rehearsed hypothesis that the followers of Jesus were so grief stricken and compelled by Jesus's kingdom movement that they envisioned him alive again. As implausible as it may seem, he even applies the same narrative to Paul! Craig, however, again exposes the various ad hoc assumptions made by Lüdemann in order to even propose the "vision" hypothesis:

> (i) The disciples fled back to Galilee on the night of Jesus's arrest. Lüdemann needs this assumption in order to separate the disciples from the gravesite of Jesus. Otherwise it becomes difficult to explain why they did not investigate the tomb. But this assumption has not a shred of evidence in its favor and is on the face of it implausible in the extreme.
> (ii) Peter was so obsessed with guilt that he projected a hallucination of Jesus. The records tell us nothing about the state of Peter's mind following his denial of Jesus. We have no reason to think that Peter's primary concern in the face of Jesus's execution was with his failure to stand by Jesus rather than with the shattering of Jesus's Messianic claims.
> (iii) The remaining disciples became so carried away that they also hallucinated visions of Jesus. We have no evidence that the other disciples, who presumably lacked Peter's guilt complex, were emotionally prepared to hallucinate visions of Jesus alive. We are simply asked to assume this.
> (iv) Paul had an unconscious struggle with the Jewish Law and a secret attraction to Christianity. Since the conflict is said to have been unconscious and the struggle secret, this assumption defies support by evidence. It is completely ad hoc.[35]

Thus the vision hypothesis is set on a house of cards and, what is more, runs completely counter to Paul's own autobiographical account in Philippians 3:4–14, where he boasts about his successful and fulfilling Pharisaical career. By Paul's own confession,

---

[35]William Lane Craig, "Visions of Jesus: A Critical Assessment of Gerd Lüdemann's Hallucination Hypothesis," http://www.reasonablefaith.org/visions-of-jesus-a-critical-assessment-of-gerd-ludemanns.

it was the miracle of a resurrection encounter that substantiated, for him, the apostolic claim that Jesus was in fact the Christ of God. And it is precisely this claim—a miraculous event of bodily resurrection—that Lüdemann rejects as an antisupernaturalist, and it is his presumed antisupernaturalism that serves as the catalyst for an alternative explanation for the phenomenon of Christian devotion to the resurrected Jesus. The vision and rhetoric of Paul and the Gospels must reference a "spiritual resurrection," according to Lüdemann, because a bodily resurrection cannot be considered. This leads him to construct a narrative about appearances that begins with entirely unsubstantiated ad hoc assumptions melded with anachronistic psychoanalysis for rhetorical plausibility. In the end, what Lüdemann's scholarship has actually accomplished is merely the exposing of his antecedent ideological commitment to antisupernaturalism, which only yields a reconstructed "Christian faith" that was itself antisupernaturalistic.

Lüdemann's Humean Skepticism

To really understand Lüdemann, we must appreciate the intellectual force of modern skepticism toward miracles. Any contemporary disputation on miracles begins with David Hume. Hume denied that we can ever confidently determine that an event, such as the resurrection, was a miracle. Rather, as Craig describes, Hume thought that identifying an event as a "miracle" was either (1) hyperbolic (that is, a description of an event that "probably wasn't really miraculous at all—just impressive and unusual") or (2) from ignorance due to an inability to have the event "explained as following from purely natural causes."[36] Hume's incredulity remains in vogue through contemporary belief in science as the final arbiter of truth.

A miracle, by Hume's definition, is a transgression of the laws of nature or an event caused "by a particular volition of the Deity, or by the interposition of some invisible agent."[37]

---

[36]David Hume, *An Enquiry Concerning Human Understanding*, ed. I A. Selby-Bigge, 3rd ed. (Oxford: Clarendon Press, 1974), X, i, 114.

[37]*Op. cit.*, X, i, note 90.

Skeptics like Hume think it is much more likely that an extraordinary event is a shortcoming in our understanding of the laws of nature than a divine intervention to break natural laws. However, this position betrays a self-defeating circularity. Hume begs the question because his process for evaluating a miracle implicitly assumes atheism. If it is impossible for God to be part of an explanation, then no amount of testimony will convince you that a miracle has occurred.

Neither the ancients, nor the medieval, nor moderns believe that people rise from the dead. "We don't need 200 years of evidence that people don't rise from the dead! We have two thousand years!"[38] We know, based on the example of every human life through history that humans do not rise from the dead. With Jesus's resurrection, however, we have an exception to that natural law, the sort of exception Hume refuses to believe if there remains any possibility of an alternative natural explanation in favor of a "divine interference."

The resurrection stands outside the process of inductive inquiry, and so miracles are explanations of last resort when we are otherwise at a loss for a naturalistic one, especially when the testimony and governing narrative clearly posit such. This is an important point. People don't rise from the dead, as human experience shows, but in the case of a resurrection of Jesus, we are at a loss for a *natural* explanation and must explore the possibility of a supernatural one. The resurrection is not a normal event—and that's the whole point, for in that one event, God's kingdom broke through nature, and what happened on earth happened as it is in heaven to bring about a new paradigm and a new order. Lüdemann dogmatically follows Hume's maxims concerning the implausibility of miracles and pursues an alternative, natural explanation.[39] However, since the New Testament evidence and postapostolic testimony decisively and unambiguously attest to a miraculous bodily resurrection, he ultimately ends up altering the narrative to cohere not with the evidence but with his own physicalist commitments.

---

[38]N. T. Wright, "Can a Scientist Believe in the Resurrection?," in N. T. Wright, *Surprised by Scripture* (San Francisco, CA: HarperOne, 2014), 56.

[39]Craig and Lüdemann, *Jesus' Resurrection*, 150.

Lüdemann does claim that he tries "to deal with the Bible in strictly historical terms."[40] But if that were the case, he would identify and evaluate Paul's antecedent intellectual commitments, but he doesn't. First-century Jews strongly believed that miracles were possible and in certain scenarios expected.[41] God had intervened in their history many times throughout the Old Testament and could do so again. Lüdemann must come to terms with this. Additionally, the Jewish faith of the Pharisees and Essenes (at least) was profoundly tactile.[42] They had a good grasp on physical reality. Thomas Howard offers perspective:

> Judaism . . . is heavy with matter. First, at creation itself, where solid matter was spoken into existence by the Word of God. Then redemption, beginning not with the wave of a spiritual wand, nor with mere edicts pronounced from the sky, but rather with skins and blood— the pelts of animals slaughtered by the Lord God to cover our guilty nakedness. Stone altars, blood, fat, scapegoats, incense, gold, acacia wood—the Old Covenant is heavily physical.[43]

Notwithstanding, Lüdemann remarks, "I am the last to deny that the Bible really says Jesus ate fish and bread. But just because the Bible says so, that doesn't mean we have to believe it or defend it."[44]

If first-century Jews wrote about someone eating and the genre was neither metaphorical nor anagogical, then there should be no confusion about what was meant when the language employs tactile referents. Ancient Judaism was notably more in touch with the materiality of the world than other philosophical traditions, especially those influenced by Plato and the ancient Greeks.[45] Lüdemann's

---

[40]Lüdemann quoted in ibid., 43.

[41]Wright, *The Resurrection of the Son of God*, 26.

[42]Eliezer Berkovits, *God, Man and History* (Jerusalem: Shalem Press, 2004), 14–17.

[43]Thomas Howard, "Recognizing the Church," in *Creed and Culture: A Touchstone Reader*, ed. James M. Kushiner (Wilmington, DE: ISI Books, 2003), 127.

[44]Wright, *The Resurrection of the Son of God*, 43.

[45]See Colin Gunton, *The Christian Faith: An Introduction to Christian Doctrine* (Oxford: Blackwell, 2002), 38–42.

methodology should take this into account as a basic condition of his research, but it does not.

It is easy to think that moderns are the first to be grounded in a material and scientific world view. We are more materialistic, certainly, but while we know about bacteria and quarks, our desire for empirical evidence is not novel. Thomas didn't ask for a hair sample of the risen Christ to see if his DNA matched the blood on the cross, but he would not believe until he had placed his fingers and hand into the wounds of his Lord.[46] Likewise, Mary Magdalene physically laid hold of the resurrected Jesus, confirming the tactile reality of what her senses already perceived to be true.[47] While he didn't know modern science, we can be confident in Paul's ability to distinguish between a bodily resurrection and the sort of spiritual experience that Lüdemann substitutes because his Jewish faith—and its climax in Christianity—were heavily physical. Second Temple Jews like Paul had a robust conception of materiality, according to which the actual physical phenomenon of the resurrection was of crucial importance to them. Paul was worried about the same things we are and was thoroughly informed about materiality, matters of evidence, and the distinction between things that are real and sensual and those that take place in the mind or the heart alone.

This is where Lüdemann's thesis fails before it has even floated. He is concerned about evidence but violates the intellectual context of that evidence. All this is compounded by the fact that the Jewish authors of the New Testament—indeed, it seems *all* Second Temple Jews whatever (including the Sadducees)[48]—were supernaturalists, though the Sadducees denied ordinary divine providence, according

---

[46]John 20:24–29.

[47]In Max Zerwick's authoritative *Analysis philologica Novi Testimenti graeci*, 5th edition (Rome: Scriptura Pontificii Instituti Biblici, 107, 1966), he unpacks Jesus' John 20:17 comment to Mary "not to touch" him by writing: "μή w[ith] pres[ent] imp[erative] forbidding continuation of an action. ἅπτου . . . *grasp*; *touch* [something]; durative, *hold on to*; μή μου ἅπτου *stop clinging to me!*" (345). Mary physically handled the resurrected Christ's transformed body.

[48]In Acts 4:16–17, the Sadducees admit that the apostles of Jesus engaged in the miraculous, saying: "We cannot deny that they have performed a miraculous sign, and everybody in Jerusalem knows about it."

to Josephus.[49] The miraculous was not precluded from their world view; it was an integral part of it. Lüdemann could hardly be more out of step with scholarly knowledge of the apostles' philosophical and scripture-tradition commitments.

Paul's Damascus Road Conversion

Paul's conversion looms large in both his persona and legacy. A man en route to prosecute Christians finds himself blinded by a bright light and confronted by a voice demanding an answer to the charge, "Saul, Saul why do you persecute me?"[50] Saul's vision on the road to Damascus was not the private inner spiritual experience that Dr. Lüdemann asserts. Saul's two traveling companions also see the light and hear the voice that speaks, though the Lukan account in Acts says that they were puzzled because they did not see anyone. Furthermore, they are there to witness the voice and the clearly external, physical effect of the experience on Saul, which eliminates the idea that this was a subjective, personal encounter. Most strikingly, Saul is physically blinded by the vision until Ananias lays hands on him and scales fall from his eyes. The witness of the companions and the dramatic physical effects of the experience suggest something wholly other than the sort of feeling of inner peace or significant emotion that would be characteristic of an internal religious experience or vision.

The multipersonal, multisensual nature of Paul's conversion on the road to Damascus gives us some insight into the nature of Paul's faith and perspective. From the moment of his conversion, he is not a believer in Christ because of a feeling of inner peace or a sense of inspiration that could help him find meaning in his life after the stoning of Stephen. (So far from feeling remorse, he was empowered to carry out greater persecutions by his own request!) Paul encountered sound waves from the voice of Jesus, overheard by his traveling companions, and his eyes were physically affected by an external blinding light. This was a multiperson drama. His experience of the

---

[49]Josephus, *The Works of Flavius Josephus*, I: 8, 14.

[50]Acts 9.

spiritual reality that Christ was the Son of God was also a physical reality. There was no dichotomy between the two realms, and this physicality is essential in appreciating how Paul understood the world—a world in which spirit and matter overlapped, time and eternity commingled, and heaven and earth were suffused together.[51]

But what did Paul mean when he described Jesus "appearing"? The answer to this question demands a mix of intellectual history and epistemology. How did Paul know that the body of Christ had been physically raised: did he know this fact in a literal sense or in a spiritual sense of feeling the presence of Christ in a personal way? Lüdemann explains, "[T]here were various notions of the resurrection around, one of which was bodily." This is why, he claims, that a Jew at the time of Jesus wouldn't immediately think "bodily resurrection" as a possible explanation for Jesus's empty tomb. He's not wrong that there was not a single Jewish doctrine on the afterlife. The Sadducees believed that the individual was extinguished at the end of life, and others thought there was a disembodied afterlife. To be sure, this diversity of thought is interesting, but make no mistake: the only salient fact is that Paul was a self-professed and credentialed Pharisee (Philippians 3:5-6) and thus believed that resurrections were bodily. So when Paul speaks about the Jesus who "appeared" to him (and a list of others, according to 1 Corinthians 15:4-6), he is always and only talking about a corporeal appearing of Christ.

Jewish Appraisement of Material Reality

The Pharisees had taken it upon themselves to resist the Hellenization of Judaism. They believed firmly that the world was good because God created it and deemed it so. Greek philosophers like Plato, on the other hand, taught that the struggle of life was to escape from the material, to free oneself from our physical bodies, which imprison us.[52] Philosophy aimed to help men and women prepare for and practice being dead, when we will finally be freed from this prison.

---

[51]N. T. Wright, *The Case for the Psalms: Why They Are Essential* (San Francisco, CA: HarperOne, 2013), 20–21.

[52]Plato, *Phaedo Dialogue*.

From the contrast between the two philosophies, it is not surprising that Platonism made few inroads into the Jewish world view of the Pharisees. And communities that were steeped in Greek philosophical outlooks needed disabusing: hence Paul writes to the Corinthians to correct their Platonic interpretations of the Jewish tradition ("But if it is preached that Christ has been raised from the dead, how can some of you say that there is no resurrection of the dead?" [1 Corinthians 15:12]).

Only a few decades before Paul, Philo Judaeus attempted to make the ancient Jewish texts and teachings compatible with Greek Platonism.[53] His Hellenizing efforts were widely rejected and sometimes violently so by the Second Temple community as unfaithful to the Jewish world view. We have good reason to believe that Paul, as a Jewish authority himself, would have understood the conflicting world views. Judaism was inseparable from the material world, and attempts to reconcile it with Greek thought failed until the Middle Ages.

We also know that Paul was conversant in Hellenistic philosophy. When preaching in Greece, he consciously contrasted the resurrection and crucifixion with Greek thought about the soul and the afterlife. In Acts, Paul debated with Epicurean and Stoic philosophers. In chapter seventeen, he even stands in the middle of the Areopagus saying, "[M]en of Athens, I perceive that you are very religious . . . what you worship as unknown, this I proclaim to you . . . Yet he is not far from each one of us, for in him we live and move and have our being."[54] Acts specifically mentions Paul defending the faith in contrast to these various strains of Greek philosophy, Stoicism, Epicureanism, and Platonism. Paul's involvement in the intellectual life in Athens confirms his familiarity with Greek philosophy and ability to confront its antipathy with the body and to do so proclaiming the bodily resurrection of Jesus Christ (Acts 17:31–32) as the fulfillment of tactile and true Judaism.

Gerd Lüdemann's claim that Paul conflated seeing a physical being with spiritual visions is a tempting alternative to a bodily

---

[53]Philo, who lived in Alexandria, Egypt, was thought to have been born circa 25 BC and died c. AD 50.

[54]Acts 17:22–29.

resurrection. But an examination of Paul's Jewish philosophical holdings gives confidence that the apostle was making no mistake about the resurrection yielding a corporeal manifestation of the once certifiably dead Jesus. His emphasis on the physical not only adds weight to the case for Jesus's resurrection as a historical event but also deepens our understanding of what a tactile and true resurrection means for the baptized, as well as for the physical world itself (Romans 6:3–5; 1 John 3:2; Revelation 21:9–27). Gerd Lüdemann's anachronistic approach and failure to examine Paul's perspective fatally undermine his conclusions and invalidate his alternative visionary "resurrection" narrative. Well intentioned though he may be, what remains after Lüdemann neuters it is unrecognizable as Christianity such that Paul and evangelists proclaimed and defended.

Recommended Reading

Bammel, Ernst, and C. F. D. Moule, eds. *Jesus and the Politics of His Day*. Cambridge, MA: Cambridge University Press, 1984.

Barnett, Paul. *The Truth about Jesus: The Challenge of Evidence*. Sydney South, Australia: Aquila Press, 1994.

Craig, William Lane, and Gerd Lüdemann. *Jesus' Resurrection: Fact or Figment?: A Debate between William Lane Craig and Gerd Lüdemann*. Edited by Paul Copan and Ronald K. Tacelli. Downers Grove, IL: InterVarsity Press, 2000.

Evans, Craig A., and N. T. Wright. *Jesus, the Final Days: What Really Happened*. Edited by Troy A. Miller. Louisville, KY: Westminster/ John Knox Press, 2009.

Gunton, Colin. *The Christian Faith: An Introduction to Christian Doctrine*. Oxford: Blackwell, 2002.

Hengel, Martin. *Between Jesus and Paul: Studies in the Earliest History of Christianity*. Eugene, OR: Wipf and Stock, 1983.

Licona, Michael R. *The Resurrection of Jesus: A New Historiographical Approach*. Downers Grove, IL: IVP Academic, 2010.

Stanton, Graham. *The Gospels and Jesus*. Oxford: Oxford University Press, 2002.

Wright, N. T. *Simply Good News: Why the Gospel Is News and What Makes It Good*. San Francisco, CA: HarperOne, 2015.

Conclusion

Adam S. Francisco

The preceding essays demonstrate, in various ways, that Jesus's resurrection is a matter of fact. This is the most basic of Christian assertions, as Paul wrote, after explaining what it would mean if he had not been raised (in 1 Corinthians 15:12–19). "But in fact," Paul writes, "Christ has been raised from the dead." And it is in this fact, as "the firstfruits of those who have fallen asleep," that the good news offered in the Gospel (namely, the forgiveness of sins and eternal life) is grounded. "For as by a man came death, by a man has come also the resurrection of the dead. For as in Adam all die, so also in Christ shall all be made alive. But each in his own order: Christ the firstfruits, then at his coming those who belong to Christ" (1 Cor. 15:20–24).

The resurrection was God's way of furnishing "proof to all men" (Acts 17:31 NASB) that the Gospel is true. It is for this reason that the defense of the resurrection is essential to the task that Peter exhorts Christians to always be prepared for: "to make a defense to anyone who asks you for a reason for the hope that is in you" (1 Pt. 3:15).

Ever since the first century, the defense of the resurrection has been the heart and soul of the apologetic task. John Warwick Montgomery writes:

> From earliest Christian history—indeed, from the pages of the Bible itself—miracles have been the mainstay of Christian apologetics. Taking their cue from Jesus' own assertion that the "one sign" to His generation of the truth of His claims would be the "sign of Jonah"

(Jesus' resurrection, Matt. 12:39, 40 *et al.*) and from Paul's catalog of witnesses to that Great Miracle apart from which Christians would be "of all men most miserable" (see 1 Cor. 15), patristic apologists such as Irenaeus, Origen, and Eusebius of Caesarea confidently argued from the historical facticity of our Lord's miracles to the veracity of His claims and the consequent moral obligation to accept them. Every major apologist in the Christian history from that day to the mid-eighteenth century did likewise, whatever the particular philosophical or theological commitment he espoused. The list includes Augustine the Neo-Platonist, Thomas Aquinas the Aristotelian, Hugo Grotius the Arminian Protestant, Blaise Pascal the Catholic Jansenist, and Joseph Butler the high church Anglican.[1]

Then came David Hume, and with him (and a host of other enlightenment thinkers) the proliferation of the naturalist world view and its critique of the miraculous. The response by many influential Christian writers of the age and throughout the modern era was to retreat to existentialism and fideism. Apologists began to take "their cue from Søren Kierkegaard's willingness to substitute for objective proofs of faith to the believer's personal, existential experience and to claim that, in the final analysis, 'truth is subjectivity.'" As Montgomery puts it, in his typically incisive manner, "Thus miracles in the heart have replaced miracles in history in the weaponry not only of theological radicals such as Rudolf Bultmann and neoorthodox advocates of the 'theology of crisis,' but also of evangelical pietists who sing with A.H. Ackley, 'You ask me how I know He lives? He lives within my heart.'"[2]

The relegation of the resurrection to the realm of private, subjective belief did not protect Christianity from its secular aggressors. In fact, it led to the claim by many twentieth-century analytical philosophers that the Gospel was—factually speaking—meaningless gibberish, and while the theology of Christianity might be different from all the other religions, it rested on the same shoddy

---

[1]John Warwick Montgomery, "Science, Theology, and the Miraculous," in *Faith Founded on Fact: Essays in Evidential Apologetics* (Edmonton, AB: Canadian Institute for Law, Theology, and Public Policy, 2001), 43–44.

[2]Ibid., 45.

epistemological foundation as other religions. Not only is its veracity outside the pale of any real critical investigation; the ability for one to know whether it was true or not was destroyed. It is no small wonder, then, that Christianity has lost its appeal in Western culture and that westerners are just as likely to pursue up-until-recently foreign religions such as Buddhism, Islam, or Wicca.

If Christianity is to be taken seriously—and not as just another private cult of belief that happened to achieve dominance in the West centuries ago—then it must show itself to be something other than another cleverly devised myth. There is no good reason to believe that the church invented the story or that the disciples were deluded into thinking they saw their master alive and well while he lay dead. The case is actually quite the opposite. The objections modern skeptics raise alleging this are not rooted in problems with the evidence. They are, instead, grounded in modern philosophical assumptions and methodological bias, as many of the previous chapters have illustrated. They therefore fall far short of undermining or weakening the foundation of the Christian faith.

The resurrection is foundational for Christian belief. It is also foundational for its defense. It is Jesus's resurrection that confirms the claims he made about himself—that he was the Son of God and coequal with the Father and the Spirit. It also, by confirming his divinity, verifies the inspiration of the Bible. He regarded the Bible in his own day—that is, the Old Testament—as the word of God (e.g., Mark 7:13, Matt. 4:4, 22:31). Also, before his ascension, he promised to send the Holy Spirit to his disciples so that they would be able to recall everything their master had taught them and to guide them in all truth (John 14:15–31, 16:4–15). Eventually, after turning the world upside down with their preaching and persuasion, they inscribed what they had been eyewitnesses of and what some of them had learned from eyewitnesses into the texts that make up the New Testament.[3] Not everything was written down, for there was too much to write about. Nevertheless, it still comprised the inspired apostolic message in all its fullness. Thus, after the generation of

---

[3] On this, see J. E. Komoszewski, M. J. Sawyer, and D. B. Wallace, *Reinventing Jesus: How Contemporary Skeptics Miss the Real Jesus and Mislead Popular Culture* (Grand Rapids, MI: Kregel Publications, 2006), 21–38.

apostles with their inspired teachings passed, God's word remained enshrined in the New Testament. Accordingly, we have good reasons derived from objective evidence to believe that the Bible is the word of God.[4]

Jesus's resurrection is Christianity's linchpin. It holds everything together and is the grounds on which Christianity's truthfulness stands or falls. Illustrating it to be a fact does not and cannot bring non-Christians to saving faith in Jesus. Only God the Holy Spirit does that. It can, however, change the minds of those who have fallen prey to bad history (influenced by bad methodology, philosophy, and theology), and it most certainly can demonstrate that Christianity is not a cleverly devised myth. God did enter time and space in the person and work of Jesus. He presented many infallible and convincing proofs (Acts 1:3) that he was the Christ, the Son of the living God. The last and final proof was his resurrection (Acts 17:31). This did not happen in some otherworldly or extrahistorical realm beyond human observation. No. As Paul put it, it did not happen in a corner (Acts 26:26). It was and is a matter of fact.

---

[4]This is the basic apologetic approach of John Warwick Montgomery. It can be found in varying degrees of detail throughout all his work, above all his *Tractatus Logico-Theologicus* (Eugene, OR: Wipf and Stock, 2013).

Index of Names

Index of the Holy Bible

Made in the USA
Middletown, DE
01 May 2022

65004979R00139